THE

CIRCUIT

THE CIRCUIT

An ex-SAS soldier's true account of one of the most powerful and secretive industries spawned by the War on Terror

BOB SHEPHERD

with M. P. Sabga

MACMILLAN

First published 2008 by Macmillan
an imprint of Pan Macmillan Ltd
Pan Macmillan, 20 New Wharf Road, London N1 9RR
Basingstoke and Oxford
Associated companies throughout the world
www.panmacmillan.com

ISBN: 978 0 330 45573 2 (HB)
ISBN: 978 0 230 71026 9 (TPB)

1 3 5 7 9 8 6 4 2

A CIP catalogue record for this book is available from the British Library.

Typeset by SetSystems Ltd, Saffron Walden, Essex
Printed and bound in Great Britain by
Mackays of Chatham plc, Kent

For Vince Phillips
A Soldier

TURKEY
ARMENIA
AZER.
AZERBAIJAN
IRAN
SYRIA
DAHUK
Mosul
Arbil
NINAWA
ARBIL
As Sulaymaniyah
Kirkuk
AS SULAYMANIYAH
AT TA'MIM
SALAH AD DIN
Samarra
Euphrates
DIYALA
Ar Ramadi
BAGHDAD
AL ANBAR
Tigris
WASIT
Karbala
KARBALA
Al Hillah
Al Kut
MAYSAN
An Najaf
Diwaniyah
AL QADISIYAH
Al Amarah
DHIQAR
An Nasiriyah
AN NAJAF
Karun
Basra
AL MUTHANNA
BASRA
KUWAIT
SAUDI ARABIA
IRAQ
200 kilometres

ISRAEL
100 kilometres
LEBANON
SYRIA
Haifa
Mediterranean Sea
Nablus
WEST
BANK
Tel Aviv
Ramallah
Jerusalem
Hebron
Gaza City
GAZA STRIP
IRAQ
JORDAN
EGYPT
SAUDI
ARABIA
Eilat

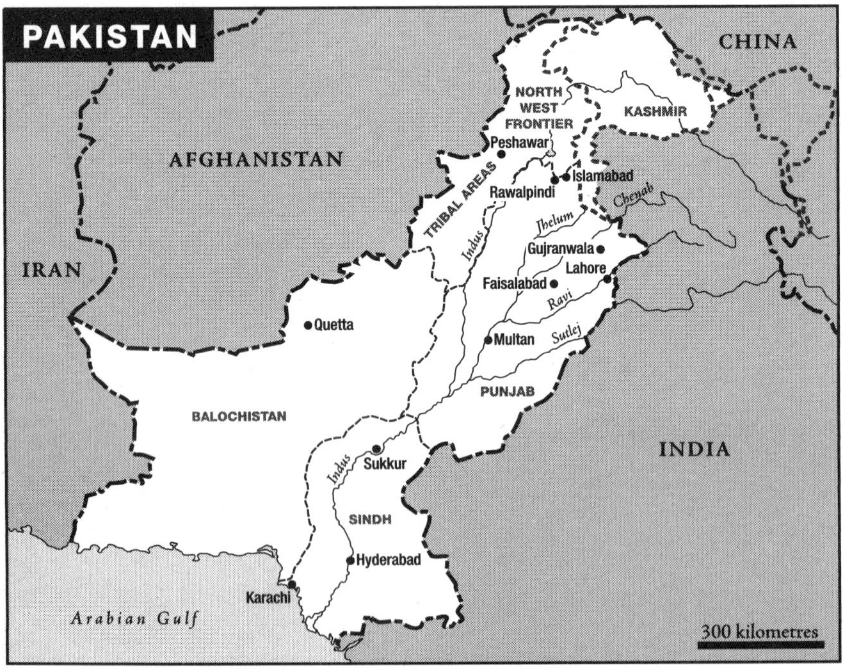
PAKISTAN
CHINA
NORTH
WEST
FRONTIER
KASHMIR
AFGHANISTAN
Peshawar
TRIBAL AREAS
Islamabad
Rawalpindi
Chenab
Jhelum
Indus
Gujranwala
Lahore
IRAN
Faisalabad
Ravi
Quetta
Multan
Sutlej
PUNJAB
BALOCHISTAN
INDIA
Sukkur
Indus
SINDH
Hyderabad
Karachi
Arabian Gulf
300 kilometres

UZBEKISTAN
TAJIKISTAN
CHINA
TURKMENISTAN
Amudar'ya
BADAKHSHAN
JOWZJAN
BALKH
KUNDUZ
TAKHAR
Mazar-e Sharif
SAR-E POL
SAMANGAN
BAGHLAN
Indus
FARYAB
NURISTAN
KUNAR
BADGHIS
BAMIAN
Hari Rud
Kabul
Jalalabad
Herat
WARDAG
HERAT
GHOWR
Khost
1 KABUL
2 KAPISA
3 AGHMAN
4 LOWGAR
5 PAKTIA
6 KHOST
7 NANGARHAR
URUZGAN
GHAZNI
FARAH
PAKTIKA
Farah
ZABUK
Indus
Kandahar
Lashkar Gah
NIMRUZ
IRAN
PAKISTAN
Helmund
KANDAHAR
HELMUND
200 kilometres
AFGHANISTAN

ISRAEL
IRAQ
SAUDI ARABIA
JORDAN
Ar'ar
400 kilometres
KUWAIT
IRAN
Duba
Persian Gulf
Al Jubayl
Ad Dammam
BAHRAIN
Buraydah
Dhahran
QATAR
Shadra
Al Hufuf
Riyadh
Medina
As Sulaymaniyah
EGYPT
U.A.E.
Red
Layla
Mecca
Jeddah
Ar Ta'if
Sea
Rub' al Khali
(Empty Quarter)
SUDAN
OMAN
Abha
Na ran
YEMEN

CONTENTS

GLOSSARY

MILITARY TERMINOLOGY

AK47 7.62 mm short, Soviet-designed assault rifle
APC armoured personnel carrier
Beaten Zone area of ground upon which the cone of fire falls
Comms communications
Contact situation in which an enemy attacks your position
Cot military fold-up bed
Drones pilot-less aircraft used for surveillance
FOB forward operations base
GPS global positioning system
LZ landing zone
M16 US-made 5.56 mm assault rifle
MSR main supply route
NCO non-commissioned officer
OP observation post
PRT provincial reconstruction team
Recce reconnaissance
RPD Soviet-designed, belt-fed, light machine gun
RPG rocket-propelled grenade
Rupert commissioned officer
RV rendezvous
Sig Sauer 9 mm automatic pistol
SOP standard operating procedure

CIRCUIT TERMS

BAPSC British Association of Private Security Companies
CP close protection
CSC commercial security company
IED improvised explosive device
Level B6/7 highest-rated armoured vehicle available commercially
SIA Security Industry Authority

TELEVISION NEWS TERMS

B-roll footage
DV camera digital video camera
Embed assignment in which a journalist or group of journalists report from inside a military unit
Fixer individual retained by the media to help out in a foreign country
Fly Away mobile satellite dish
Live Shot live report
Live Truck vehicle with a satellite dish
Minder government official who oversees journalists
Phoner live report delivered over a phone
PAO public affairs officer
Presser press conference
Snapper stills photographer
Stand-Up brief, on-camera commentary by a correspondent
Shooter cameraman or camerawoman
Soundbites on-camera quotes; also known as voxpops

OTHER

ANA Afghan National Army
ANSO Afghan NGO Security Organization
ISAF International Security Assistance Force
NGO non-governmental organization

PREFACE

I thought it would be useful to explain why I've selected and omitted certain terms from this book, starting with the title. 'The Circuit' is shorthand for the international commercial security circuit, an industry which caters to government, military, commercial and individual clients. The Circuit's activities encompass a vast array of services including, but not limited to, the following: protective services, asset tracing and recovery, employee screening, counter-surveillance and anti-surveillance, Kidnap & Ransom response, information security, political and security risk analysis, business and intelligence investigations, fraud awareness and investigation, crisis management and security audits.

The core of this book is the biggest growth area for The Circuit in recent years: the market for protective services in hostile environments. These services include Close Protection or CP (bodyguards in layman's terms) for commercial clients and outsourced military jobs including CP for government personnel, securing government installations, running convoys and security sector reform (i.e. training national military and police in places such as Iraq and Afghanistan).

The Circuit uses several terms to describe firms which provide security services: PMCs (Private Military Companies), PSCs (Private Security Companies) and PMSCs (Private Military and Security Companies). Though they appear similar, each of these acronyms is politically charged. For instance, the British Association of Private Security Companies, a trade group of

British security firms with operations abroad, refers to its charter members as PSCs due to what it terms 'cultural reservations' surrounding the term PMCs.[1]

As for myself, I take issue with applying the term 'private' to security companies. Though technically accurate – we are talking about private sector firms as opposed to government owned – it can be misleading because 'private' can refer to non-profit companies.

Throughout this book, I will refer to the firms comprising The Circuit as CSCs, Commercial Security Companies. CSCs don't exist to do good works in the world. They are not fundamentally noble in nature. The primary goal of CSCs is to make money. They are above all *commercial*, profit-driven enterprises and should be referred to as such.

That's not to say that the people doing the actual work on the ground in hostile environments place financial gain above all other considerations. This is why you will also note a conspicuous absence of the term 'mercenary' in this book. I have often heard the media refer to the men and women working on The Circuit as 'mercenaries'; a label as offensive as it is inaccurate. Let me explain.

Mercenaries are hired guns who sell their services to the highest bidder. They have no national loyalty, no sense of duty to country and no moral foundation. They'll take up arms against their own government if the price is right.

Security advisers, by contrast, are a relatively new phenomenon (and by 'advisers' I mean the people putting their lives on the line in the field, not the managers and executives sitting in plush offices back in London). Security advisers first appeared in the 1970s, when The Circuit was still very much in its infancy. Today, the vast majority of advisers work on contracts servicing their own governments, governments closely allied to

---

1 *The Regulation of the Private Security Industry and the Future of the Market*, by Andrew Bearpark & Dr Sabrina Schulz.

their own or industries regulated by their home countries, their allies or international law. Many security advisers have served in the military or supported their communities as police officers. They regard their employment on The Circuit as a continuation of their public service, not an end to it.

In fourteen years on The Circuit, I have never accepted an assignment that I felt ran counter to Britain's national interests. I served my country proudly as a soldier for twenty-three years and continue to serve it through my work in the commercial security sector. I see myself as a patriot and a security adviser. Never call me a mercenary.

PART ONE

A STEEP LEARNING CURVE

CHAPTER 1

'I told you to STOP!'

I could tell by the accent that he was Russian. His voice certainly matched the rest of him. He was a blond-haired, blue-eyed monster. Even with half of his body hidden in the hatch of his APC, he looked about six foot tall. All in all, a stereotypical Russian soldier – except for his weapon (an American-made M16) and his uniform (IDF, Israeli Defence Force).

Only in Ramallah.

It was April 2002. I had arrived in the West Bank just two weeks earlier to look after a CNN crew reporting on the largest incursion of Israeli troops into Palestinian lands since the 1967 Six Day War. It was a typical spring morning in that part of the world; drizzly and cold with the heavy scent of wet concrete dust hanging in the air. The pavement had been reduced to rubble, chewed up by Israeli tanks ploughing through everything in their paths. Flattened cars, like pages from a book, and piles of rubbish waiting to be burned lined the silent, undulating streets. The residents of Ramallah were battened down indoors observing the Israeli-imposed curfew that promised to shoot on sight any Palestinian – or anyone mistaken for a Palestinian – who disobeyed.

The Russian climbed down from the APC, all the while keeping his M16 aimed towards me.

'Who are you?' he asked.

I had dressed to blend in with my journalist clients: nondescript shirt and trousers, Timberland boots, body armour with the letters TV taped across the front flap, and a ballistic helmet also with the letters TV taped on the sides.

'Journalist,' I said.

'Liar,' barked the Russian. 'Where are you from?'

'Scotland,' I said, unable to contain the shit-eating grin that spreads across my face whenever I say the name of my country out loud.

'This isn't fucking Scotland,' said the Russian.

'This isn't fucking Israel either,' I replied.

Not the answer he wanted to hear. The Russian looked over his shoulder and nodded to one of his mates; another blond monster in an IDF uniform, no doubt Russian as well. The next thing I knew, he was sprinting towards me, his M16 elevated as if he were charging into battle. The pair of them grabbed me and dragged me behind the APC. A small group of Israeli soldiers, non-Russians, were there. When they saw what was happening, they moved away towards the front of the vehicle, leaving the Russians alone with me.

Meanwhile the CNN crew I was looking after were well out of view. If they'd followed my instructions to the letter, they'd be on their way back to the hotel.

I briefly considered trying to overpower the Russians and escape but they probably would have shot me in the back. The lead Russian slammed my head against the APC. His henchman shoved his rifle into my temple. I could feel the flash eliminator at the end of the barrel sink into my flesh. I was scared, probably the most scared I've ever been in my life – not exactly the position I expected to find myself in as a civilian.

When I retired from 22 SAS Regiment in 1994, I was certain that dangerous adventures in far-flung places were behind me. I had spent twenty years in the Regiment, achieving the rank of Warrant Officer. I'd fought some good wars and taken part in plenty of operations: Oman, the Iranian embassy siege in London, Northern Ireland, the Falklands War, the First Gulf War, Bosnia, and many little skirmishes in between.

I was offered a commission to stay with the Regiment as an officer but turned it down. Though I couldn't have asked for a better military experience, I promised myself as a young recruit that I'd leave at the age of forty, the natural end to a soldier's career. I didn't want to be a hanger on. So, four months shy of my fortieth birthday, I gathered my belongings from camp in Hereford and walked out of the gates for the last time. I cried like a baby.

The international commercial security circuit, or The Circuit as it's known, was a natural place for someone with my background and skills to land. Plenty of retired Regiment lads had led the way before me. Back then, The Circuit was a cottage industry catering primarily to the oil and mining industries and to high-profile individuals such as celebrities, royalty, businessmen and the super rich. Most of the lads on the ground were like me; former Regiment or SBS (Special Boat Service), as well as some very good people from other military backgrounds. Many of the advisers were highly skilled individuals, but as with any industry there were a handful of bluffers who could talk themselves into a job.

When I first joined The Circuit, my assignments were well paid and confined to non-hazardous areas. I spent my first five years working as part of a Close Protection team for an American billionaire and his family. Though busy, the job required me to spend a lot of time in five-star hotels and on private Caribbean beaches. In half a decade, the gravest threat my client encountered was a playful seal in the Galapagos Islands that swam a bit too close. At the time, it was the best job going on The Circuit. My client was a tremendous man to work for and I learned a lot. Sadly it ended due to budget cuts.

I went on to work as a security adviser for a major oil company with operations in Algeria. After that, I headed a thirty-man security detail for a Swiss family based in the south of France. Cushy as these assignments often were, I refused to let myself go or allow my military training to deteriorate. I never drank on the job; I kept myself in good physical condition and seized every opportunity to sharpen my proactive security skills. I didn't know it at the time, but my discipline would pay off handsomely.

My days of looking after rich people in glamorous locations ended when al-Qaeda hijackers crashed two planes into the World Trade Center. That day, 11 September 2001, marked the beginning of The Circuit's transformation from a niche business into a multi-billion-pound industry. As the War on Terror intensified, so did the demand for security advisers, especially in hostile environments; media, diplomats, civilian contractors; suddenly everyone needed looking after.

When I got the call to go to Ramallah to work with a team of CNN journalists, I jumped at the chance. It had been years since I'd had a real adventure and I missed the adrenalin rush of being in a hostile environment (technically Algeria was a hostile environment but I spent all of my time there looking after workers inside a secured cordon). I relished the chance to apply skills I hadn't used since the military in a commercial environment. Ramallah also held out the fascinating prospect of being able to do what I never could as a soldier: mix with the local population as a real civilian.[2]

The only question mark over the job was the actual clients. I hadn't worked with journalists before and wasn't sure what to expect. More importantly, media was a new market for The Circuit so it was likely that the journalists I'd be assigned to had never worked with a security adviser. I was warned during my pre-deployment briefing that many media clients resented having advisers around. As far as the journalists were concerned, they'd covered plenty of conflicts without our help and they

2 I had posed as a civilian on covert operations during my time in the Regiment.

didn't need it now. Much of this resistance was due to ignorance. The journalists thought security advisers were nothing more than tick-tock ex-soldiers who would get in the way of their stories. The possibility of difficult clients didn't put me off going to Ramallah. I was confident that if I did my job well I'd win over even the most stubborn journalist.

Israel launched Operation Defensive Shield in March 2002 in retaliation for a wave of Palestinian suicide bombings that killed over a hundred Israeli civilians within a single month. As part of the operation, Israeli tanks surrounded Yasir Arafat's presidential compound or Mukhata in Ramallah, effectively imprisoning the Palestinian leader in his own office. By the time I got there, the situation had reached a stalemate and nerves on both sides of the conflict were raw to the point of bleeding.

Meanwhile, I was having a ball. That is, until I met the Russians.

Some journalists had armoured cars but only CNN had both an armoured vehicle and security advisers on the ground. The majority of the press corps had no choice but to spend most of their time indoors while CNN roamed around Ramallah getting stories. That really pissed off the Israelis. Usually, they showed their displeasure through basic harassment; stopping us willy-nilly and telling us to leave Ramallah; closing off streets when we were in the middle of filming; threatening to break our equipment – in short, tactics meant to drive us out.

That changed when we ran into the Russians. The siege had just entered its fourth week with no resolution in sight. I had set out with a stripped-down crew (a cameraman and correspondent) to recce the streets. As we slowly navigated the city in our armoured 4x4 I did my best to skirt the known Israeli checkpoints. Sure enough, as we drove up a hill towards the Manara, Ramallah's main square, a tank was waiting at the top; its gun barrel was pointed right at us.

I had already established a procedure for this type of situation and my clients knew the drill. I stopped short of the checkpoint, left the engine running and got out. I wanted to keep the Israelis as far away from the vehicle as possible. My biggest worry, aside from them shooting one of my clients, was that they would confiscate the vehicle, leaving us stranded and unable to get stories.

I had positioned the correspondent in the passenger's seat. It was his job to keep tabs on me once I left the vehicle. If the Israelis became aggressive or attempted to detain me in any way, the correspondent was to slide behind the wheel and drive back to the hotel. That way if the Israelis kicked me out of Ramallah, he and his crew would still be able to report from inside the city. I could always find a way back in later.

As I walked towards the tank I spotted a group of soldiers gathered around two APCs parked up a side road. It was a cold, wet, windy day and some of them had taken shelter under a piece of corrugated tin roofing they'd propped against their vehicle. I continued on past the side road and advanced slowly towards the tank. The gun barrel was still pointed directly at my clients. Finally, an Israeli commander poked his head up from the turret. The markings on his uniform indicated that he was a captain.

'Who are you?' His accent was American.

'Journalists,' I answered.

'Where are you going?' he asked.

'To a primary school at the other side of the Manara,' I said.

He looked over my shoulder at my clients and then back at me. 'Have a nice day,' he said and disappeared back into his tank.

It looked as if we would get off easy. I turned and started walking back to the vehicle. I had nearly made it to our 4x4 when the Russian decided to get involved.

'Stop!' His voice came from the side road where I'd spotted the APCs. I looked at the Russian's uniform. The captain who'd just let me go outranked him, so I continued on my way.

'I told you to STOP!'

That's when I learned that rank counts for nothing in the IDF. The Russian pointed his rifle towards me and ordered me up the side street. I didn't want my clients to lose visual contact with me but the Russian had a weapon. I, on the other hand, was unarmed.

At that moment, I should have recognized the crucial difference between operating as a member of the military in a hostile environment and operating as a commercial security adviser. No matter how skilled the adviser, soldiers will always have the upper hand; they have superior firepower, superior equipment and superior backup. Had I been thinking like a civilian that morning, I would have appreciated just how weak my position was. But I was thinking and acting as if I was still in the Regiment. Rather than keep my big mouth shut and walk away with only my pride wounded, I mouthed off to a well-supported, well-armed soldier and ended up with an M16 digging into my temple.

My head was still sandwiched between the APC and the barrel of the Russian's M16. I scanned the area as best I could and fixed on a block of apartments three storeys high. I was looking for signs of life, anyone who might see what was happening. I wanted a witness, someone to tell the tale because I was convinced the Russian would shoot me in the head.

'Who are you!' the lead Russian demanded again.

'I'm a field producer for CNN.'

'No you're not,' he screamed. 'You're a spy.'

'If I was a spy working in Ramallah wouldn't that put me on your side?' I argued.

The Russian, in a moment of clarity, considered my answer. 'Show us some ID!'

I asked them if I could get my ID out of my back pocket – I didn't want to provoke them with unannounced movements. I reached into my pocket and handed the lead Russian my press card. In the left corner was my picture. In the right, the official seal of the Israeli Press Office.

The Russian looked over the card, smiled smugly and threw it in the mud.

At that moment, I was certain he was destroying my credentials so he could claim – after he killed me – that he hadn't realized I was a member of the media. I looked at my muddied press card like a drowning man watching a life-raft drift out of sight. It seemed like an eternity.

'Pick it up!' the Russian ordered.

I wasn't sure of his endgame but I did as instructed. As I scooped up the card the Russian slammed the heel of his boot down on my hand. I felt the bones in my fingers snap.

'Fucking hell,' I muttered through clenched teeth.

'If we see you on the streets of Ramallah tomorrow, you're a dead man,' he said. 'Now fuck off.' The lead Russian nodded at his mate to withdraw his weapon. I took the cue to get the hell out of there.

My hand throbbing, I walked away thinking just how stupid and arrogant I'd been. I thought my twenty-three years of military experience had fully prepared me to negotiate a hostile environment as a security adviser. I was wrong. By failing to realize the crucial differences between operating as a civilian and operating in the Regiment, I'd unnecessarily compromised my safety and, in doing so, failed to serve my clients to the best of my ability. I was lucky to have got away with only two broken fingers.

CHAPTER 2

I never gave much thought to politics when I was in the Regiment. I was a soldier, not a politician. As far as I was concerned there were two kinds of characters in the world: goodies and baddies.

When I joined The Circuit politics still weren't at the forefront of my mind. I read the newspapers regularly (*Daily Telegraph* and *The Times*) and watched news on television to keep myself informed. When the Israelis launched Operation Defensive Shield, I thought I had a pretty good grasp of the Arab–Israeli conflict: the Israelis were the good guys and the Palestinians were a bunch of terrorists led by the filthiest terrorist of them all, Yasir Arafat.

As a soldier, I'd come to admire the Israelis. When I was a young lad in the Regiment, IDF Special Forces conducted the legendary Entebbe raid in July 1976 to free Israeli hostages held by Palestinian terrorists on an Air France flight at Entebbe airport in Uganda. At the time the Ugandan leader Idi Amin was backing the terrorists, so the Israelis had to conduct the raid in utter secrecy. The Jewish commandos carried out their operation with all the professionalism and guile of any first world force, freeing all one hundred hostages and losing only one of their own.

The Entebbe raid was a source of inspiration for me throughout my military career. It was at the forefront of my mind during the Falklands War, when I was sent to Port Stanley to carry out a similar task with the Regiment.[3]

---

3 That raid didn't happen though I did go on to take part in an even more daring operation which I'm not at liberty to discuss.

Obviously, I held the Israelis in very high esteem. My feelings about the Palestinians were equally as strong, albeit not in a positive way. The western media had always referred to Arafat as a 'terrorist' and his multi-party confederation, the Palestine Liberation Organization, as a 'terrorist' organization. The label meant only one thing to me. The old adage of 'one man's terrorist is another man's freedom fighter' was a load of liberal crap as far as I was concerned. Having fought the IRA, I'd seen first hand just how ruthless they could be. IRA, PLO, it didn't matter; they were all gutless bastards who killed and maimed innocent civilians to achieve their aims.

Operation Defensive Shield was entering its second week when AKE, a commercial security company owned by a former Regiment mate of mine, sent me to Ramallah to look after CNN. AKE already had a cracking lad in situ, Will Scully. An era behind me in the Regiment, Will and I worked together many times on The Circuit in the 1990s. As advisers go, Will is top drawer. If I had to put a team together, he'd be one of the first people I'd call.

I talked to Will prior to leaving to get a better idea of the assignment. I was heartened to hear that he was revelling in it. The only reason he was coming home was because of a family commitment. The job wasn't all giggles though. Will warned me that the toughest part initially would be getting into Ramallah; the Israelis had locked it down and, though journalists were allowed to leave, no one was allowed to enter.

As it turned out, the hurdles went up as soon as I landed in Israel. I was singled out immediately by security at Ben Gurion International Airport in Tel Aviv. Mind you, it's not as if I blended in. A forty-seven-year-old man travelling alone must have stood out among the families and groups of religious tourists. I felt like all eyes were on me as I walked to passport control. I knew I was about to be picked on.

A big fat man in his late twenties and a skinny young woman plucked me out of the passport line and ushered me to one side. Without so much as a 'Welcome to Israel' they started grilling me: what was I doing here? I handed them a covering letter CNN had given me prior to departure and told them I was a field producer temporarily assigned to the Jerusalem bureau. They asked to see my passport. Luckily, I'd recently renewed it and there were no incriminating stamps from Arab countries. The pair then asked me a string of questions, repeating many of them to see if my answers varied. Two questions in particular could have landed me on the first flight back to the UK. They asked me several times if I spoke Arabic. I do speak respectable colloquial Arabic having studied it in the 1970s for operations in Oman, but I kept my language ability to myself. They also wanted to know if I planned to travel to the West Bank or Gaza during my stay.

'Not me,' I said. 'It's far too dangerous.'

I eventually cleared security and went to the arrivals terminal where CNN had arranged for a driver to meet me. There were hundreds of people milling around with name boards, but none for me. I called the number I had been given for the driver but there was no answer. I then rang the CNN bureau in Jerusalem to get a physical description of him. The woman on the other end of the phone told me 'Ahmed', my driver, was approximately five foot eight with a large belly, thinning hair and a moustache. Over half the men in the terminal fitted that description.

Fortunately, the woman in the bureau was able to tell me Ahmed's vehicle make and plate number. I headed out to the car park with my bags, a black canvas duffel and a day sack slung over each shoulder. Normally, I never leave the reception area of an airport until I'm met by my point of contact. But I'd already learned first hand that the airport had fairly good security. Moreover, my flight had been lousy and I was keen to get on with it.

I walked up a row of vehicles sixty yards long and back down another. On my third pass I found Ahmed's sedan with Ahmed inside, stretched out in the passenger's seat and out for the count. I stood by the door and rang his phone. I could hear his catchy Arabic ring tone through the window but he slept right through it. I had no choice but to hammer on the windshield with my fist. Ahmed nearly launched through the roof. When he saw me he opened the door with such haste that a cold cup of coffee he'd rested on his lap shot out into the parking bay.

'Are you Bob?' he asked.

'Aiwa' (yes), I answered in Arabic.

Ahmed drove me straight to my hotel, the American Colony in east Jerusalem. Just a few minutes' walk from the Old City, the hotel is a favourite with the international press corps. Built as a palace in the late nineteenth century, it was taken over by a group of Americans who remained neutral towards the city's various factions. To this day, the American Colony remains something of a little Switzerland where Arabs and Jews can mix over drinks or a meal in the beautiful gardens or inside in the bar and restaurant.

I booked in at reception and was shown to my room. When the porter opened the door, my eyes widened with delight. The room was a palace within a palace; the ceilings were at least fourteen feet high and decorated in hand-carved, nineteenth-century Ottoman motifs. The furniture was hand carved as well in traditional Arab designs and the bed could have accommodated a platoon. No wonder journalists flocked to the place.

I enjoyed my opulent surroundings to the fullest knowing that the next day I'd be facing some Spartan conditions in Ramallah. I dropped my bags, ran the water in the enormous bathtub and bounced onto the bed.

The rest of my day involved meeting with the CNN bureau chief in Jerusalem, getting my Israeli press pass and calling Will on the phone to arrange an RV for the handover.

That evening, I sat down to a monster dinner of surf and turf in the hotel restaurant. The place was full of journalists who looked like they spent most of their time in a pampered environment like the American Colony. Hostile environments were another matter. I'd never seen members of the media up close before and had always assumed that war correspondents would look the part; characters like Sandy Gall who were mature but fit enough to travel over the mountains of Afghanistan. Most of the journalists I saw were smoking and drinking and looked very unhealthy, including the young ones. I imagine that if any of them had to run three hundred yards to get away from an incident they'd probably drop down dead. I certainly couldn't see them engaging in E&E (escape and evade) for a protracted period over a given distance. But the people-watching didn't put me off the assignment. I was still excited by the prospect of returning to a war zone for the first time since retiring from the Regiment.

The next morning I was up at seven (a long lie-in by my standards) to shower, dress and arrange for transport to Ramallah. The Jerusalem bureau had given me the number of a taxi driver who worked frequently with CNN. I was told he could find his way around the West Bank blindfolded.

The driver said it would only take twenty minutes to get from the hotel to Ramallah and he'd collect me at nine. It seemed strange that someone working regularly for a news organization operating in and around a hostile environment should be on such a relaxed schedule. Ramallah is only ten miles due north of Jerusalem but Will had warned me that IDF checkpoints can add hours to the journey. The driver was waiting outside the hotel at 9 a.m. sharp. Since Ramallah was under military lockdown, we bypassed the main route leading north into the city where the fixed Kalandia checkpoint is located and travelled by a back road to bring us in from the east.

We arrived only to discover that the IDF had set up a checkpoint east of the city as well. It was manned by an armed

Israeli patrol that didn't appear to be letting anyone through. We watched them turn away three vehicles in quick succession. When our turn came, I was ready with my credentials. I held my passport and Israeli press card against the window for the soldiers to see. One of them leaned over, looked at my documents and stepped back. I expected him to wave me away. Instead, he lifted his M16 and fired a short burst on the ground near the side of our car. Firing at us was a scare tactic and it worked on my taxi driver. He practically shit himself. The driver turned the car around and started heading back towards Jerusalem. I offered him 200 US dollars to get me into Ramallah via another route, but he refused. 'Those fuckers shoot at anyone,' he said. 'I go back to my family in east Jerusalem and you go back to hotel.'

I called Will to let him know what had happened and told him I'd try to get to Ramallah the next morning – with a different driver. I booked back into the hotel and went outside to the taxi stand to see if I could find a willing candidate. I found a group of drivers standing around. I asked them if anyone was up for driving me into Ramallah the next morning. A young, slim lad with a broken nose and cheeky expression stepped forward.

'I do it,' he said.

His name was Walid and he claimed to know several back routes into the city. I asked him if he would get scared if Israeli soldiers tried to stop us.

'Nobody scare Walid. Walid brave man,' he said, thumping his chest.

'You've got the job, mate,' I said and we shook on it.

I woke early the next morning after a restless night's sleep. In my mind, I couldn't stop replaying the incident with the soldier at the checkpoint. It was the first time in my life I'd been fired on without having the ability to fire back. I had never operated in a hostile environment without a weapon. It felt like my arms had been cut off. It was a strange and horrible experience but one I'd get used to soon enough.

I loaded my black duffel bag into the back of the 'brave' Walid's taxi but kept my day sack containing my medical kit with me up front. I wanted self-aid at hand in case we ran into any more trigger-happy IDF soldiers.

We travelled the route I'd taken the day before, approaching the city from the east. The checkpoint was still up and a queue of cars had formed. As we inched towards it, I studied a large chalk quarry beside the road. It appeared to stretch right into Ramallah. I asked Walid if there was a track in the quarry that led to the city. He said if there was then the IDF surely would have blocked it off with one of its giant armoured bulldozers.

As we neared the checkpoint, it was apparent from the vehicles turning around that the Israelis weren't letting anyone through. When it was our turn to try, we were told to leave as well. I got out of the taxi and asked the checkpoint commander why I couldn't get into the city when I held an Israeli press pass.

'The town is a closed military area,' he said.

It was an answer I'd hear again and again.

I got back into the taxi and asked Walid to drive a mile back up the road and let me out.

'Why? What are you going to do?' he asked.

I pointed towards the quarry. 'I'm going to walk through there into Ramallah.'

Walid smiled. 'Bob, you are fucking crazy. The soldiers, they will shoot you.'

I asked Walid to pull off the road and into a lay-by. I paid him the agreed fare and told him if he waited there until Will arrived, there'd be an extra two hundred dollars in it for him.

'If the soldiers come, drive off and come back an hour later,' I said.

Walid took the money and shook my hand.

'Bissalama,' he said. 'Have a safe journey.'

I threw my day sack over my back and my black canvas duffel across my shoulders. From the lay-by, I could see Ramallah in the distance about two miles away. I stepped off the road and the ground dropped away. The quarry path dipped and rose at steep inclines and was pocked with holes just the right size to twist an ankle. The sun was bouncing off the white chalk, making it very difficult to see clearly. After a mile or so I came across a cluster of buildings that looked like the quarry company's administration area. I stopped and crouched against the wall of one of the smaller buildings to call Will and let him know where I was and what I was planning.

Will asked me if I could see a large wall where the quarry backed onto the city.

'I see it, mate,' I said.

'Great,' he said. 'Can you see the minaret on top of the mosque?'

I scanned the skyline . . . one, two, three . . . 'Will, mate, I see nine minarets.'

Will paused for a second. 'I think I know where you are. Can you see the big blue minaret? I'm about three hundred metres left of it behind the wall.'

I located the blue minaret. 'OK, mate, got that. I'm on my way.'

I only had about half a mile to travel, but most of it was over open ground. I took a couple of minutes to survey the landscape with my binos; about six hundred yards to my left I spotted a group of IDF soldiers on a patch of high ground. Glints of light were bouncing off their position, indicating that they were looking through optics of their own. I couldn't see their weapons so I wasn't sure whether they had the firepower to target me effectively given their distance.

I had just tucked my binos into my day sack when I heard children's voices approaching from behind. I looked back and saw a group of ten of them, boys and girls aged about eight to twelve, come into view. They were all carrying book satchels and appeared to be headed in the same direction as me – Ramallah. I greeted the children in Arabic. One of the older girls responded in English. I asked her where they were going. She pointed towards Ramallah and explained that the only way they could get to school during the Israeli lockdown was through the quarry. I warned the kids about the soldiers I'd spotted on the hillside and told them to be careful. The girl said the Israeli soldiers were always there and had shot at them on several occations. Before the kids headed off, the girl showed me the route they intended to follow. Though I was going in the same direction as the children, I didn't want to walk with them. If the Israelis were onto me, my presence alone could draw fire and endanger the kids unnecessarily.

The kids hadn't gone more than a hundred yards from me when the IDF soldiers on the hillside opened up. I could tell by the sound of the gunfire that the kids were out of range of the bullets. High-velocity bullets like rounds from an M16 travel faster than the speed of sound. If you're in range when fired upon, you first hear the sharp crack of the round travelling past you followed by the thump of the bullet leaving the barrel. In the military it's referred to as 'crack and thump'.

I estimated the bullets were dropping fifty or sixty yards short of the children. The kids, meanwhile, simply glanced over at the high ground where the soldiers were positioned and carried on on their way to school. To them, it was just another day. They were seasoned veterans, and I was new to the game. I watched the kids for another five hundred yards until they disappeared into a small hollow. When the soldiers stopped shooting, I went on my way. Sure enough, as soon as I was in the open, the soldiers started firing their weapons again. The rounds were falling well short of my position and I couldn't be sure whether they were targeting me or the kids further up the path. My life wasn't in immediate danger but I was concerned that the gunfire could alert other IDF patrols in the area; patrols that might be in firing range.

The sun was cresting in the sky and the light reflecting off the chalk was now blinding. It was very hot and sticky and the air was heavy with the smell of wild herbs. As I neared the wall, there was no place to take cover and make a call so I rang Will on the hoof to see if he had me in his sights yet. Will said he could see me and directed me towards a break in the wall. I climbed through the wall and found Will waiting there with a big, cheesy grin on his face. We hugged each other like two lost souls. I asked him why the fuck he was smiling when he'd have to travel back along the same route I'd just taken. At six foot with blond hair, Will made a much bigger target than me.

For the next fifteen minutes, Will gave me what still stands as the best quick briefing I've ever received. When he finished, he handed me a list of written notes and the keys to CNN's armoured Land Rover. 'It's got three bullet strikes in it,' he said. 'Every time we go somewhere, the Israelis shoot at us.'

'I'll see if I can match that,' I said.

'Seriously, mate,' he said. 'Keep your body armour and helmet well advertised with the letters TV. The IDF shoot at anything.'

He didn't have to remind me. I'd already been fired on twice in twenty-four hours just trying to get into Ramallah.

CHAPTER 3

Some people never change. Others do, though it usually takes one hell of a catalyst. In my case, it was seeing Israeli soldiers take pot-shots at those kids on their way to school. Within forty-eight hours of arriving in Tel Aviv my long-held beliefs about the Arab–Israeli conflict had been dealt a serious reality check. It never occurred to me that the Israeli military would be anything less than 100 per cent professional. At forty-seven, I was starting to realize that my political views weren't my own; I had allowed others to dictate them to me. When I was in the military I was fed a certain bias in order to fulfil an operation and I never questioned it. I guess the habit stuck when I retired to civilian life.

My assignment in Ramallah placed me in the role of observer rather than participant in a conflict. For the first time in my life, I was on a fence looking down on both sides. Suddenly the media reports I'd trusted to inform me about serious issues including the Arab–Israeli conflict didn't seem so reliable. My intention from then on was to stay on top of that fence and seek the truth for myself. It was the start of a long-overdue political education.

I wished Will all the best as he headed down into the quarry and out of Ramallah where hopefully Walid the taxi driver was still waiting for him. I walked to the Land Rover and introduced myself to the CNN producer in the passenger seat; a young woman I'll call Nihal.

During the handover, Will explained that I'd be working with women. I believe my response was something like, 'You're fucking kidding, mate.' I had seen female war correspondents on TV but having spent nearly two decades in the Regiment, I never envisaged working alongside a woman in a hostile environment. In my view, war zones were for men only.

The women of CNN would soon set me straight. Nihal was an old hand at navigating Ramallah during Israeli lockdowns. Before I'd even got the vehicle into gear, she was giving me directions. The key to getting around, she explained, was to avoid IDF armoured checkpoints. I followed her instructions to the letter as she talked me through a series of twists, turns and backtracking right to the doorstep of our destination: Ramattan Studios, home to Ramattan TV, the main Palestinian news services in the West Bank and Gaza. Occupying one floor of a simple eight-storey building in the heart of Ramallah, it had become a temporary office/home to dozens of journalists of various nationalities covering the siege of Arafat's Mukhata just a mile down the road.

When I walked into Ramattan, it was apparent that the siege mentality had migrated from Arafat's compound to the press corps. Tapes, cameras, editing gear, tripods, bags, body armour, helmets, old scripts, water bottles and personal items littered the place. The air reeked of cigarette smoke and stale sweat. Everyone's eyes were ringed in dark circles and their clothes were wrinkled and dirty.

Nihal introduced me to the rest of the CNN crew including Margaret Moth, a New Zealand camerawoman who Will had spoken of very highly indeed. The crew was getting ready for a live shot, so I left them to get on with it while I settled in.

No sooner had I put my gear down than I was intercepted by a man introducing himself as Wakil. A short, stocky lad with a heavy beard and booming voice, Wakil was Ramattan's unofficial cook, administrator and welcoming committee. His official job was less warm and fuzzy: Wakil was a correspondent for

Hezbollah TV – as in Hezbollah the Iranian-backed Shiite organization the US and UK label as terrorist. Over a cup of tea, Wakil filled me in on everything that had happened at Ramattan since the start of Operation Defensive Shield. One incident really grabbed my attention. A few days before I arrived, the IDF attacked the building housing Ramattan Studios, sending armed soldiers up the stairwell. CNN was the only network using security, so Will was the only adviser in situ. He shouted down to the soldiers that the building was full of journalists and single-handedly covered the stairwell until everyone, clients and their competitors, was safely evacuated. Will's actions undoubtedly saved a lot of lives.

While Will left some very big shoes to fill, his accommodation was another matter. I took over Will's old 'room'; a four-and-a-half- by three-foot broom cupboard where I slept curled up with my feet against the wall. I don't know how Will managed it; I'm only five foot nine and like I said, he's six foot. I swear he slept standing up. Cramped or not, I was grateful to have my own private space where I could get away from the cigarette smoke.

It wasn't long before I'd settled into a daily routine. Throughout the night I'd hear explosions and gunfire. Then around 5 a.m. there'd be a lull. The silence was my alarm clock. I'd get up, put the kettle on and head to the shower. There was only one bathroom in Ramattan to accommodate forty-odd journalists. It would have resembled a cow field were it not for Wakil; every morning he'd get up before me and clean it. No one asked him to – he just took it upon himself. Regardless of what you may think about Hezbollah TV, their correspondent in Ramallah is the most immaculate journalist I've ever met.

After a shower, I'd make a brew for myself and the rest of the CNN team. I'd then head downstairs to check the armoured car to see if it had been tampered with overnight. I'd also check the fuel, oil and lubricants to ensure it was roadworthy for a day's wandering around Ramallah. If the crew didn't have an early shoot scheduled, I'd load up my medical pack and take a drive around Ramallah on my own to see if the Israelis had changed their checkpoints overnight or moved in sniper positions or more tanks. When my recce was complete, I'd return to Ramattan, meet up with the CNN crew and map out what they wanted to achieve for that day.

Most of my time was spent helping the crew evade Israelis while they gathered elements to turn into stories. A lot of the reports focused on how Ramallah's residents were coping with the curfews and lockdowns, some of which lasted more than a week. Basics such as food and medicine were constantly in short supply. At one point, a United Nations food convoy bound for Ramallah was turned back by the Israelis.

Many of the Palestinians featured in the reports were determined to carry on with their daily lives as normally as possible. I really admired how quickly they tidied up when the Israelis pulled back. During the lockdowns, I'd see Israeli tanks and APCs rolling over cars and smashing through pavements. As far as I could determine, the practice didn't accomplish anything strategically but it did have the psychological impact of creating one hell of a mess. As soon as the tanks backed off, however, the Palestinians would emerge from their houses armed with brooms and dustbins to clear the rubble. Sometimes their defiance took a humorous turn: one Palestinian artist created a sculpture from a pile of flattened cars.

All in all, I found working with the media immensely satisfying and very insightful. One thing I hadn't realized before was just how hard journalists work to get a story out. Three correspondents and crews rotated through Ramallah during my first assignment there. When they weren't on the ground gathering elements for a story, they were back at Ramattan Studios doing live shots that lasted well into the night.

I was also learning to appreciate what women can bring to the table in a hostile environment. Margaret Moth, in particular, seemed like she was born to be a war photographer. Her energy for the story was relentless. She thrived on the long hours and never missed an opportunity to get a great shot. Whenever we'd head out in the armoured car, she'd sit in the middle of the backseat with her camera facing the front window, ready to roll. It came as no surprise when I learned that 70 per cent of CNN's international promos at that time used b-roll shot by Margaret Moth.

In addition to being extremely talented, both Margaret and Nihal were incredibly brave. One episode in particular stands out. It was mid-morning, just after curfew. I had accompanied a CNN crew to Ramallah's old town to shoot a story. We arrived to find an armed Israeli unit dispersing a crowd of Palestinians, many of whom were upset and wailing. When Nihal asked what was happening, she was told that the Israeli unit had shot dead a ten-year-old boy.

Nihal learned that the boy had been sent by his parents to buy bread at the local shop. He'd left his house two minutes before the curfew ended to be first in the queue. He was running – alone – along a wall on his way to the bread shop when the Israeli unit fired on him from approximately thirty yards away with a general-purpose machine gun (at that distance, there's no mistaking a ten-year-old for an adult). By the time we arrived on the scene, the boy's body had been taken to hospital but his blood was still splattered on the pavement and the wall along with bits of his skull and flesh. One of my sons was ten years old at the time. I tried to imagine him running to buy bread for the family only to be blown away by a group of soldiers.

Later that afternoon, we returned to the incident area to shoot some b-roll for a story wrapping the day's events. As we got out of our vehicle, the Israeli unit that had shot the little boy trundled down the road in their APC shouting at us in a very aggressive manner to move off the street. When they pulled alongside our vehicle, Nihal, out of nowhere, let fly a barrage of angry words – in Hebrew. I didn't know what she was saying. I didn't know she could speak Hebrew. But it was clear from her expression and the look on the soldiers' faces that she was really letting them have it.

As much as I relished watching Nihal stand up to the soldiers, having recently survived the incident with the Russian I knew that things could turn nasty quickly. One of the soldiers on top of the APC began to dismount the vehicle. Nihal, still yelling, tried to climb up to meet him. I grabbed her by the neck of her flak jacket and pulled her back into our vehicle. She was fuming. As we drove back to Ramattan, I told her she was brilliant, but if she kept on that way she'd get herself shot.

'If you want to beat the Israelis, do it by telling great stories,' I said.

CHAPTER 4

As Operation Defensive Shield passed the thirty-day mark, pressure was mounting worldwide for the Israelis to pull back from Yasir Arafat's Mukhata and leave Ramallah. There was growing concern at the time among the international community that the Israelis would kill Arafat – and any hope of restarting the peace process along with him. Though the Palestinian President had given phone interviews from inside his compound, cameras couldn't penetrate the ring of Israeli armour. No one knew for sure how Arafat, who looked frail before the siege, was coping physically with his imprisonment. The press corps was foaming at the mouth to get that all-important, on-camera interview with him.

At the start of the siege, Will Scully had managed to get CNN an exclusive with Arafat by concealing a crew amongst a group of peace activists who were allowed past the Israeli cordon surrounding the Mukhata. The ruse was brilliant in its simplicity and totally effective. I wanted to match it.

In between working with Margaret, a second cameraman I'll call Samir rotated in for CNN. Though Samir held a Jordanian passport, he was originally from Bethlehem, which made the West Bank his home. After a couple of days on the ground with Samir, I asked him if he'd be interested in getting in to see Arafat, provided I could find a way. He was well up for it.

From that point onward, I took every available opportunity to recce the Israeli troops surrounding the Mukhata. It soon became apparent that during bad weather – and there was plenty of it – the Israelis were happy to batten down their hatches and stay put. On a few occasions I was even able to weave in and around Israeli armoured positions without being stopped. I'd determined that, given the right weather conditions, getting a crew in to see Arafat was achievable.

I was up on a rooftop overlooking the Mukhata when I saw an opening. It was a very cold, wet and windy evening and Samir and his correspondent were shooting b-roll for a story. Around 11 p.m. local time, an Israeli patrol arrived in two jeeps to tell us to leave the roof. After a bit of negotiating, they agreed to let us stay so long as we didn't move from our location.

'Things are changing,' they warned.

An hour later, I heard what sounded like the revving of engines coming from the western end of the Mukhata. At first I thought the Israelis might be mounting an offensive. Then I saw a long convoy of tanks pulling back. There was still a heavy flank of Israeli armour hemming in the Mukhata from the east, north and south, though I was fairly certain the tank redeployment had left a major hole in the cordon. Only a recce could confirm my theory. I told Samir and his correspondent to stay on the roof while I took the Land Rover out for a look. Sure enough, when I reached the far western edge of the Mukhata there wasn't an Israeli tank in sight.

I rushed back to the roof and told Samir that if he was up for it, I reckoned I could get him in to see Arafat. Not only was Samir willing to give it a try, so was the correspondent. The three of us jumped into the armoured car and drove back to the western edge of the Mukhata. The gap was still wide open. We drove past the outer wall right up to the central building where Arafat was holed up. I couldn't believe how easy it was!

We dismounted our vehicle and knocked on a large steel door surrounded by sand bags. A viewing hatch slid open. The man peering through recognized Samir immediately. The door swung open and all three of us were pulled in by PLO bodyguards. The building was dimly lit by candles and the odd torch. At the start of the siege, the Israelis cut all electricity and running water to the Mukhata. My euphoria at having successfully evaded the IDF was smothered by the stench of 150 PLO men who hadn't bathed in over a month. The guards meanwhile were thrilled to see us. They knew better than anyone the risks involved in running the gauntlet of Israeli positions. They appreciated our efforts and were eager to get their side of the story across to the world. One huge man grabbed me as if I was his best mate. As he crushed my face into his armpit, I thought the heavy tracks of an Israeli tank going over my head would have been a more favourable outcome.

We were shown upstairs to a small room and told to set up for an interview with 'President Arafat'. While Samir got his camera ready and the correspondent went over his notes, I admired the only decoration in the room: Arafat's presidential flag. It was rather spectacular; three layers of silk the size of a double bedspread with the Palestinian national colours and Arafat's coat of arms embroidered in gold and black threads.

The word 'souvenir' popped into my mind.

Samir must have read my thoughts.

'After the interview,' he said grinning.

A few minutes later two PLO men armed with AK47s burst into the room followed by the man himself. Given his infamous reputation, you'd think Yasir Arafat would have been a towering man mountain. Instead, in marched this slight, five foot two cartoon character with a greying beard, huge grin and eyes that had really seen life. Arafat was full of praise for CNN coming to interview him. His manner was very warm and genuine. His command of English was excellent and none of his wicked dry humour was lost in translation. He decided to give CNN an interview in English – something he rarely did. The Israelis may have had the upper hand militarily, but Arafat knew that world opinion, not firepower, would determine the true winner of the siege. Giving the interview in English was a calculated move on his part to garner greater support from the international community.

The correspondent asked Arafat the obvious questions: how are you feeling? How long do you think you can survive like this? Arafat answered each question with trademark passion. After the interview he shook all our hands and exited with his bodyguards, leaving us alone in the room. While Samir folded up his tripod, I asked the correspondent to keep a watch on the door and let me know if anyone was coming. Samir looked at me and laughed.

'What's going on?' the correspondent asked.

'I'm taking that flag,' I said.

The correspondent's eyes widened like saucers. 'You can't do that. They'll kill us!'

'I'll kill you if you don't watch that door,' I joked. 'And I just got you a world exclusive. I can do anything I want.'

Samir laughed again. I looked at the correspondent, and he laughed as well.

'Well, be quick then,' he said.

I pulled the flag off its plinth, folded it up and tucked it inside my body armour.

Arafat's bodyguards had lined the staircase to see us out. The correspondent led the way, followed by Samir and then me. I was halfway down when one of the guards stopped me. He put his hand on the top of my vest and patted my chest. The ends of his fingers touched the flag. My arse almost hit the floor. How on earth did he know?

'What's your name?' asked the guard. His voice was deep and grisly and his breath stank of strong coffee and cigarettes.

I squared up to him. 'Bob,' I said.

'Well, Bob, when this is all over you can come back to see us anytime,' he said and shook my hand.

Thirty-six days after Israeli tanks rolled into the West Bank, they turned around and rolled back out. Yasir Arafat emerged from his Mukhata completely unscathed, flashing the Churchill two fingers victory sign. It was an appropriate gesture. Before the siege, Arafat was contending with heavy domestic criticism. Afterward, he was more popular than ever with his people. Even Palestinians opposed to Arafat had rallied around him – albeit briefly.

The Israelis didn't seem to fare so well. They launched Operation Defensive Shield to root out terrorist elements within the Palestinian community. But from what I saw, instead of curtailing extremism, the Israeli military's overly aggressive tactics only seemed to fuel it. Many innocent Palestinian civilians were killed during the siege. It cost Israel the goodwill of the international community, not to mention a sizeable investment of military resources. And for what? The deadly campaign of Palestinian suicide bombings continued. Sadly, it was a pattern I would see repeated elsewhere in the not-so-distant future.

As for me and my clients: CNN came out of Operation Defensive Shield with six bullet strikes on its armoured Land Rover (three on Will's watch, three on mine – all of them courtesy of the IDF) and two world exclusives. I left the West Bank with one very nice souvenir and an insatiable desire to learn more about the conflict I'd witnessed first hand. I'd been to see Arafat and got his flag to prove it. Now it was time to meet the militants behind the suicide bombings.

CHAPTER 5

I used to think there was no difference between Palestinian groups: PLO, Hamas, same people, different acronyms. Working with CNN in the West Bank taught me otherwise. Yasir Arafat may have been President of the Palestinian National Authority, but he did not enjoy universal support among his people. Arafat's power base was the PLO and its secular, political wing, Fatah.

At his core, Arafat was a fierce warrior and not at all the type to sit down with his enemy and work things out over a brew. It was remarkable that he'd ever sought a negotiated settlement with Israel. Even during his more militant periods, though, Arafat had boundaries. He never asked his followers to go and blow themselves up for the cause.

That distinction belonged to Arafat's most bitter political rival: Sheikh Ahmed Ismail Yassin, co-founder and spiritual leader of Hamas (the Movement of Islamic Resistance), and the father of the Palestinian suicide bomber. Yassin was based in Gaza, a good hour's drive from the West Bank but a world away ideologically. Unlike Arafat's Fatah, Hamas refused to negotiate with Israel. For Yassin, armed struggle was the only way forward.

In July 2002 I took another assignment working with CNN's Jerusalem bureau. By then the focus of the story had shifted from the West Bank to Gaza. The day after I arrived in Gaza, Hamas militants attacked an Israeli settlement with al-Kazan rockets. Anticipating an Israeli response in the form of an armoured incursion into Gaza, Hamas planned to lay landmines to slow the advance of Israeli tanks and APCs. The militants invited CNN to film the operation.

The offer was made to CNN's Gaza producer: a twenty-four-year-old woman I'll call Noor. Despite her youth, Noor had impeccable credentials within the Palestinian community; her uncle had been assassinated in North Africa by agents of Israel's Intelligence Agency, Mossad. Noor called a meeting in our hotel to discuss the Hamas offer with the team. The correspondent refused to do the story outright, saying it was far too dangerous. The camerawoman, Margaret Moth, disagreed; she thought it was an amazing opportunity and CNN would be crazy to turn it down. With the correspondent and camerawoman divided on what to do, they turned to me to cast the deciding vote. All that mattered from my point of view was whether they could get the story safely. I told them I'd have an answer by dinner. I needed to be alone and free from individual agendas to run the scenarios in my head.

I went to the hotel restaurant to have a think over a cup of coffee. I found a quiet spot overlooking the beach leading out to the Mediterranean. It was twilight and the lanterns from the fishermen's boats in the distance glowed against the darkening horizon.

Though I hadn't let on to the team, I was as intrigued as Margaret by the offer. It was very rare for Hamas militants to be filmed during an operation. I wondered what kind of equipment they used and how professional they were. I was also curious to see whether the operation was legitimate or just an orchestrated media stunt; it would reveal a lot about how much world opinion mattered to the militants.

As I watched the lights dance on the water, I thought about the run of luck I'd had with CNN in Ramallah. It would have been all too easy to sit back and follow the roll without thinking about when and how it might end. Complacency is a security adviser's worst enemy.

I put my personal interests to one side and focused on what could go wrong. My main concern was that the Israelis would find out about the Hamas operation in advance and launch an attack while we were filming. It was well known that Israeli Intelligence had its touts inside the Palestinian community. One loud-mouthed militant was all it would take for word of the operation to spread like wildfire.

The correspondent was justifiably cautious. Even if we did go ahead with the story, technically, he didn't need to be there while Margaret filmed, nor would I want him there. He'd made his position clear and I respected that. He was a very good journalist and a brave man to stand by his limits. Good on him. That would leave Noor, Margaret and me. In theory, I could have let the two of them go on their own, but I'd never have let that happen. I didn't trust Hamas with their lives. Not because I thought the militants would harm them deliberately. My worry was that Hamas lacked the skills to determine whether the Israelis were observing them, waiting to attack.

I had been told that Hamas operated on the assumption that unless they could physically see them, the Israelis weren't a threat. It reminded me of my children when they were very young. They would hide by covering their eyes, reasoning that if they couldn't see me, I couldn't see them. Surely, operatives of a notorious militant group such as Hamas were more sophisticated than that. After all, it was common knowledge that the Israelis sent pilot-less aircraft called drones over Gaza and areas of the West Bank to gather intelligence.

Israel's technical surveillance was so pervasive, in fact, that I had reason to believe it extended to my clients. Before entering Gaza, we were stopped at an Israeli-controlled checkpoint and led away from our vehicle to be questioned. Normally, we'd be questioned inside or near our vehicle. I was 95 per cent certain that while CNN's Land Rover was out of our line of vision it was daubed for surveillance, probably with colourless paint only visible to a night vision camera attached to a drone or helicopter. After the checkpoint, I scrubbed the roof and bonnet of the Land Rover and re-arranged the large TV stickers just in case. I also stripped the vehicle to search for technical surveillance equipment that could have been hidden inside while we were being questioned.

I had no doubts that if we went ahead with the story, the Israelis would be watching all right; if not CNN then certainly Hamas. The concern therefore was whether the surveillance would lead to an attack. I really couldn't see the Israelis deliberately whacking a missile into a CNN crew. Even if they pleaded ignorance, it would be a huge PR headache for the IDF. Frankly, I didn't see why they would go to all the trouble. But I couldn't dismiss the possibility completely. Journalists don't wear body armour in Gaza and the West Bank because it's fashionable. If the Israelis did go after Hamas and – by default – us, the easy option would be for them to position an attack helicopter two or three kilometres away; close enough to target our position with surgical precision but far enough that we might not hear it hovering.

I finished my coffee and felt much better for it. I decided that as long as we limited the number of people on the ground and kept our ears and eyes open – wide open – we could go ahead with the story.

Noor arranged a RV for the following evening at ten. Two Hamas members would wait for us up the road from our hotel and then escort us to the area where they planned to lay the anti-tank mines.

I wanted to recce the operational area in advance but obviously Hamas wouldn't disclose it beforehand. So the next morning I took a detailed drive around Gaza. It was a stab in the dark, but I thought if I familiarized myself with enough landmarks and buildings then I might recognize something when we got to the operational area. If I could determine where we were, then I'd know where to move to cover if the need arose.

The next evening, before leaving our hotel, I gave Margaret and Noor a thorough security brief. I told them to keep an ear open for aircraft, and to wrap the shoot as quickly as possible; the sooner we moved off the ground the better. I then distributed three radios among us. If things went pear-shaped and we got separated, I didn't want to lose contact with my clients. We loaded our gear into the Land Rover and waited for the militants to show. I drove, Noor rode in the passenger seat and Margaret sat in the back, camera as always at the ready. As usual I was unarmed. If the Israelis found a weapon on me or in the vehicle, they'd classify my clients as combatants and lump them in with Hamas.

The militants arrived on schedule at ten o'clock. After a brief word with Noor, they beckoned me to follow them into Gaza's narrow, winding streets. It was soon apparent they were trying to disorientate us rather than lead us directly to our destination. After thirty minutes of twisting and turning we arrived at a track junction surrounded by fifteen-foot-high sand mounds. One quick scan of the area and I was delighted to discover that I knew exactly where we were; the entrance to a refugee camp on the outskirts of Gaza City. My recce that day had paid off handsomely. We were only about twelve minutes from our hotel.

The Hamas car switched off its lights. I did the same. As we slowed up, six hooded figures stepped out of the darkness. They were all carrying AK47s and backpacks; three with RPG rounds sticking out the top. I presumed the other three backpacks contained anti-tank mines. Two of the hooded men wore military helmets with sprigs of foliage coming out the top. It struck me as really amateur, especially as there's very little foliage on the streets of Gaza.

The Hamas car turned down a side street and parked up. I

followed their lead, only I turned our car around to face out. I couldn't see through to the end, but I knew from my recce that we were in a cul-de-sac. Should a situation arise, I didn't want to be facing a dead end. I cut the engine and got out of the vehicle. Normally, I would have kept the engine running but I was keen to listen for Israeli drones flying above us in the darkness. As far as I could tell, the skies were clear as was the immediate area. I told Noor and Margaret they could get out, but asked them to hold off on shooting until I was certain the area was reasonably secure. The details of the street which I'd committed to memory that morning took shape in the moonlight. There were a couple of empty buildings on either side and the concrete shell of a partially built petrol station near the corner.

Noor introduced me and Margaret to the escorts and the group of hooded men. The formalities sorted, I had Noor ask one of the militants to keep an eye out for any Israelis patrolling the area. By that point, we'd taken every possible precaution. Our aim now was to get the story and get out of there.

From what I could tell, the militants were laying anti-tank mines in the hope of stopping Israeli armour from bulldozing through the sand mounds at the entrance to the refugee camp. They started with the mound at the top of the cul-de-sac where we'd parked up. Working in pairs – one man to handle the explosives, the other to give cover – they pulled a round-shaped anti-tank mine approximately nine inches in diameter from one of the backpacks. I couldn't be sure but the mine looked like it was Russian made. The militants dug a hole in the back of the mound about one foot off the ground, placed the mine inside and covered it over with sand. They finished by brushing over their footprints with leafy twigs before moving on to the next mound.

The militants were working swiftly, which eased my mind a bit. Then, as they finished laying the second mine, my ears picked up the sound of something in the distance. My brain switched into high alert; it was the low purr of an attack helicopter and it sounded like it was heading in our direction.

The Hamas militants ignored it and continued working. I called Margaret over in a low voice. I knew from previous assignments that she is partially deaf in one ear and oblivious to anything happening outside her lens when the camera is rolling. I told her about the advancing helicopter. She was worried about it as well. I wasn't there to be an adviser to Hamas, but in the interest of keeping my clients safe I decided I'd better share my concerns with the hooded men. I grabbed the one closest to me and told him in Arabic that an Israeli helicopter was hovering nearby.

'Mafi mushkila' (No problem), he said. 'Shoufna tayara kull-yawm' (We see aircraft everyday).

I told him this helicopter was heading towards our position and could very well be targeting us.

'Mafi ashoof tayara. Mafi mushkila' (I can't see the helicopter. It's not a problem), he said.

I couldn't believe it. They really were that naïve. My Arabic wasn't good enough to explain the danger and I didn't want anything lost in translation through Noor, so I asked the hooded men if any of them spoke English.

'What's the problem?' one of them asked.

'Your English is good?' I asked.

'I studied English at University in Cairo,' he said.

I explained to him that even though the helicopter was a long way off, it could still see us. 'You've got to realize they can catch you picking your nose two kilometres away – at night,' I said.

'No way,' he said laughing.

'I'm serious. Just because you can't see or hear them doesn't mean they can't see you. We have to be careful,' I said.

I suggested we take cover in the half-finished petrol station at the entrance to the cul-de-sac. The concrete shell would block our heat signatures from the helicopter's thermal imaging equipment. We waited under the shell until the helicopter moved off. When I was satisfied it had flown further away, as opposed to higher up, I let Margaret resume shooting.

The militants worked quickly laying the third and final anti-tank mine. When they finished, I told Noor it was time to say our goodbyes. I had Noor and Margaret get in the vehicle ahead of me. I wanted a moment's silence to listen again for drones. The skies were still clear.

As I climbed into the driver's seat, one of the militants told me to wait a minute and he'd lead us back to our hotel.

I started the engine. 'No worries,' I said. 'I know the way.'

CHAPTER 6

Meeting the Hamas militants in the flesh was a real eye-opener. I had thought the movement's foot soldiers would be nothing more than a gang of ignorant street kids. Not so. At least one of the hooded men laying anti-tank mines was university educated. I also thought they'd be somewhat savvy when it came to guerrilla tactics. Wrong again. Far from a group of formidable insurgents, what I saw that night was nothing more than a band of militarily clueless youths playing with explosives, trying to get a little of their own back.

Put simply, Hamas wasn't the highly trained insurgent organization I imagined it to be – which made them even scarier in my book. What those hooded youths lacked in skill they more than made up for in determination. I'm sure in their hearts they knew they'd be lucky to throw a track on an Israeli tank with those mines, yet they were willing to put themselves at risk to lay them.

The IRA had displayed similar resolve when the Regiment operated against them in Northern Ireland. But Hamas took the terror game into a realm where even the IRA wouldn't go. Hamas used suicide bombers.

I wanted to – and, given my line of work, needed to – understand what had led Hamas down that path. A lot of my curiosity was fuelled by my own fear. Forget smart bombs and laser-guided missiles; in my view, nothing is more terrifying than a suicide bomber with a crude, homemade explosive device.

Many people have the false impression that suicide bombers

are crazy, drugged up or brainwashed and that they are exclusively male, young, poorly educated and fanatically religious. I learned during my time in the West Bank and Gaza that suicide bombers come from all walks of life: male, female, rich, poor, young, old, ignorant, well educated, religiously moderate, fundamentalist. The question in my mind, therefore, was not what kind of person commits such a heinous act. I wanted to know what was driving such a diverse group of people to the same violent end.

I got the chance to find some answers, thanks to Noor. As if the anti-tank mine story weren't enough, while I was in Gaza she pulled off another major coup for CNN: an interview with the mastermind of the Palestinian suicide bombing campaign against Israel; Sheikh Yassin, co-founder and spiritual leader of Hamas.

Sheikh Yassin was a reclusive figure who rarely gave interviews to western journalists. A nearly blind quadriplegic, Yassin may have been physically weak but he was a towering figure among Palestinians disillusioned with the peace process. Yassin inspired dozens of Palestinians to 'martyr' themselves in suicide bombing missions that killed hundreds of Israelis.

Needless to say, Yassin was a prime target for the Israelis. My major concern with the interview was that CNN could find itself in the wrong place at the wrong time, so two days before the shoot was scheduled to take place, I went with Noor to recce the location. It was rather unremarkable: a sleepy hollow with one-storey buildings and no proper roads. I checked to see if there were any IDF patrols snooping around or undercover agents. I also determined a safe place to run to in the event of an attack.

Two days later a Hamas escort led us back to the same area. I expected things to look less sleepy this time around. Surely the security surrounding Yassin would be airtight. But instead of a beefed-up cordon, the only security we encountered was a group of bodyguards sitting outside Yassin's house playing backgammon. They were so switched off they didn't even see us until we were within twenty yards of them.

After a cursory check of our bags and equipment the guards led us inside the house. I knew then that Yassin was living on borrowed time. Good thing he was a religious man; given the poor security surrounding him, Yassin's fate really was in the hands of Allah.

We were shown to a large tiled room and told to set up for the interview. The room was sparsely furnished with four bed frames at one end and a bookcase at the other. It reminded me of a giant loo; not what I expected as the backdrop for an interview with a notorious militant leader.

Twenty minutes later, Yassin was wheeled in by one of his bodyguards. He looked the same in person as he did in the posters plastered around Gaza. He reminded me of a wizard with his long thin nose and flowing white beard. I'd read that he'd been paralysed in a sporting accident during his youth. Even after all those years, you could see how he'd once been physically strong.

Yassin greeted us in the thin, soft voice of someone with limited lung capacity. I couldn't imagine him delivering a sermon his followers could hear, let alone one that would inspire them to commit suicide. Once the interview got under way, however, I started to understand how Yassin could appeal to the disillusioned, frustrated and hopeless.

Yassin's self-belief was the exact opposite of his physical state; powerful and unyielding. He spoke with tremendous confidence and I could see how desperate people would gravitate to him. When he was asked why he sent out suicide bombers, Yassin answered without skipping a beat that the Palestinians had their backs against the wall. The Israelis had attack helicopters, fighter aircraft, tanks and artillery while the Palestinians had nothing. The suicide bomber, he argued, was the only way to even things up.

When he was asked why he condoned the killing of innocent civilians, Yassin answered that there were no civilians in Israel. In his view, every Israeli was a legitimate military target; the old had served in the military, the young people were in the military and the children would be one day. Yassin also justified his actions by arguing that the Palestinians had no superpower backing on the world stage; in his words, the west is quick to condemn a suicide bombing in Israel but nothing is said when the Israelis bomb a Palestinian neighbourhood.

The irony wasn't lost on me. Yassin was justifying suicide bombings by evoking a scenario straight out of the Hebrew Bible: David versus Goliath. But in Yassin's version, Goliath was the Jew, David the 'Philistine' and the slingshot had been updated to an explosive vest.

Almost two years after that interview, the Israelis finally assassinated Yassin, but his violent legacy lives on. His followers continue to sacrifice themselves in order to kill others. Perhaps that's because like the biblical David, Yassin was convinced that religious superiority would allow him and his supporters to triumph over a stronger enemy.

I'm not religious, so I'll never understand that way of thinking, but seeing Yassin speak in person gave me a newfound respect for the power of religious conviction. Yassin's brand of radical Islam had already inspired the 11 September hijackers. Soon, it would spread to nearly every frontier of the War on Terror, creating security challenges that would change The Circuit beyond recognition.

CHAPTER 7

In September 2002 I ventured on a third trip to Jerusalem, again advising CNN. The day I landed, a Palestinian suicide bomber attacked a bus in Tel Aviv, killing half a dozen people and injuring more than fifty. Israel responded by immediately launching another incursion into the West Bank. That evening, I met with CNN's Jerusalem bureau chief to see what he needed security-wise to cover the story.

The timing of those events couldn't have been worse for the bureau chief. He had no available shooters to send to Ramallah, his backup correspondent had just rotated out of Jerusalem and a replacement wouldn't arrive for several days. CNN was in a bind. If the network didn't establish an immediate presence in Ramallah, it risked falling behind its competitors in terms of coverage. Moreover, if the Israelis locked down the city, which they almost certainly would, it would be extremely difficult to get a crew in there without someone in situ to help them negotiate the checkpoints.

I suggested to the bureau chief that as an interim measure I go to Ramallah with a live truck and engineer and work with a cameraman from TV Ramattan. That way CNN could have live pictures of what was happening and an adviser on site to help a crew get in safely, once one became available. The bureau chief told me to leave for Ramallah first thing in the morning.

Fortunately, Nihal, the young female Palestinian producer I'd worked with during Operation Defensive Shield, had been visiting relatives in Ramallah when the IDF armour started rolling in. We linked up in Ramattan Studios where she'd already finalized arrangements for a cameraman to be loaned to CNN.

We'd been in Ramattan less than thirty minutes when news filtered in that the Israelis were attacking Arafat's compound. The story was confirmed by our own ears; we could hear the sound of heavy machine-gunfire coming from the location of the Mukhata. It was looking like Operation Defensive Shield all over again.

Nihal had a great idea of where to set up operations. She knew a woman who owned a house approximately two hundred yards from the centre of the Mukhata. After a bit of negotiating, Nihal convinced the woman to rent CNN her rooftop for two hundred dollars a week. It was money well spent. The rooftop position allowed us to see the Israeli security cordon in incredible detail. For the next forty-eight hours, CNN owned the story. The cameraman, a young Palestinian lad, worked day and night without a break, filming Israeli tanks and bulldozers laying siege to the compound. The live truck engineer also worked tirelessly feeding out pictures.

On the second night, the Israelis suddenly floodlit the area. Bulldozers began chipping away at some of the perimeter buildings, but the reason for the lights wasn't immediately clear. Then, around 3 a.m., the tanks backed off and IDF engineers wired one of the buildings with explosives. I was just about to phone the Jerusalem bureau with the information when there was an almighty explosion. Debris from the blast went flying over our heads. When the smoke cleared, the building was gone. It had been levelled to the ground. From a clinical standpoint I had to admire the skill with which the Israeli engineers had placed the explosives; the building dropped like a stack of cards. CNN was over the moon with the pictures.

By day three, the bulk of the international press corps was attempting to enter Ramallah. The IDF was patrolling the streets aggressively and many journalists were turned away.

Once again, CNN's leading-edge reporting hadn't won it any

friends in the IDF. Several Israeli patrols tried to kick us off the roof. Each time we were harassed, I'd produce the 'lease' to prove that we were legitimate residents who had every right to be there.

Naturally, other news organizations tried to ride CNN's coattails. I lost count of how many snappers (stills photographers) and crews from other organizations tried to climb up on our roof. Some had the cheek to walk up there without even asking first. I'd show them right back down. I'm all for helping other networks and especially snappers (photojournalists usually work alone and for very little pay compared to their paparazzi counterparts), but I didn't want other journalists compromising our position. The IDF had already escorted two rival news crews off the rooftops of nearby buildings and out of Ramallah.

By day four, CNN was finally able to get a correspondent and shooter to Ramallah, not that there was much of the Mukhata left to film by that point. Most of the compound had either been blown up or knocked down. Even the main building housing Arafat had sustained structural damage.

Once again there was tremendous world pressure for the Israelis to back off. As the siege dragged on I thought for sure Arafat would either be killed outright or kidnapped and forced out of the country. Israel's tactic of cutting power and water to the Mukhata also posed a graver threat to Arafat's health, given the time of year. September is very hot in that part of the world and the searing midday heat would make the crowded, primitive living conditions inside the Mukhata that much more unbearable.

On day ten of the siege CNN got word that the Israelis had bowed to world pressure and were planning to pull back from the Mukhata. Ramallah was absolutely buzzing with press by that point so if CNN was going to be the first network in to see Arafat, we'd have to move fast.

CNN had learned that a United Nations envoy was in Ramallah waiting to meet with Arafat as soon as the Israelis withdrew. I figured that if we could find the UN convoy we could latch onto the back of it and beat everyone else to the punch.

I loaded the correspondent and the cameraman into the Land Rover. After searching a few streets, we found the UN convoy; it was fronted by an Israeli escort vehicle. I stayed back until the convoy moved off, at which point I crept up behind the UN vehicles. I tailed them as inconspicuously as possible until the Mukhata was in sight. Just before we reached the entrance, I hit the gas and overtook both the UN vehicles and the Israeli escort. As far as the IDF knew, we were just part of the convoy. We drove straight past the Israeli security cordon and right up to Arafat's front door. For CNN, the story ended just as it had started; with the rest of the press corps playing catch-up.

This time, there would be no exclusive with Arafat. He held a press conference though he did throw out the first question to CNN. Once the dust settled and the cameras stopped rolling, Arafat walked over to me. He took my hand firmly in both of his and looked at me with a big grin on his face.

'Bob, have you got my flag?' he asked, keeping his hands locked on mine.

I looked down at him and smiled. 'What flag, General Arafat?'

When I retired from the Regiment, I thought I was saying goodbye to the most exciting era of my life. As it turned out the Regiment was just a warm-up; working with the media in the West Bank and Gaza was more exhilarating than anything I'd done in the military.

I didn't take for granted how rare it is for a man approaching fifty to experience a professional renaissance. I felt enormously fortunate and was delighted by this new market opening up for The Circuit. I couldn't see myself looking after billionaires ever again.

Over a six-month period, I'd advised my clients through two

Israeli incursions into Palestinian territories, one Hamas operation and interviews with Yasir Arafat and a notorious Islamic radical. With each assignment I learned something new about my job, my clients and the nature of insurgency.

I couldn't have known it then, but those lessons would resonate through every assignment I'd accept from 2002 onwards. I would have been perfectly content to continue working with the media in Israel and Palestine but by the start of 2003, The Circuit's attention was turning elsewhere. I started getting calls asking if I'd be interested in working with the media in Iraq – should the need arise.

PART TWO

THE BOOM YEARS

CHAPTER 8

We knew instantly that it wasn't just the Americans who had fired on the ITN journalists. The scorched chassis of the crew's 4x4 had incoming bullet holes on both sides; clear evidence of a two-way contact. It didn't take a genius to figure out they'd been caught in crossfire.

Back in Hereford, we wanted to believe that we were heading to Iraq on a rescue mission. Despite the wreckage in front of us, we couldn't rule that out, nor did we want to. We had signed on to this job with the intention of finding the men alive and returning them home safely to their families. That alone was enough to keep us going. But time was working against us. It had been nearly a fortnight since the men had vanished in a hail of gunfire and the trail that could lead us to them grew colder with each passing minute. If we were to have any hope of finding them alive we'd first have to suss out exactly what had happened. We needed to conduct a thorough and meticulous forensic investigation of the incident area; which in this case, happened to be in an active war zone sandwiched between the British Army and Iraqi troops loyal to Saddam Hussein.

Five days earlier, the Iraqi desert was the last place I expected to be. I was on home leave watching the opening days of Gulf War II unfold on TV. It was the first time in my adult life that my country had gone to war and I wasn't a soldier. Admittedly, I made a lousy spectator. I was so hacked off by the reporting that I spent most of my time shouting at the television. The major networks were plastered with coverage from correspondents 'embedded' with military units in Kuwait and Iraq. Some of the embedded journalists were giving the impression that they were right where the action was, but at the start of Gulf War II most of the broadcasters at least were miles behind the front lines. I couldn't believe how many reporters were using military phrases out of context or big-timing it like they were combat soldiers themselves. It was like watching actors on a film set, not genuine journalists covering a real war.

There was a handful of established correspondents on embeds but many appeared to be young and very green. Not that it seemed to matter. The embed was a novelty so, experienced or not, embedded journalists got the most airtime. Meanwhile, many veteran war correspondents who could offer serious analysis were left struggling for something compelling to report.

Terry Lloyd fell into that category. A highly regarded ITN war correspondent, like many un-embedded journalists, Terry and his crew had been sitting in Kuwait City waiting for British troops to invade the southern Iraqi city of Basra.

The invasion of Iraq began on 20 March 2003. The next day, Terry and three ITN crew members crossed the border from Kuwait into Iraq. The following day, 22 March, Terry and his crew attempted to enter Basra unilaterally ahead of British forces. They never made it. The ITN crew were attacked on the outskirts of Basra. Terry was killed. One member of his crew, Belgian cameraman Daniel Demoustier, managed to escape to safety. The two remaining crew members, cameraman Fred Nerac and translator Hussein Osman, were missing.

I was as surprised as anyone by the news. Not because Terry was a so-called 'seasoned' war reporter (I'd worked with the media long enough by that point to know that 'seasoned' meant little more than 'lucky'), but because what he and his crew had attempted struck me as nothing short of foolhardy. As I watched the various media outlets turn the story over and over, I kept wondering about the two missing men. Were they alive? Had they been captured? Were they riding it out in a safe house in Basra? I'd never met Fred Nerac or Hussein Osman, but I felt for them and their families.

Fred and Hussein had been missing for five days when I received the call at home from AKE asking if I would go to Basra as part of a two-man team to investigate what had become of them.

I wanted to say yes immediately, but before I committed to anything, I needed to know who I'd be working with. My partner would definitely need to know his way around a hostile environment. At that stage, Basra hadn't fallen to the British and irregular Iraqi forces known as the Fedayeen were proving far more formidable than the coalition had bargained for. It was also important that whoever I teamed with was physically capable of handling the assignment. I knew first hand how challenging the Iraqi desert could be having spent six consecutive weeks there during Gulf War I undertaking operations with the Regiment.

AKE told me I'd be working with a highly regarded lad I'll call Martin. I accepted the assignment, though I had my doubts about what Martin and I could accomplish given how much time had already passed. It was imperative we get on the ground ASAP.

Ten days after Terry Lloyd and his crew were attacked, Martin and I boarded a flight from London to Kuwait. Before take-off, I bought a newspaper to see if anything new about the incident had hit the headlines. As I flipped through the pages, I came across an article that knocked me for six; a huge double-page spread featuring Daniel Demoustier, the only member of Terry's crew who made it to safety. In the article, Daniel gave a blow-by-blow account of what took place on the outskirts of Basra that day. Topping it off was a huge photo of Daniel, posing on the balcony of his Kuwait City hotel room. Cuts and bruises were visible on his face.

I was stunned. Coverage of the Terry Lloyd story had died down but that interview threw it right back into the spotlight, a highly dangerous development from my perspective. Martin and I had to assume we weren't the only ones interested in finding Fred and Hussein. If Iraqi hardliners wanted to get their hands on the men, that story would give them an excellent reference point to start looking (assuming they weren't holding them already). I ripped the article from the newspaper, folded it up and tucked it in my shirt pocket.

We landed in Kuwait City at midday local time and headed straight to the hotel where ITN had set up a temporary bureau to coordinate its war coverage. We needed to talk to Daniel personally to see if there were any additional details he could offer that he hadn't already discussed with the press.

We were met in the lobby by an ITN senior producer who led us to a suite where Daniel was waiting to speak to us. Martin and I were anxious to get the briefing over with as quickly as possible. We desperately wanted to get across the Iraqi border and to the incident area before sundown. Also, the hotel was very plush and I didn't want to get too comfortable. For five days I'd been gearing up mentally to live rough in a desert hellhole.

The producer began the brief, calmly relaying information ITN had been able to gather behind the scenes. She told us that Terry's body had been identified in one of Basra's main hospital morgues by a news crew working for the Arab television news network al Jazeera. ITN was working with the Iraqi Red Crescent to repatriate his remains. As for information on Fred and Hussein, ITN had nothing.

Throughout the producer's brief, Daniel remained remarkably composed. When it was his turn to speak, however, his unruffled façade grew more and more agitated. What Daniel told us was almost word for word what I'd read in the paper that morning. On 22 March, he and the rest of his team headed towards Basra believing the city's fall was imminent. The crew were travelling in two Mitsubishi 4x4s, clearly marked with the letters TV. Daniel drove the lead vehicle with Terry as passenger, while Fred and Hussein followed behind. Anticipating a long assignment, the crew had mounted extra stores of petrol, food and water on the roof of the front vehicle.

En route, the crew were stopped at a British military checkpoint and warned not to go any further. They were told that battles were going on and it was very dangerous. The crew ignored the warning and pressed on towards Basra.

Daniel recalled that as the crew neared the outskirts of the city, they passed a US mortar position to the right off the main highway they were travelling along. Half a mile further up on the left, he remembered seeing a row of tanks and APCs set 100–200 metres off the road. Both military units were facing north towards Basra.

The crew pushed past these positions and continued towards Basra. Approximately one kilometre outside the city, they came to a hump bridge that crossed a canal (Basra is built on marshland with small canals criss-crossing reclaimed areas). According to Daniel, it was at that point he and Terry saw armed Iraqi men coming towards them. The Iraqis were on foot and riding in vehicles including a white pickup truck with a large machine gun mounted on the back. The occupants of the pickup were waving their hands. Daniel thought they were trying to surrender to them.

Daniel and Terry didn't like the look of the situation, so they did a U-turn. Daniel was certain Fred and Hussein followed suit. The Iraqis pursued them. After two hundred metres or so, Daniel recalled seeing Fred and Hussein's vehicle slow or possibly stop before speeding up again.

As Daniel and Terry drove back down the main highway, the white pickup truck pulled up along their left side – an action which effectively sandwiched them between the Iraqis in the pickup and the US armour positioned off the main road. The Iraqis in the pickup were waving at Daniel to stop; he still thought they wanted to surrender.

Daniel described what happened next as an explosion of gunfire, windows shattering and the sound of bullets ripping through the vehicle. Daniel remembered seeing Terry's passenger door open; Terry wasn't there anymore. Daniel ducked down and tucked his body underneath the steering wheel until the vehicle came to a stop. The next thing he remembered was the petrol cans on the roof exploding. He abandoned the vehicle and scurried for what little cover he could find on the ground.

Daniel said he lay low while machine guns fired all around him. He was sure that the Americans were the ones doing the firing, not the Iraqis. While he was taking cover, Daniel spotted Fred and Hussein's vehicle stopped about thirty metres away from his position on the same side of the road. Daniel said he saw Fred wave to him from a piece of shallow ground.

I interrupted and asked him whether he thought Hussein would have stood a chance of escaping the vehicle and finding cover as well.

Daniel said it was entirely possible but he didn't recall seeing any sign of Hussein. He was convinced, however, that the US military were the only ones firing at the vehicles. On this point Daniel seemed adamant: the Yanks had shot Terry.

I took everything Daniel said with a grain of salt. I didn't think he was trying to mislead us, but I was very much aware of the fact that Daniel was a civilian who had suddenly found himself in a combat situation. It would have been nothing short of remarkable if his recollections were 100 per cent accurate. It must have been horrendous for him; a series of flashes and bangs, the shock of looking to the passenger seat and discovering Terry wasn't there, the terrifying prospect that he himself might not survive.

I knew Daniel had been traumatized but I had to press him for the sake of Fred and Hussein. I asked him if he was absolutely certain he had seen Fred wave to him. The question must have struck a nerve; Daniel snapped at me from across the table 'Of course it was him! We've known each other for years. He's my best friend!'

I apologized but told him that Martin and I were about to go forward and risk our lives in much the same manner as he and his team had done; unilaterally and without immediate backup if things turned ugly. I also reminded him that we too had families waiting for us back home.

Recalling the incident in detail had clearly left Daniel shattered, but we had one last point to cover with him. I took the newspaper clipping from my pocket, unfolded it on the table, stared him right in the eye and asked him why he had given an interview. He said, rather defensively, that he had told a media friend what had happened and that he never intended for the story to be published. When I pressed him about the photograph, he claimed that it was just an innocent snapshot.

I wasn't trying to harass David. The only reason I had brought it up at all was to make the point that, from a security perspective, the more the incident was discussed in the press, the more it could compromise our mission and possibly the safety of Fred and Hussein.

At the end of the briefing the producer handed us a stack of 'missing' posters with pictures of Fred and Hussein and captions underneath in Arabic and English. Martin and I thanked her and told her we were sure the men's families would appreciate her efforts.

After the briefing, we lost no time preparing to leave for Iraq. ITN had hired us a soft-skinned Mitsubishi Shogun which they'd kindly stocked with plenty of food, water and spare fuel. They'd also included baby wipes which more than likely would be our only means of personal hygiene for the foreseeable future. Martin and I promised each other we'd refer to them as 'man wipes' for the duration of our assignment.

We checked over the vehicle and changed a few things around to suit our requirements such as fitting our GPS and satellite communications and taping the letters TV to the sides and bonnet. Our thinking was that all foreigners operating around Basra would be thrown into two categories: military and press. Though technically we weren't either, we were working in the service of the media. By taking on the appearance of journalists, we could maintain a lower profile.

Next, we checked all our communications equipment: mobile phones, a set of two-way hand-held radios and satellite phones. We made sure our medical grab bag was handy as well as our helmets should we drive into mortar fire or any such dramas. Finally, we performed one final check of all the equipment and vehicle ancillaries, fitted our body armour and headed towards the border. In some respects, it was like being a soldier again, with one crucial exception; we were heading into a war zone unarmed.

I had a feeling of déjà vu as we drove through the desert, especially as we approached the border with Iraq. The smell of wild herbs growing on rocky outcrops and the brilliant orange of the late afternoon sun reminded me of the first Gulf War. Back then, however, I crossed into Iraq from Saudi Arabia in the middle of nowhere under cover of darkness.

My entrance this time would prove much more bureaucratic. Martin and I were forced to queue at a border checkpoint with loads of other vehicles. Driving around it through the desert wasn't possible as the border was lined with a fifteen-foot-high berm that ran as far as the eye could see. APCs and other armoured vehicles were spread intermittently along it, all of them facing north towards Iraq.

I looked at my watch. We still had a couple of hours of

daylight left; enough time to get to the incident area for a quick sweep. Unfortunately, the Kuwaitis couldn't give a toss about our timetable. They refused to let us cross, saying we didn't have 'official' clearance.

As fate would have it, a convoy of British Royal Military Police came along. We explained our situation to them. They understood the urgency of our mission and put in a call to their Colonel back in Kuwait City. After a few nerve-racking exchanges between the British Colonel and Kuwaiti border officials we were cleared to go.

We cracked over the border and drove as fast as we could towards the incident area. Time was now very much against us. The desert highway was initially very quiet but as soon as we hit a small village we encountered hostile crowds along the roadside. We had no time for dramas, so we pulled off the road and drove through the desert. Only when the village was well behind us did we return to the main highway.

The sight of the aggressive crowds left me feeling a bit unsettled. It was a stern reminder that we were travelling in a war zone unarmed and in a soft-skinned vehicle. There was little we could do about our transport, but it was down to us to rectify our 'unarmed' status soonest.

By the time we reached the incident area, there was only ten minutes of daylight remaining; not nearly enough to leave our vehicle and examine the site up close. Through our windscreen, we could see the burnt-out wreckage of the incident lying virtually undisturbed on either side of the highway. Even from a distance, the violence of the encounter was brutally apparent. To the west was the charred chassis of Daniel and Terry's vehicle stuck in the mud twenty yards from the road. To the east lay the remains of the Fedayeen pickup truck with the machine gun monopod mounted on the rear. We also identified a burnt-out saloon car. There was no sign of Fred and Hussein's vehicle.

It was an incredible let-down to have waited so long and come so far only to have to postpone our investigation yet another day. At least we'd got our bearings to give us a running start in the morning.

CHAPTER 9

With twilight descending, we turned around and headed for a holding area or 'hub' the British military had set up for the press corps approximately four miles south of the incident area. ITN had alerted the hub commanders about our mission and got permission for us to stay there.

Roughly the size of a football pitch, the hub housed around a dozen journalists and a mix of about three dozen full-time troops and part-time Territorial Army soldiers. The first thing Martin and I did when we arrived was check in with the commander to make sure he was OK with us staying there. He told us it wouldn't be a problem. We were chuffed to bits. We were prepared to sleep rough in the desert on our own. Now we had the luxury of sleeping rough surrounded by barbed wire. For the media, however, the hub's facilities – tents, trailers and no showers – must have seemed dreadfully basic.

We set up camp in the car park on the ground next to our vehicle. That way, if the hub was attacked in the middle of the night, we could move off quietly and crack on with our assignment. It may sound harsh, but we couldn't afford to get side-tracked into a battle between the Fedayeen and the troops at the hub. Our sole reason for being there was to find Fred and Hussein. We had to stay focused on our mission for their sakes.

The temperature had plummeted to near freezing by the time we settled in for the night. The Iraqis had set fire to oil pipelines around Basra to deter missile strikes from coalition aircraft and the smell of burning oil polluted the crisp night air. As I crawled into my sleeping bag, images of the incident area flooded my head. I wondered if Fred and Hussein were alive somewhere behind the fires encircling Basra. I dearly hoped so.

Martin and I woke just before first light. We'd spent the night in bivvy bags; Gortex covers that can serve as one-man tents or as an extra layer over a sleeping bag. They were just the ticket for protecting us against the freezing climate. Thankfully, I knew what to expect weather-wise. During the first Gulf War, Iraq had one of its coldest winters on record. I spent six weeks with my squadron sleeping and operating in the open air; no tents, not even covered vehicles. The conditions were so bitter that the skin on our hands cracked and bled to the point where we found it difficult to cock our weapons.

I only wished that this time we had weapons to handle. Not every assignment on The Circuit calls for an adviser to be armed. I've worked in places for example where local law wouldn't allow me to carry weapons. Arming in the West Bank and Gaza made no sense; it would have increased the risk to myself and my clients by classing us as combatants.

On this assignment, however, weapons were a must. Not only were we in an active war zone, but Terry's fate had demonstrated that the Fedayeen regarded all westerners, including journalists, as targets. We needed to be able to defend ourselves effectively. That's not to say that if we did manage to procure weapons we'd flaunt them or abandon our TV cover. We wanted to move around as inconspicuously as possible.

The night before, we'd asked one of our military hosts at the hub if he could find us some weapons. He said he'd see what he could do. Martin also phoned one of his infantry contacts operating in our vicinity to see if he could help us out.

After a quick wash with the 'man wipes' Martin and I headed to the canteen for a brew and breakfast. The hub kindly supplied us with ration packs; something I hadn't tasted for nine years. Sadly, they hadn't changed. After breakfast, our lot improved quickly. One of our hub 'hosts' came through with two 9 mm pistols with magazines and ammunition. I told Martin I felt better but I'd feel a whole lot better if we could get our hands on assault rifles. Someone's ears must have been burning because no sooner had I said it than Martin got a call on his satellite phone; it was his contact, an ops officer operating locally with a British military unit. He told Martin he had something for him.

We drove a couple of miles north of the hub to where the British military had set up a FOB, forward operations base. The ops officer was very busy but he found time to shake our hands and chat briefly about the war. We asked him when he thought Basra might be taken. He said the Brits could have done it already but politics, specifically American agendas, were dictating the timing of the invasion. He said he hoped it would be a matter of days and not weeks, then handed us a heavy blue mail bag.

I looked inside the bag; there were two AK47s in very good condition with twelve magazines full of ammunition. I felt like a kid on Christmas morning – Martin and I were beaming. We thanked the ops officer profusely. There he was busy fighting a war with his own lads to look after, and he still found time to help us out. He was a very good Rupert (officer) indeed.

We were anxious to get out to the incident area to start our investigation, but first, we had to test-fire our new weapons. There was a track off the main highway near the area which we wanted to recce, so we decided to kill two birds with one stone and fire our weapons there.

The track was made of gravel and dirt and moved east in a straight line from the highway to a small industrial park three miles away. The first third of the track was bordered by irrigation ditches which by that point had become filled with pools of thick, black tar that had seeped in from the canals surrounding Basra. In addition to setting the oil pipelines on fire, the Iraqis had also dumped oil in the canals with an eye towards igniting them once the British launched a full-scale invasion.

Driving down the track, I felt like we were slicing through two realities; to our left the billowing soot from burning oil pipelines consumed the sky like a creeping black cancer. To our right, the sky was big, blue and blindingly clear. After about half a mile, we passed a group of Red Crescent volunteers whom we identified from the crimson emblems on their shirts. They were pulling dead Iraqis out of the irrigation ditches. The oil-soaked corpses were a gruesome sight, but I thought at least the bodies had fallen into shallow pools where they could be seen and recovered. Had they been disposed of in deeper canals, no one would ever know for sure what had happened to those people.

After two miles we pulled over onto a patch of broken ground. We got out of our vehicle and scanned the area to ensure that no one was in viewing distance. It looked good. We couldn't even hear the traffic from the main highway. Improvising targets from tufts of weeds and debris, we test-fired our weapons and magazines and zeroed the sights to our eyes. To our delight, everything worked perfectly. I tucked my pistol inside the front flap of my body armour where it would be hidden from view but close at hand. Martin and I then positioned the AKs inside the vehicle where we could get to them quickly. Finally, we wrapped the extra magazines in small grab bags and tucked them between the seats.

The weapons sorted, we headed back up the track. Before we reached the highway, we decided to stop and search the irrigation ditches. We couldn't rule out the possibility that the bodies of Fred and Hussein had ended up there. Martin scanned the murky water to one side of the road while I trolled the other. After a few minutes, we noticed dust rising from a vehicle driving towards us from the highway. There was no activity at the industrial park so it was very possible that the vehicle had turned down the track for the sole purpose of checking us out.

I stayed on the road while Martin returned to our 4x4 to cover me with the AK. As the vehicle got closer I could see it contained four passengers, all male. I wondered what they were up to. If their intentions were innocent perhaps they'd be willing to talk. They could have information that could help us.

The vehicle slowed to a crawl twenty yards short of where I stood. The men were sizing me up, as I was them; they were all dressed in black and ranged in age from early twenties to mid-thirties. All the windows in their vehicle were rolled down.

I looked at Martin and he nodded back at me. I felt a whole lot safer knowing he had me covered. I kept my arms at my side and away from the flap of my body armour; I didn't want the men to think for a second that I might be armed.

As the vehicle drew level with me, I offered a traditional Arabic greeting. 'Sabah al khayr. Salam alay khum.' (Good morning. Peace be upon you.)

The men looked at me without smiling and greeted me back. My heart was thumping as my eyes bounced between them, searching for any hint of a weapon. If I saw one, I was ready to drop to one knee, take out my pistol and fire. With my magazine of thirteen rounds I could double-tap each one of them and still have five rounds left.

The vehicle passed me and crawled to Martin's position. They gave him a short wave, then picked up speed and continued down the track until they disappeared into a patch of dead ground.

I returned to our vehicle and asked Martin what he thought of the men. Martin said they didn't look friendly and it wouldn't surprise him if they were Fedayeen out on a recce.

Our first potential surveillance by the Fedayeen underscored just how challenging our investigation would be. Inspecting the scene of an incident in an active war zone is infinitely more difficult than conducting a forensic investigation in non-hostile circumstances. For example, there's no police tape to prevent people from tampering with evidence, not to mention looting it. The biggest difference, however, is time. When you're operating in an active war zone, you don't have all day to do your job. The longer you're on the ground the more you expose yourself to danger.

Martin and I reckoned we'd be operating in the same defined area for several days. Though we were trying our best to remain low profile, two Brits driving around in a well-supplied 4x4 on the outskirts of Basra still stuck out. It looked like the Fedayeen could already be observing us, assessing our movements, possibly with the intent to kidnap or kill. Martin and I were in Iraq to look for the missing, not to join them. With that in mind, we estimated we could spend fifteen to twenty minutes tops per day at the incident area without compromising ourselves or our mission.

The day before we'd done an initial cast thirty metres out from Terry's vehicle. Today, we wanted to get a good look up close, not only at Terry's 4x4 but at the Fedayeen truck as well. We also wanted to push out on both sides of the highway to see if there were any blood trails or signs of the missing men's bodies.

We pulled off the main highway across from Terry's vehicle. The road was busy with traffic; lorries, cars, people on bicycles going about their business. At times it was hard to believe there was a war on. Down the road, some forty metres south, a group of kids aged six to sixteen were playing around the burnt-out hulk of an Iraqi military truck. It looked as if the truck had been bombed from the air, and Iraqi artillery shells were strewn around the area. Some of the kids were playing with the live ammunition; kicking it, picking it up and aiming it at each other. That ammunition was incredibly delicate, having been burnt and then lying around in the hot sun. I said to Martin if one of those kids drops a shell the ground is going to shake. The kids were completely unaware of the dangers involved in what they were doing. It pained me to watch them. Martin and I desperately wanted to intervene but we were in no position to wander down the road and sort out a bunch of reckless kids. We had a job to do and we were already attracting enough attention just sitting by the side of the road.

We needed to be as inconspicuous as possible so we made the call to leave our AKs in our 4x4 and walk to the incident area armed only with concealed pistols.

We began by focusing on Terry's 4x4. It was so bullet ridden, it looked like a sieve. As we walked toward it, we noticed many fresh footprints on the surrounding ground, indicating that we weren't the first people to check it out. Being so badly shot up, the vehicle must have been a magnet for looters and curious onlookers. We approached our investigation systematically, beginning with a 360-degree survey of the wreckage. We found the number plate. Although badly burnt, enough remained for us to positively identify the vehicle as Terry's.

As we circled the 4x4, I kept two lists in my head; one containing details of Daniel's version of events and the other what I was seeing with my own eyes. We noted scorch marks on the roof of the vehicle which supported Daniel's description of the fuel cans exploding. But there was one key element of Daniel's story that wasn't adding up. He had seemed adamant that only the Americans had fired on them. But the vehicle before us had clearly been fired on from more than one direction.

We were beginning to build up a picture of what had really happened but we needed more evidence. Martin and I aligned ourselves with Terry's vehicle facing west where the US tanks would have been positioned some two hundred metres away. The remains of the Fedayeen pickup truck were right behind us. That placed Terry's 4x4 in a direct line between the Fedayeen and American forces. From where we stood, it looked like Daniel had definitely got it wrong; it wasn't just the Americans who had shot at them; the poor ITN lads had got themselves caught in crossfire.

We found further evidence of crossfire inside the vehicle. On the floor we picked up 7.62 mm long and 5.56 mm bullet heads – standard American issue. We also found 7.62 mm short bullet heads, a Russian-made calibre used by the Iraqis.

It didn't surprise me that Daniel could have got such a crucial detail of the incident wrong. The odds of surviving brutal crossfire are poor indeed. Martin and I were astonished Daniel had managed it. The whole episode must have left him in a state of deep shock.

With the clock moving against us we walked across the highway to see what the Fedayeen vehicle could tell us about what had really taken place. The Fedayeen pickup truck was only partially burnt. The wheels had been stolen but, as we'd noted already, it still had a Russian-made medium machine-gun monopod mounted on the back. The angle of the monopod was aimed through Terry's vehicle directly at the American tank position.

As far as we could tell the Iraqis had fought fiercely before succumbing to the Americans' superior firepower. There was still a lot of dried blood on the ground near the pickup truck. Inside, we found bits of flesh and bone along with 7.62 mm long and 5.56 mm bullet heads. Loads of empty ammunition cases and link littered the back of the pickup and surrounding ground. That showed us that the Fedayeen machine gunner had managed to put down a fair weight of fire before they were taken out.

We extended our search beyond the pickup along the east side of the highway. There were sections of large drainage pipes big enough for a man to walk through running north intermittently along the road. In between the pipes was a series of partially dug trenches.

We searched the pipes and ditches for the bodies of the missing lads but found nothing; no blood trails, no clothing. We also kept an eye out for wildlife that feed on decaying flesh, such as vultures, dogs, etc., but there appeared to be no animals like that in the area.

We still had one more vital point of Daniel's story to check out – one which we hoped would prove correct. We crossed back to the west side of the highway to search the area where Daniel had told us he'd seen Fred wave to him. There was a piece of dead ground where Fred could have taken cover; the area had a shallow puddle of water and scrub reaching eight feet tall. We searched the area as thoroughly as we could in the time we had remaining. We found nothing that could either prove or disprove what Daniel had told us.

By this point, we'd spent forty-five minutes on the ground; thirty minutes longer than we should have. We'd pushed ourselves to the limit for the sake of the two missing men, but it was time for us to get going.

CHAPTER 10

Day three of our investigation began with a heated exchange with a Rupert at the hub. Martin and I had spent another night sleeping on the ground next to our 4x4 in the vehicle holding area; which happened to be twenty yards from the communal toilets (upwind of course). Makeshift military toilets don't offer a great deal of privacy. They're basically a trench divided by screens tall enough to shield the lower half of the body. Not once in my entire twenty-three-year military career had I ever experienced a problem with this set-up. As far as I was concerned, any kind of toilet is a luxury in a war zone. A half-screened trench is better than a plastic bag (which was often my only option during Regiment operations).

Martin and I had just sat down to breakfast when a Territorial Army major started having a go at us. Apparently, a female soldier – also TA – had complained to him that we'd been staring at her while she went to the toilet that morning. The major told us we'd have to move from the car park and sleep in a tent with the rest of the media.

I was outraged and not just because Martin and I had been accused of being peeping Toms. We were sleeping in the car park because we felt it was vital to ensuring the success of our mission.

'I thought we were in the middle of a war,' I said to the major. 'If that lassie feels uncomfortable, why don't you put the men's toilets at one end of camp and the women's at the other, instead of picking on us?'

'We're all in the army together,' said the major, as if reading from an officer's manual. He then reminded me that we were lucky to be staying at the hub in the first place.

I was about to take his head from his shoulders when Martin grabbed my arm. I knew I'd better not say anything else or we wouldn't have a place to stay and army rations to eat. The entire episode, however, reinforced a belief that I'd held throughout my military career and still hold today: the TA infantry doesn't belong in war zones. Individually, most TA soldiers are well-meaning people. For some, the TA is a stepping stone to the regular army. And there are parts of the TA that work well in conflict areas, such as doctors and medics back at the rear, away from the front line. But in my view, a part-time soldier has part-time skills; a war situation requires full-time soldiers with full-time, up-to-date skills. You can't be a supermarket under manager one day and a front-line infanteer the next. I could never understand how over the past three decades, the government could disband or amalgamate great regular British Regiments while keeping TA units intact. It may have saved money and won some generals who dropped their pants for the politicians a few medals, but it ultimately weakened our armed forces.

Before leaving the hub for the incident area, Martin and I finalized our plan of action. The day before had given us a clearer picture of what had taken place on 22 March. We now wanted to get a good look at where the US mortar and tank positions had been, but our priority was to gather intelligence that could lead us to Fred and Hussein. It was imperative we widen our investigation to the bridge leading to Basra and possibly beyond. We had to determine whether it was feasible to probe into the outskirts of the city and make contact with locals. It was entirely possible that someone inside Basra had information about the missing men.

Our first stop was where Daniel recalled seeing the US mortar unit. We pulled off the main highway, drove forty metres east and got out of our vehicle. The ground was littered with empty mortar bomb boxes. We concluded that the unit must have been protecting US tanks probing towards the main bridge into Basra.

Next, we headed to where the US tanks would have been located. A west-bearing road branched off the main highway approximately fifty yards south of where the burnt and bullet-ridden remains of Terry's vehicle lay. We drove one hundred yards down the road and got out. Tank tracks were etched into the sand indicating that a group of five armoured vehicles had been positioned thirty metres apart. Ammunition containers and empty American ration packs were spread across the desert floor.

On closer inspection we could see empty cases and link from where the US troops had fired machine guns. The calibres corresponded with the bullet heads we'd found in Terry's vehicle and in the Fedayeen pickup truck. We took bearings with a compass from the different tank positions. Terry's vehicle sat smack in the middle of the line of fire.

Everything pointed to what we'd already established; there had been a firefight between the Americans and the Fedayeen. The only thing we couldn't work out was who had fired first. In the end, however, there was a war on. The Americans had been in a great position to see the Fedayeen pickup flanked by the ITN 4x4s driving towards them. It didn't matter that ITN had put TV stickers on their vehicles. What the Americans would have homed in on was the machine gun sticking out the top of the Fedayeen vehicle. The Americans would have concluded, and rightly so, that they were about to be attacked.

Having checked out the mortar and armoured positions, we headed up the road towards the bridge where Daniel had told us they'd been confronted by the Fedayeen. We stopped to talk to a British reconnaissance unit stationed a couple of hundred yards short of it. Some of the lads warned us that they'd been taking mortar fire that morning from Iraqis stationed on the other side of the bridge and that we shouldn't go any further. The lads didn't know exactly who was targeting them: regular Iraqi troops, Fedayeen or both. Whoever it was they weren't letting up. While we were talking, a group of Iraqi civilians travelling out of Basra drove past us screaming 'Midfa huwaan! Midfa huwaan!' (Mortars! Mortars!)

Soft-skin vehicles are no match for mortars, so Martin and I decided to leave the bridge until later and go back to the incident area to regroup. When we got there, we pulled up on the east side of the highway and turned our vehicle towards Basra to monitor the situation. The bulk of the traffic on the highway was heading south – away from Basra and the mortar fire. As Martin and I sat discussing what to do next, two vehicles with 'TV' taped to the sides drove past us heading north; right into the fighting.

We shook our heads in disbelief. Hadn't the media learned anything from what had happened to Terry Lloyd? Basra was still under Iraqi control and there was another group of journalists trying to get ahead of the situation with no concept of the danger involved.

Not long after they passed, the TV vehicles had turned around and were heading back our way. They pulled off the road and stopped right in front of us. They probably assumed from the TV letters on the side of our 4x4 that we were press as well. I got out to talk to them (I felt like I was about to discipline my children).

The two vehicles contained four Scandinavian journalists and two Kuwaiti translators. The Scandinavians had Arab shamaghs wrapped around their heads and necks. I asked them what they were doing. As I suspected, they were trying to get into Basra. I asked them if they were aware of what had happened to Terry Lloyd. They had no idea what I was talking about.

A quick glance inside their vehicle confirmed that they were indeed clueless about the environment in which they were operating. Their body armour and helmets were stashed in bags in the back of their truck. When were they planning to put them on? After shrapnel ripped through their flesh?

When I asked why they'd stopped, they said it was to warn us about a 'road accident' up ahead. I told them that they were mistaken; there was no road accident. Traffic was turning around to avoid mortar fire.

'What mortar fire?' they asked.

I told them that the Iraqis had been firing on British positions that morning. Then I pointed to Terry's vehicle and gave them a sobering blow-by-blow account of what had happened to him and his crew. The Scandinavians were speechless.

When I asked if they had security, I wasn't surprised to hear they had none.

'Medical facilities?' I asked.

None, they replied. But they did have two cases of beer.

'Fellas, go back to Kuwait and drink your beer,' I said.

I watched them drive south down the highway. I never saw them again. I hope they took my advice and didn't stop until they reached Kuwait.

As I walked back to our vehicle, Martin called to me. 'Over there,' he said, pointing across the highway.

An old white 1970s sedan had pulled off the highway and come to a full stop. I watched as a short, round, middle-aged man climbed out of the driver's side, walked to the front of the car and put up the bonnet. I counted three others inside the vehicle: two men and a boy who looked about twelve. They were all staring at me.

The round man smiled and waved. I returned the gesture. He took that as an invitation to walk across the highway and say hello.

I stayed on my side of the road to meet him, safe in the knowledge that Martin had me covered from our vehicle. I greeted the man in Arabic.

He replied in English and introduced himself. I'll call him Tariq. 'Do you need help?' he asked.

I looked at his vehicle. 'You're the one with the bonnet up. Can we help you?'

Tariq laughed. 'We have to keep bonnet open so people think we broke down.'

'Aren't you?' I asked.

'No,' he said. 'We see you stop at side of road and come to help. You are TV?'

Tariq didn't seem to be angling for a set-up. Perhaps he really did think we were in trouble. Or maybe he was curious. Either way, if he was from Basra, he could be a potential contact.

'Are you from Basra?'

'Yes,' said Tariq. 'I am marine engineer. I fix boat on Shaat al Arab (referring to the Shaat al Arab waterway). Come with me to my working place or you come with me to my house. My wife cook for you.'

He wasn't kidding. He really was inviting me to dinner.

'There's a war on, Tariq,' I said. 'I wouldn't be welcome in Basra.'

'But you are not American?'

'I'm British.'

'We like British!' he said.

I gestured towards his car on the other side of the highway. 'Who's the little boy?' I asked.

'My son,' he said. He nodded to the front seat. 'And they are my work partners. You can trust us all.'

'Are you in the Baath party?' I asked.

'Of course,' said Tariq.

He must have sensed some apprehension on my part. The Baath party was Saddam's eyes and ears in Iraq. 'Not all Baath party are bad,' he continued. 'If you want good life here, you join Baath party.'

Fair enough, I thought. Under Saddam, it was impossible to

do anything in Iraq without the approval of the Baath party. There had to be a fair amount of people who had joined out of convenience rather than conviction.

Still, a second opinion never hurts. My gut told me Tariq was legit, but I wanted to see what Martin thought of him. I walked Tariq over to our vehicle, introduced him to Martin and then – with Martin watching – explained that we were looking for two journalists who'd gone missing in the area.

'Do you know anything about that?' I asked.

Tariq said he'd heard there were 'problems' the other week between the Fedayeen, Americans and a group of British journalists. 'I have many friends in Baath party. Also Fedayeen,' he said. 'Come with me now and we find out together what happen to your friends.'

I explained that it was far too dangerous for us to go to Basra at present. But if he could go, I'd pay him two hundred US dollars if he'd meet us tomorrow with the information.

'I don't sell information,' said Tariq. 'I here to help.'

I asked him to meet us at the same location the following morning at ten. If he did manage to find anything out, we'd take it from there.

Tariq agreed and we shook hands.

'We think these missing men are still alive,' I said. 'We desperately want to find them.'

'Of course,' he said. 'Inshahallah.' (God Willing.)

Tariq walked back across the highway and closed the bonnet of his car. His little boy waved to us through the back window as they drove off.

'What do you think?' asked Martin.

'If I went with my heart we'd be following him to Basra,' I said. 'But I'm going with my head. We need a while longer to trust him.'

CHAPTER 11

We woke the next morning with a renewed sense of urgency. The night before ITN Kuwait called to tell us that Terry's body had been collected from the morgue in Basra and was being repatriated to Britain. Tragic as Terry's death was, at least his family and loved ones wouldn't have to wonder what had become of him. With his body returned home they could say their final goodbyes.

I could only imagine the torment Fred and Hussein's families must have felt by that point. It had now been a fortnight since the incident and there was still no word on the men's whereabouts. I wanted to find answers for those families, even if those answers were tragic. I wanted them to have closure.

Martin and I were anxious to hear what Tariq had found out about the missing men. We arrived at the RV area an hour ahead of schedule to recce it. Though Martin and I were both of the opinion that Tariq was probably above board, we weren't willing to bet our lives on it.

There was a small track running east of the incident area that allowed us to lay off the main highway and view the RV through binos. We scanned the area, looking for signs of anyone lying low with the intent to ambush us. We were also worried about the possibility of someone planting an IED (improvised explosive device) in the area and detonating it upon our arrival (a precaution which at the time some people regarded as paranoid; it turned out we were way ahead of the game in terms of security concerns in Iraq).

At two minutes to ten, Tariq pulled up in his white sedan. I joked to Martin that I'd never thought I'd see the day when an Arab would show up two minutes early to a meeting instead of two hours late. Through my binos, I could see that he'd brought the same gang as the day before including his wee boy.

Tariq and one of the co-workers got out of the car. They assumed the same 'cover' as the day before, lifting the bonnet as if they had engine trouble.

It took only thirty seconds for Martin and me to drive the short distance up the road to meet Tariq. His little boy waved to us from the back window as we pulled up behind them. What an awfully big adventure for such a young lad.

Unlike the previous day, Martin and I decided beforehand that we'd both stay in our vehicle with the engine running for the duration of this meeting. We wanted the ability to get away quickly. I still didn't think Tariq had it in for us, but for all his good intentions, the Fedayeen could have pressured him into setting us up.

Tariq walked towards us and I rolled down the window to speak with him.

I wanted to cut to the chase. After a quick greeting I asked him if he'd learned anything about the two missing men.

'There is dead body of British or Russian man in Basra hospital,' he said.

I assumed he was talking about Terry.

'We're aware of that body, Tariq, and the situation is being dealt with as we speak,' I said. 'Did your contacts tell you anything else?'

'I meet with friend of mine,' Tariq continued. 'My friend Baath party associate with Fedayeen contact. He tell me the two journalists you look for – they taken from truck and shot dead.'

My heart sank as soon as the words left his mouth.

'Why did the Fedayeen shoot them?' I asked.

Tariq explained that the Fedayeen had stopped the men on the Basra side of the bridge just up the road from us. They

Another violent day in Ramallah. West Bank, 2002.

above An IDF patrol rests on a street corner in Ramallah. The Russian-Israeli soldier put the gun to my head approximately 600 metres from this location. West Bank, 2002.

Palestinians rally in support of Yasir Arafat during Operation Defensive Shield. Ramallah, 2002.

My favourite photograph. One of Arafat's PLO bodyguards stands inside a large hole punched into the Mukhata by Israeli forces during the ten-day siege of Arafat's compound. Ramallah, 2002.

The bridge leading to Basra where ITN's Terry Lloyd and his crew were apprehended by the Fedayeen. Basra, 2003.

The destroyed Iraqi ammunitions truck where young children were playing with live shells. Basra, 2003.

Statues of Iraqi generals who commanded during the Iran–Iraq War lining the Shaat al Arab waterway. The statues were torn down by the British following the 2003 invasion. Basra, 2003.

A motorway sign indicating we're not far from Baghdad city centre. I first saw this sign driving to Baghdad from Amman, Jordan, when doing so was still considered reasonably safe. Abu Ghraib, 2004.

OPPOSITE PAGE

top First light outside the Palestine Hotel, surrounded by rings of physical security. Baghdad, 2004.

bottom A view of a mosque from behind the security of the Palestine hotel. The statue on the right replaced the statue of Saddam Hussein that was pulled down by US troops following the fall of the Iraqi capital. Baghdad, 2004.

An old man dressed in traditional Kurdish clothing. Northern Iraq, 2004.

What remained of Nabil's restaurant, a favourite among westerners, including journalists, after it was attacked by a suicide car bomber. The incident was a wake-up call for internationals who believed they were somehow immune from Baghdad's escalating violence. Baghdad, 2004.

CNN Senior International Correspondent Nic Robertson and me on a hilltop overlooking the Afghan capital. Kabul, 2004.

A diversion on the Kabul to Kandahar road, one of many possible ambush locations. Afghanistan, 2004.

The left side of our convoy drivir
across the desert to Lashkar Gah.
We opted to drive off-road in
order to avoid Taliban and bandi
Afghanistan, 2004.

Our local drivers and guards blov
out air filters during one of sever
stops on the way to Lashkar Gah
Afghanistan, 2004.

Sculduggerers-in-arms: poppy
farmers, Afghan police, drug
lords and Taliban gather for the
eradication of a poppy field outsi
Lashkar Gah. Afghanistan, 2004.

wanted the journalists' vehicles to use as cover to attack American troops.

'What about the bodies. Where are they now?' I asked.

Tariq said he didn't know and that he'd asked his friends that same question. He was told the bodies could have been burnt, buried or dumped in the canals.

'Do you think you could find out what happened to them?' I asked. 'It's important we find out.'

'I don't know. I try,' said Tariq. 'Through my friend in Baath party I try to talk to Fedayeen man. He may know where to find bodies.'

I asked him if it would be possible for Martin and me to meet with the Fedayeen man. 'Would he come to see us?' I asked.

'He will not leave Basra,' said Tariq. 'But I go to Basra with you and you meet him there.'

At that moment, two attack helicopters flew overhead and fired missiles at targets inside Basra.

'Tariq, we can't trust the Fedayeen. I know you think Basra is a great place but for me and Martin it's very dangerous right now.'

Tariq looked up at the attack helicopters and then back at me. 'I understand.'

'Thank you, Tariq, for finding out what you did,' I said. 'It's dreadful news. We were really hoping the two men were still alive.'

'Sadly not,' said Tariq.

'Let's meet again tomorrow.' I pointed up the road. 'Do you see that track to the north of here on the right-hand side?'

'Yes, I know it,' said Tariq.

'We'll meet you there tomorrow at twelve o'clock,' I said. 'Please, if you can, try and find out from the Fedayeen man what happened to the bodies.'

'I try. I talk to man directly.' Tariq shook my hand and smiled. 'Tomorrow you be late again?'

Martin and I were left in a very difficult situation. Had Fred and Hussein really got shot? All we had at that point was the evidence we'd gathered from the incident area and an unconfirmed story from a local informant. We had established more or less what had happened to Terry and Daniel but until we had concrete proof, we had no way of knowing for sure what had become of Fred and Hussein.

It was frustrating to think that the clues had run dry. Martin and I looked down the highway towards the bridge. If Tariq was lying or his information was wrong and the two lads were alive, then it was possible they were being held captive or holed up in a safe house in Basra.

If Tariq was right, and Fred and Hussein had been shot where he said, then their bodies had to be somewhere in the vicinity. Our searches through the ditches and dead ground around the incident area had turned up nothing. We didn't have the time or equipment to drag the oil-soaked canals. That left the hospital morgues in Basra.

The problem was, of course, that the city had yet to fall to the British. The Brits had the ability to take Basra at any time but as we'd learned through our conversations with the military, politics not military imperatives were dictating the timing of the invasion. The Yanks were calling the shots and their priority was Baghdad. It could be weeks before the Americans gave the British Army the green light. In the meantime, more and more people were dying in and around Basra either through direct targeting or collateral damage. The bodies would be piling up in the morgues and Iraqis throughout the city would be searching for their missing loved ones.

Dead or alive, one thing was certain; our chances of finding Fred and Hussein were very remote by that point. We didn't have the luxury of waiting for the British to capture the city. We needed to go to Basra now.

Having made up our minds to give it a go, Martin and I drafted a strategy. We agreed that we'd travel slowly with the modest intention of penetrating the outer edge of the city. We would advance further towards the centre only if circumstances allowed.

If either of us felt at any point that we were being compromised, we'd pull back immediately – no discussion.

We drove down the highway and pulled over two hundred yards south of the main bridge where Terry and his crew had been apprehended by the Fedayeen. The bridge rose in an arc over the canal. At its apex, it stood thirty feet above ground level. That meant that we'd be blinded driving up the bridge but have an excellent point from which to assess the road ahead once we reached the top.

I pulled out my binos and surveyed the landscape across the waterway. It was very similar to the incident area; flat desert broken up by patches of scrub and burned-out Iraqi armour. The road connecting the bridge to the city was approximately a mile long and flanked on both sides by metal telegraph poles and the odd building.

Attack helicopter blades clubbed the air above us as I folded away my binos. The sky was still clouded with soot from burning oil pipelines, punctuated by darker plumes drifting up from deep inside the city where the odd air strike had hit. There was no mistaking this was a full-scale war zone.

I stopped for a moment to think about what we were about to do; two unsupported civilians travelling in a soft-skin 4x4 through hostile territory hoping magically that we'd see a sign or meet someone who could lead us to the missing lads. I felt nervous, more nervous that at any other point during our mission.

It was late morning and traffic was moving steadily over the bridge. Martin and I agreed it was a good time to get going because we could merge with the flow and not stick out too much.

We turned onto the main highway just as two British military armoured recce vehicles drove past in the opposite direction. They were returning from a probe inside Basra and had strike marks on the sides and front where they had been hit with RPGs. Even with their superior firepower, the Brits weren't getting it all their own way. The Fedayeen may have been outnumbered, but they were tough – and often lethal.

My nerves grew raw as the bridge drew closer.

'Well, mate, here we go,' I said.

We kept up with traffic as we ascended the bridge, blind to any potential dangers lurking on the other side. When we hit the apex, the road into Basra spread out before us; I could see the outline of the city in the distance. To our right lay a burnt-out Iraqi tank with a fully loaded, heavy machine gun still mounted on the turret. The tank must have just been in a battle because the Iraqis hadn't stripped it yet for parts.

We cleared the apex and descended into the outskirts of Basra. There were no signs of Iraqi authorities as we advanced towards the city; no police, no military, no Fedayeen. We continued up the highway, passing pedestrians and the odd house and shop. I couldn't believe the buildings were still occupied. As we drove, Martin and I looked everywhere for possible clues; buildings, people, the landscape in between.

The glances from the faces we passed grew increasingly suspicious the closer we got to the city. People were paying very close attention to the road and our vehicle in particular. About five hundred yards short of the city's edge, we approached a shop where five men were gathered outside. As we drove into their line of vision, the men stopped talking and stared directly at us.

At that point, I knew we were pushing our luck. We drove forty yards past the shop and pulled over on the hard shoulder of the highway. We were so close to the city, we could have hopped there on one foot.

Martin and I looked at Basra as if it were a jewel dangling in front of us, but until the city was taken, it was too dangerous to go cold-calling on people when we couldn't be certain of their loyalties. Desperate as we were to get on with our investigation, we'd have to turn back.

By our fifth day on the ground, the morning chill had all but vanished from the air. The weather had locked step with the war; both were heating up.

We headed out early again for our meeting with Tariq. The day before had been enormously frustrating for Martin and me and we both had fingers crossed that Tariq would come back with a promising lead for us.

On our way to the meeting, we saw a British unit holed up away from the highway in a battered university complex. We pulled over to see if they could tell us anything about when the Brits would finally make their move. Talking to the soldiers, it was obvious they were frustrated by the delays. They knew that the longer they waited to launch a full-scale invasion, the more they exposed themselves to death and injury. They told us that the probes in and out of Basra were very hazardous. One light-tank commander described an ambush in which a Fedayeen soldier played dead on the side of the road, only to jump up and whack an RPG into the side of his tank. 'The Fedayeen are maniacs,' he said.

The suicidal tactics of the Fedayeen weren't their only worries; several of the more experienced soldiers we spoke with felt the Brits needed more boots on the ground to secure the city after the invasion.

The consensus was, the sooner the Brits invaded the better for everyone. One tank commander was fairly certain they would get the go-ahead within twenty-four hours.

I asked one of the APC commanders in the unit, an Irish lad, if Martin and I could get a ride with him into the city once the invasion started.

The commander looked at me like I was barking mad. Then he realized I was serious. 'I'd have to get top cover to run that one by,' he said. [4]

It looked like Martin and I would have to go in alone. We wished the unit good luck and good hunting.

---

4 Four years later I ran into that same lad in Afghanistan. He was heading up a CP team for a British diplomat. He reminded me of our conversation outside Basra and told me that he'd decided to join The Circuit to 'get a fraction of the adventure' Martin and I seemed to be having that day.

I poked my head out the window as we drove away. 'Don't run over our soft skin with your tank!' I shouted.

'You'll be fine so long as you wear your helmet,' the commander shouted back.

Tariq was bang on time for our meeting. Once again, he was accompanied by his son and business associates. Martin and I were desperate to hear what he'd learned overnight.

Tariq looked sullen as he walked towards our vehicle. I braced myself for a blow.

'I have bad news,' he said. 'The Fedayeen man I want to meet, the one who know about your friends, he killed last night in fighting with British.'

It wasn't just bad news – it was the worst possible news.

'What about his family and associates? Would they know what happened to the men we're looking for?' I asked.

Tariq said he'd already talked to the man's friends and family. Some knew that two journalists had been killed by the Fedayeen, but no one had a clue where the bodies might be. He had managed to pick up a few new details about 'the white person' who'd been wounded during the incident; he was told that the man had been put on a green minibus and taken towards Basra. Again, Martin and I assumed Tariq was referring to Terry.

We thanked Tariq for the information, gave him our contact numbers and asked him to call us if he learned anything new. Martin and I watched again as he headed back to the city which for the time being was off limits to us. We were stumped. What could we do next? It was gut wrenching to think we'd come this far only to have to sit and wait for our phones to ring.

CHAPTER 12

Trying to keep an operation under wraps when you're surrounded by dozens of journalists is next to impossible. Every night at the hub Martin and I were barraged with questions from overly inquisitive correspondents wanting to know how we were getting on with our search for the two missing ITN lads. We'd offer bits and pieces for them to chew on, but never the whole story.[5] A handful of journalists were genuinely concerned about the missing men. Some, however, were digging for something to report. Sitting in the desert day after day with nothing to do was having a corrosive effect on them. The press corps was tired of waiting for Basra to fall. On that point at least, Martin and I could empathize with them.

Day six of our investigation began with the news we were all waiting for: the main assault on Basra was finally under way. Martin and I learned of it from one of our military contacts who told us the city was taken almost without a fight. Word of the invasion spread to the hub through various channels. Journalists were foaming at the mouth to get inside the city and start reporting. The British military, however, was not eager to accommodate them. The last thing they needed were a bunch of journalists thrown into the mêlée of victory before the city was secured.

Martin and I threw our stuff into our vehicle and raced up

5 ITN Kuwait was the exception to this rule. Each night we'd send our contact at ITN's Kuwait bureau a detailed report of our findings.

the road towards Basra. Our priority was to get inside the city and start searching the hospital morgues for any sign of Fred and Hussein. We knew we'd have a very narrow window in which to act. If the morgues were overflowing, it wouldn't be long before unclaimed bodies would be shifted to mass graves.

The Brits were still rooting out the last pockets of resistance inside the city and as we drove we could see helicopters whacking the odd rocket into targets. The sky, already poisoned by days of burning oil pipelines, had grown even darker with the smoke of burning buildings.

On the main highway, we passed a British convoy heading towards the city. The hatches on the armoured vehicles were open and the soldiers were smiling and waving to people as they passed. It was definitely the British Army at its professional best; they'd only just taken Basra and already the soldiers were moving from a battle stance into a more relaxed posture meant to calm the Iraqis. I was so proud of those young soldiers I was moved to tears.

British tanks lined the main road all the way into the city centre. They reminded me of dinosaurs the way they dwarfed nearly everything around them. Many residents had come out of their houses to wave to the Brits as they drove past.

The day was young and the mood on the streets, for the most part, was one of overwhelming relief. After weeks of anticipation on both sides, the inevitable had happened. For the city's mostly Shiite residents, Saddam's brutal, dictatorial grip had been shattered. For the first time in decades, people could take a deep breath.

Our first stop was the main hospital where Terry Lloyd's body had been recovered. Though technically Basra had fallen to the British, the central hospital at least was still firmly under Baath party control. Martin and I had no choice but to deal with the Baath party colonel still in charge.

We explained to the colonel that Terry Lloyd's body had been found in his hospital and asked if it was possible that the bodies of the other two men – one Lebanese, one French – had ended up there as well.

The colonel's response was cold and curt. 'We have many casualties. You are welcome to join the queue and see what bodies we have,' he said.

Martin and I spent hours looking at dead Iraqis; from Fedayeen and civilians, right the way down to body parts and lumps of meat. Of the bodies that were identifiable, none matched the description of Fred and Hussein. As for the lumps of tissue, none revealed any identifying marks. We soon realized that if the rest of our search went the same way, ITN would have to bring in DNA experts at a later date.

There was still a slim possibility that Fred and Hussein were alive somewhere in the city. With that in mind, Martin and I left the hospital and began plastering telegraph poles and walls around the city with the 'missing' posters we'd been given in Kuwait. The posters generated a lot of interest as we taped them up. The downside was many people claimed they could tell us where the missing men were – for a price.

The people looking to make a quick buck were fairly easy to spot. But when one man told us he'd seen two men resembling Fred and Hussein in a hospital near Saddam's palace on the east side of Basra, we had to check it out. We asked the man to take us there. He jumped into our vehicle. I didn't want to rely on him to translate for us, so I called Tariq and asked him to meet us. Tariq was waiting at the hospital gates when we arrived. We thanked our 'guide' for his help and told him we'd take it from there. Just as we'd feared, he demanded money for his services. I gave him bottles of water and food for his family instead. He seemed satisfied enough.

Even though we'd probably been led there on a lie, Martin and I still felt the hospital was worth searching. Tariq waved us through the gates to the main car park. The place was heaving with angry, desperate people trying to find missing loved ones. A group of six doctors in white coats was engaged in a very heated, emotional exchange with a crowd of no fewer than fifty local residents. The doctors were struggling to maintain order. Voices were getting louder and louder, arms were flailing and people were pushing one another.

We showed one of the doctors a poster of Fred and Hussein and asked him if he knew anything about them. The doctor hadn't seen them but said we were welcome to search the morgue. He accompanied us to the back of the hospital. Even before we turned the corner, Martin and I knew we were in for a grisly task. The stench of decaying flesh was overpowering. When we got to the morgue, we understood why. The hospital's cold storage unit was big enough to accommodate only about a dozen bodies and the overflow had been placed in two unrefrigerated, twenty-foot sea containers. The stench from the corpses baking inside was so intense it seeped through the metal doors.

Rows of people were lined up to look for their loved ones. The doctor explained our situation to the morgue keeper, a little old man with an expressionless face who was kind enough to let us jump the queue. He led us to one of the sea containers and opened the door. The stench hit us like a rugby scrum; it nearly had us on our backs straight away. Martin graciously volunteered to have the first look. I was happy to oblige him. He put a handkerchief to his nose, inhaled deeply and ducked inside. After three minutes Martin emerged, blue from holding his breath and gagging from the stench. 'That was horrendous,' he said, doubling over like he was about to vomit. 'There's no need for you to go, Bob. They're not in there.'

'I believe you,' I said, slapping him on the back. 'I'll give it a miss.'

We spent the rest of the afternoon visiting other locations but found nothing. As the day dragged on, general elation gave way to lawlessness. Chaos gained traction with each passing hour and by late afternoon full-blown anarchy had broken out in neighbourhoods around the city. Basra was no place to be after nightfall. We made our way back to the hub, still no closer to finding Fred and Hussein.

At the hub, Martin and I tried to avoid the press corps and keep ourselves to ourselves. By that point, I, at least, had given up hope of finding Fred and Hussein alive. I had seen dozens of dead bodies that day and watched dozens more Iraqis looking for missing loved ones. The desperate faces, the smell of death and lumps of lifeless flesh rammed home what Tariq's intelligence had already suggested; Fred and Hussein were dead and no one could tell us what had happened to their bodies.

I was depressed. I had always felt like we were racing to catch up, having landed in Iraq ten days after the incident. In my mind, our main goal had been to bring Fred and Hussein back alive. I knew the only way we could succeed with the assignment was to tackle it aggressively – which we did. From probing the edges of Basra before the invasion to cultivating Tariq as a contact, we'd pushed our skills and luck to the limits.

Yet, despite all our efforts, we hadn't even succeeded in finding the missing men's bodies. That was the toughest blow of all – not being able to offer Fred and Hussein's families some sort of resolution.[6] It was difficult to accept that we'd come away with nothing. The only concrete accomplishment we could point to was that we'd clarified what had happened to Terry and Daniel.

More details of the incident have come to light since my involvement in the early days of the investigation. Tariq's intelligence that Terry Lloyd had been loaded into a green minibus was spot on. It was eventually determined and widely reported that Terry was wounded by the Iraqis in the initial contact and fatally shot in the head by US troops as they fired

---

6 In June 2004, ITN released a statement saying that tests on remains retrieved from Iraq matched the DNA profile of Hussein Osman. Fred Nerac is still missing, presumed dead.

on the minibus. In 2006, an Oxfordshire coroner ruled that Terry was killed unlawfully.[7]

What happened to Terry and his crew was horrendous and my heart goes out to the men's families. It was a terrible tragedy, one which I dearly hope others will learn from. In my view, journalists should never attempt to report unilaterally from war zones without taking along a properly trained and skilled security adviser.

Let me be clear; I do recognize the need for journalists to report from conflict areas independently and away from the restrictions of military embeds. But those assignments must be approached with the utmost caution. Nine tenths of a unilateral operation's success hinges on the planning. The ITN lads had thought to bring extra stores of food and petrol but they didn't take a security adviser, someone who could have proactively kept them out of trouble. Perhaps an adviser would have alerted them to the limitations of taping the letters TV to the sides of their vehicles. An adviser could have interpreted the Fedayeen waving as a sign of aggression and not, as Daniel thought, a gesture of surrender (if indeed an adviser would have allowed the clients to go that far forward in the first place).

Would the outcome have been different if Terry had taken a security adviser? It's impossible to say. At the very least, Terry's tragic ending was a wake-up call for the ITN crew stationed at the hub. They were very anxious to go to Basra and start shooting stories, but they were wise enough not to attempt it alone. They asked Martin and me if there was any chance we could take them into the city. We were happy to help them out.

Later that night, we called the bureau in Kuwait and they confirmed that they would like us to shift focus temporarily to looking after the hub crew. That night, I took some comfort in

---

7 Chris Tryhorn, 'ITN Reporter Unlawfully Killed', *Guardian*, 13 Oct. 2006. In his findings, the coroner determined that the US troops hadn't fired in self-defence.

the thought that perhaps Terry hadn't died in vain. ITN had learned the value of enlisting the help of security advisers in hostile environments. Surely Terry's death would have convinced other British media organizations to do the same.

CHAPTER 13

As soon as I saw her, I knew there'd be hell on. The scene before me was utter bedlam: hundreds of people in the street; most of them young men, hauling away whatever they could get their hands on: furniture, carpets, paintings, appliances, refrigerators, TVs; you name it. The sound of AK47 gunfire cracked from the smoke-filled windows of the upper floors. Below, looters poured out of the burning building like cockroaches. Some ran away with what they could carry while others formed spontaneous clusters as they fought over the best spoils. Carving a path through the middle of this mayhem was an old man sat atop a tractor, sparks flying everywhere as he dragged an industrial-sized generator behind him.

The British 'liberation' of Basra was entering its third day and the people were letting their hair down, to put it mildly. The mostly Shiite residents of Iraq's southern capital had suffered some of the worst atrocities doled out by Saddam and his Sunni regime. The preceding twelve years had been especially brutal. Not only had the people endured harsh reprisals for the failed Shiite uprising in the wake of the First Gulf War, they'd also lived with the crushing deprivation of economic sanctions.

The fear that had suffocated the people of Basra lifted with the arrival of the British Army. There once was a time when invading armies pillaged. In Basra, the liberated were the looters.

Of course, nothing attracts the attention of the international media like a lawless free-for-all and Basra was no exception. ITN had asked us to break away from our assigned task of looking for Fred Nerac and Hussein Osman and accompany a correspondent and crew as they filmed around the city. I for one welcomed the diversion. By then I was fairly certain that the missing men had been killed. The sweeps of Basra's hospitals and morgues had turned up nothing and for the moment the investigation had stalled.

Martin and I were well positioned to help a crew of enterprising journalists. We had already searched every corner of the city for the two missing lads. We also had Tariq, our local contact. We asked him to alert us if he saw anything he thought might be of interest to a news crew. Our primary aim was to keep the ITN crew safe but with Tariq on our side we could take it a step further and hopefully help them trounce the competition.

The morning after Basra fell, Martin and I transferred ourselves and the ITN crew to Saddam's palace complex on the east side of the city. The gaudy splendour of our new accommodation couldn't have been a starker contrast to the Spartan conditions of the hub. The crew weren't content for long, though, to film the palace's gilded staircases and gold-plated loo fittings. They wanted to hit the streets of Basra and get stuck in, but there was no way Martin and I could take them there without doing a recce. By way of compromise, we agreed to take a camera so they'd at least have some b-roll for their broadcast that night.

Many of the streets on the city's perimeter were relatively quiet. At that point, the liberation was being measured in hours, not days. The majority of the population still weren't convinced it was genuine and many were staying behind closed doors waiting to see what would happen.

One of the first things Martin and I encountered was a British foot patrol dumping boxloads of weapons and ammunition abandoned by the Iraqi military into an oil-slicked canal. It wasn't an efficient disposal method; the tides would wash the boxes back up on shore and some were already floating to the top. I'm not criticizing the lads who were doing it. I'm sure if they'd had a choice, they would have loaded the weapons and ammo onto a truck and driven them to a non-populated area for decommissioning. But the Brits didn't have the manpower or equipment to do that.

A few miles up the road, we encountered our first sporadic outbreak of violence; two rival Iraqi factions shooting at each other across a roundabout. There was no way of telling whether their dispute was ethnic, clan based or a business deal gone wrong. Blood or treasure, Martin and I weren't going to hang around and find out.

The next scene we drove past was another sign of things to come in Basra: a small riot outside a bank building. Later we found out that a group of locals who'd robbed the bank had been apprehended by a British foot patrol. In the ensuing mêlée, a British soldier had been shot in the stomach.

Amazingly, just two hundred yards further up the road, we stumbled upon a completely opposite scene: a British patrol wearing their regimental berets and no body armour handing out water and food to a very large crowd of obviously grateful locals. It was another example of the British Army moving swiftly from an aggressive posture to one aimed at winning hearts and minds. Hundreds of people had gathered round and the soldiers were working hard to maintain some kind of order. It was like trying to feed the five thousand without the aid of a miracle. Despite the turmoil, I got the impression that the majority of Basrans were glad to see the Brits. After all, they represented the only organized authority left in their city.

Our recce completed, we headed back to the palace with a few minutes of daylight to spare; the situation was far too unpredictable to be on the streets after dark. While driving to the palace we were suddenly caught out by a huge fireball thundering above our heads. It shot out of the upper windows of a building like dragon's breath. Below, we saw a group of Iraqi children darting in and out of the entrance. Children are fearless by nature and rarely know when enough's enough.

Before, when Martin and I had seen a group of Iraqi youths playing with unexploded ordnance near the Terry Lloyd incident area, we couldn't afford to intervene. This time, however, we could. I got out of the vehicle to investigate while Martin kept the engine running in case we needed to move quickly (there's nothing scarier than an angry child with a loaded weapon and some of those kids could have been armed). I told the kids in Arabic to stay away from the building.

'La, la' (No, no), they said, pointing towards a ground-floor window.

I looked inside and saw rows of boxes stacked five deep containing high-explosive mortar shells. Sooner or later, the heat of the fire would set them off, possibly triggering a chain reaction that could take out the entire block.

'Mushkilla, mutafajeraat!' (Problem, explosives!) I said to the kids.

They didn't listen to me, perhaps because I was a foreigner, but probably because I was an adult. Luckily, an older boy who'd been watching from across the street came over to ask me what I was doing. After explaining the situation to him, he cracked one of the kids on the back of the head and ordered the whole lot out of there.

Martin and I stayed until the kids had cleared the area.

Back at the palace, the ITN crew were chuffed with the b-roll we'd shot on our recce. I don't think they used it because the camera work was amateur, but it gave them a good feel for what was going on. That night Martin and I tried to rest up for the next day but it was like trying to sleep through ten bonfire nights rolled into one. The locals were making a hell of a racket, firing AKs and heavy machine guns well into the wee hours.

*

The next morning, Tariq called to tell us that the Sheraton hotel was on fire and people were ripping the place apart. We thanked him for the tip and roused the ITN crew. It was exactly the kind of story they were after. We headed out in two vehicles; I drove the crew's armoured Land Rover with the correspondent, cameraman and producer as passengers, while Martin backed us in the soft-skinned Mitsubishi. Even though our vehicle was armoured, I insisted the crew wear body armour as well. I set an example by wearing mine; both for my protection and because the front flap was a perfect place to conceal my 9 mm.

The Sheraton was located on the Shaat al Arab waterway approximately two miles west of the palace. As we wound our way through the streets towards the waterfront, it was soon apparent that the sporadic outbreaks of violence we'd witnessed the day before had broadened. Scores of government buildings had been ransacked and torched overnight. The Mukhabarrat building, a concrete monolith which had housed Iraqi Intelligence, was still on fire. A wild-eyed crowd of locals was stoking the flames with anything that would work as kindling – furniture, tyres, clothes – determined to see the place burn to the ground.

Everywhere we looked, there were defaced portraits of Saddam; some had the eyes scratched out, others were painted over or burnt with petrol. Saddam's wasn't the only face that had changed. The day before, the majority of locals we'd seen had greeted us with looks of kind curiosity. Now, more sinister elements were appearing. Friendly waves were giving way to fists shaking defiantly. Scores of people pointed their thumbs towards their mouths; the universal sign for water. It wasn't out of the question that someone would shoot us for our supplies if given the chance.

Martin and I had recced the area housing the Sheraton the day before. It was the closest thing to 'upmarket' you'd find in Basra. There was a time – back when the west found it more in its interest to embrace Iraq as an ally rather than invade it – when Basra was a prime destination for international businessmen looking to profit from the country's oil wealth. During the boom years of the 1970s Basra flourished; state-of-the-art medical facilities, an international airport and palaces for Saddam's private use.

The mile-and-a-half-long stretch of land bordering the Shaat al Arab waterway reflected those once promising times. Lined by statues of Iraqi generals who'd commanded during the Iran–Iraq war,[8] the waterfront housed government compounds, wealthy residences, exclusive restaurants, stores and, of course, the nicest hotel in town.

In many ways, the Sheraton was a symbol of Iraq's graduation into the club of industrialized nations. Before it was even completed, however, Iraq plunged into an eight-year war with Iran. Then came the Gulf War, followed by twelve years, finally, of economic sanctions and, finally, Gulf War II. Each conflict ate away at the city's lustre until none of its former brilliance remained. Just as the Sheraton was a product of Basra's rise, it had been a witness to its long decline.

Wave after wave of black smoke engulfed our vehicle as we headed down the waterfront towards the hotel. It was like driving through a funfair thrill ride; each time the curtain of smoke lifted, we'd get a glimpse of the scary drama playing to our front and periphery.

Only when we pulled up across the street from the hotel did we get the full view. Gangs of men were running riot.[9] Law and order had been cast aside; there was no Saddam, no police and everything was fair game. It was like watching an army of

---

8 The British military later tore down the statues. I always felt that was an insult to the Iraqi people, as the generals were considered national heroes from Iraq's eight-year war with neighbouring Iran. The decision to remove the statues should have been left to the residents of Basra.

9 It was an all-male scene; the women of Basra had retreated indoors for their own safety.

medieval barbarians sack a civilized city. In the middle of this pandemonium was the pathetic figure of the Sheraton's general manager. He was pleading with the crowd but the poor man was powerless to stop them from trashing his hotel.

The ITN crew asked if they could get out of the Land Rover and get some soundbites from the locals. I told them it would be OK so long as I got out with them and everyone kept within ten feet of the Land Rover. It may seem odd that I'd let them leave the safety of the armoured vehicle given the state of anarchy. But I knew from my work in Gaza and the West Bank that the camera can have a profoundly calming effect on people. As soon as it starts rolling even the most disorderly individual will usually strive to put his best foot forward.

The smell of burning rubber nearly knocked me flat as I climbed out of the sealed environment of the armoured cab. The acrid fumes from the fires on the top floors, mixed with the heat and humidity of the day, forming a thick residue that burned my eyes and the back of my throat.

While the crew got down to business, I scanned the vicinity for potential threats. Two things struck me immediately: first, the gunfire coming from the top floors of the hotel. It was probably celebratory, but there could be a sniper lurking, waiting for his chance to pick off a western target. Secondly, and of greater concern to me, was the large group of around 150 men who'd gathered on the street outside the hotel. Ranging in age from early teens to mid-twenties, the unruly gang were busy showing off their booty to each other. A stocky, clean-shaven youth appeared to be the ringleader. I could tell from the way he was dressed – shirt unbuttoned to the navel, exposing a hairy and rather paunchy middle – that he was out to prove a point.

I kept a close eye on the group, marking their movements to make sure they came nowhere near the ITN crew. Everything appeared manageable until the ringleader started shouting. He pointed and all heads turned in one direction. I followed their lead and that's when I saw her.

Never in all my years as a professional soldier or as an adviser on The Circuit had I seen anything like it in a war zone; a woman, obviously a western journalist, dressed in tight trousers and a snug top that had ridden up to reveal a patch of flesh around her middle. A woman dressed that way in London would hardly warrant a second glance. But in Basra, even under normal circumstances, it was highly provocative. The unruly gang must have thought Allah was rewarding them for their years of suffering by delivering one of their seventy afterlife virgins ahead of schedule. Add in the fact that there was no authority around to keep their impulses in check and it was obvious where the situation was headed.

The most astounding aspect of this unbelievable scene, however, wasn't the men; it was the female journalist. She appeared to be completely unaware that she had become the object of desire for dozens of undoubtedly undersexed men. I couldn't believe it. She was just standing there, seemingly clueless. And when she did finally notice the group of youths, what did she do? Did she run? Did she hell. She waded right into them, notebook in hand, to conduct interviews!

The men parted like a shoal of fish then closed around her. I'm sure they wanted to give her much more than a soundbite. She was trapped and she didn't even know it. I looked around, hunting for anyone who might be attached to this woman. Across the road, about thirty yards from the gang, I saw a cameraman shooting b-roll of the Shaat al Arab waterway. If indeed he was with her and they were a team, they should have been told never to lose sight of each other. I searched the area for a security adviser. I thought surely her network would have assigned her one before sending her into a hostile environment. But there was no one to be found. She was alone.

By this point, some of the men who'd been firing rifles inside the hotel had come out and joined the unruly gang. I wondered how I could possibly intervene to help her should anything happen. My first priority was to look after my clients, the ITN crew. There was also the small matter of numbers. Could I possibly deliver her safely from the clutches of 150-odd sex-crazed young men?

The ringleader was getting louder and louder, whipping the gang into a simmering frenzy. The female journalist still seemed none the wiser to his intentions. Then the inevitable happened; the ringleader made his move. He grabbed the woman's arm with one hand and her waist with the other. Her expression quickly changed from professional indifference to total shock. At long last, the penny had dropped.

'Ureedik! Ureedik!' (I want you! I want you!) shouted the ringleader.

There was nothing left to think about. I radioed Martin to keep an eye on the crew while I went in after her. He must have been watching the scene closely as well because he required no explanation for my actions.

I shouldered my way through the outer rings of frenzied men, all the time conscious of the pistol I had hidden in my body armour. My nose filled with the stench of dozens of dirty armpits. When I finally reached her, she looked like a fox cornered by a pack of hunting dogs. She was frightened and desperate to get out of there.

'Where's your crew?' I shouted to her.

She pointed to a saloon car parked on the kerb outside the hotel. The cameraman I'd seen earlier was throwing his gear into the backseat. At least one of them had their shit together.

With one hand on her back and the other poised to grab my pistol, I pushed her towards the edge of the crowd. The ringleader lurched forward to grab her. I threw myself between him and the girl and looked him directly in the eye.

'LA! LA!' (NO! NO!) I shouted.

It was now a stand-off between him and me. He had more

than a hundred men to back his claim to this woman. I had Martin, which just about equalled things out in my mind.

I searched the mob with my eyes. I didn't see any knives or pistols but I knew that somewhere in the crowd were the young men who'd been firing rifles from the top floors of the hotel. As I inched the woman towards her car, the gang of men moved with us. They were swarming all over the vehicle like insects by the time we reached it. I opened the door and told the terrified cameraman to drive the hell out of there as quickly as possible. The weight of the crowd nearly overwhelmed me as I struggled to keep the woman shielded while she climbed into the passenger seat. Before she could close the door, the ringleader dived under my left arm and shoved his face into her lap.

The woman screamed as the dirty bastard ground his face into her crotch. I grabbed the waistband of his trousers and pulled him off her. He managed to grab a pack of cigarettes from the dashboard before he tumbled backwards out of the car.

I slammed the door shut and banged the roof with my fist. 'Go! Go! Go!' I shouted.

The cameraman floored it and the car sped away, leaving me to deal with the ringleader and his disappointed gang.

I was standing toe to toe with the ringleader. He didn't look pleased, neither did his friends. I reached into my body armour and placed my hand on my pistol. I had no intention of drawing it unless necessary – which seemed very likely.

Then, to my tremendous surprise, the ringleader smiled and extended his hand. I released my weapon and shook his hand in return. 'La, la, la' (No, no, no), I said to him, as if he were a child who'd misbehaved. The ringleader slapped my right shoulder, laughed heartily and shook my hand again. He then turned his back on me and shared out the cigarettes he'd grabbed as if he were the grand conqueror. Given all that could have happened, I was happy to let him have his moment.

CHAPTER 14

'Put your body armour on and keep your helmets right next to you,' I said.

The journalists rolled their eyes. 'Why?' said the older of the two, an American producer in his early thirties. 'We do this several times a week.'

'Well, then you should know the amount of incidents that happen on this route,' I said.

The less senior of my clients, a female producer in her late twenties, joined in. 'You're not wearing body armour,' she squeaked.

'Yes, I am.' I tugged at the neck of my coat. 'Underneath my clothes, like the two of you should be doing.'

The male producer looked at his younger colleague like a peacock poised to spread his feathers. 'Tell you what,' he said. 'We'll put on our flak jackets if anything happens.'

'Putting it on after an incident won't do you much good,' I said.

He stared at me defiantly.

'If you insist on not wearing your body armour then at least put it up against the sides of the door to give you some protection,' I said.

The female producer finally listened to reason and wedged her body armour between the seat and the side of the vehicle. The male producer folded his arms and didn't budge.

I couldn't get my head around his attitude. My client had

been in Baghdad for weeks, whereas I'd been there less than twenty-four hours.

It was January 2004. Nearly nine months had passed since George W. Bush had infamously declared an 'end to major hostilities' in Iraq. The short-lived, post-invasion honeymoon period was over and any goodwill which may have existed toward the international press corps had evaporated. The number of journalists killed in Iraq was mounting. They'd become prime targets for insurgents looking to notch up western deaths and for bandits searching for western booty.

The changing climate was underscored on 31 December 2003 when a suicide bomber targeted Nabil's, an upscale Baghdad restaurant popular with western journalists. One of the few restaurants in the Iraqi capital to serve alcohol, a large crowd had gathered at Nabil's to attend a New Year's Eve party. The celebration ended in carnage when the bomber drove a vehicle laden with explosives into the side of the restaurant. At least five people were killed in the attack and dozens injured.

Some media had woken up to the new reality. News organization no longer plastered their vehicles and body armour with the letters TV and PRESS – hence the reason I was wearing my body armour underneath my clothes. Yet despite growing evidence to the contrary, there were still those who clung to the belief that journalists in Iraq were 'untouchable'. The hard-headed male producer in my vehicle appeared to fall into that category. As we prepared to get under way, I hoped his attitude was the exception rather than the norm. I had just signed on for a two-month assignment with AKE looking after CNN in Iraq.

That particular morning we were making a very short run, from the well-guarded Sheraton/Palestine hotel complex in Baghdad to the Green Zone – an even more heavily fortified area. The journey from point A to point B was approximately two miles, but they were dangerous miles. The Sheraton/Palestine was where most of the world's media had based themselves along with scores of American contractors working on Iraqi reconstruction projects. It was, in my view, the second biggest target in all of Baghdad. The only bigger draw for insurgents was our destination that morning: the Green Zone, headquarters of the Coalition Provisional Authority, or CPA, and the seat of American power in Iraq.[10]

CNN had a large presence in Baghdad and I was one of a handful of advisers assigned to look after the various correspondents and crews. The task of running CNN staffers from their bureau at the Palestine to 'pressers' in the Green Zone was carried out several times a week. Perhaps that explained the attitudes of the two young producers. The more someone makes a journey without incident, the more likely they are to become lax about security. My clients probably thought I was being overly cautious, but I didn't care what they thought of me. I wasn't there to be their buddy. I was there to keep them safe.

We turned out of the secured parking area of the Sheraton/Palestine with a local driver at the wheel, me in the passenger seat and my clients in the back. As a passenger, I lost the ability to immediately control the vehicle but I gained a wider window to spot potential trouble and avoid it; an advantage given that we were travelling in a soft-skinned 4x4. The situation at the time was such that people were getting their arses in gear to get proper armoured vehicles but there was a backlog of demand. I took comfort in the fact that I was armed with my preferred weapons: a 9 mm concealed in a pouch buckled around my waist (there was no point in tucking it into the front flap of my body armour when I was wearing it covertly underneath my clothing) and an AK47 short for the vehicle. Both weapons were handed to me by AKE as soon as I'd crossed the border into Iraq.

From the hotel we headed north-west along Abu Nuwas, a street which parallels the river Tigris. The road was lined with small shacks housing cafes. The cloud cover was dense and

---

10 The Green Zone remained the centre of international activity following the handover of power from the CPA to the Iraqi Government in June 2004.

people were dressed in heavy coats to shield themselves from the damp morning mist. As we drove, I noticed dozens of vehicles parked on the sides of the road; many were old. By that point, anyone advertising their wealth and status by driving a flash car around Baghdad was asking to be car-jacked or abducted.

But the Iraqis still took pride in their beat-up cars and trucks. I spotted three men pushing an old Toyota to a washing point which was no more than a long hose coming from a cafe. At the same time, from the corner of my eye, I noticed a vehicle driving the wrong way up a one-way street.

Your mind is always racing when you're travelling from A to B in a hostile environment. Things that seem completely innocent under normal circumstances can suddenly appear menacing; a group of men gathered round a vehicle could be insurgents conducting surveillance. A car driving the wrong way could be a suicide bomber closing in on a target.

I looked at the grey skies stretching over the city. The weather conditions would make a suicide bombing or IED attack that much more lethal. Detonating an explosive in overcast conditions is like placing a bomb in a biscuit tin; the pressure becomes trapped below the clouds, magnifying the force of the blast. As my eyes scanned the road ahead, my ears filled with the sound of the two producers chatting away in the backseat.

'Keep a lookout for anything that appears suspicious or unusual,' I told my clients. 'I need your eyes and ears.'

They seemed to ignore me and kept on talking.

We crossed under an overpass where Abu Nuwas Street turns into Rashid Street; a very downtrodden road lined with old, traditional brick buildings that are primarily used for storage. My eyes skipped between the windows and alleys, searching for signs of movement. It was a great place for snipers to lay up and for insurgents to initiate IEDs. From Rashid Street we turned right and drove to a roundabout circling Tahrir Square; the pre-war heart of Baghdad and home to the Monument of Liberty, one of the capital's most famous landmarks. Measuring twenty feet by fifty feet, the concrete sculpture commemorates the 1958 overthrow of Iraq's British-backed monarchy. As we swept past, it reminded me of something out of the Soviet Union with its heroic silhouettes symbolically reaching towards a glorious future.

From where I was sat, it was difficult to imagine that kind of optimism having existed in Iraq. On the north side of Tahrir Square is the Thieves Market; a huge open-air bazaar where you can buy all sorts; from cheap trinkets to rare antiques. I saw vendors getting ready for the day, laying out bits and pieces to sell or barter. Since the invasion, the Thieves Market had become a very dangerous place to do business. Fatal shootings were common. But that didn't put people off from going there. For many Baghdad residents, selling possessions had become their only means of support. Before the March 2003 invasion, Iraqis enjoyed near universal employment thanks to a large military and bloated Baath party bureaucracy. One of the first things the CPA did when it took over was disband Iraq's military and blacklist former Baath party members from working in government. Practically overnight, millions of Iraqis were thrown out of work with no prospects for the future. For insurgents, it was a bonanza. Every unemployed youth in Iraq was a potential recruit.

We followed the roundabout from Tahrir Square onto the Jumhuriya Bridge, one of nearly a dozen linking the city's halves. It was still early and there wasn't much traffic, pedestrian or otherwise; precisely the kind of conditions to inspire a false sense of security. As we drove, I looked to either side, mentally mapping the locations of violent incidents that had happened since the US-led invasion. To my left, I could see as far as the Karada District where Baghdad University is located. The University had become a prime spot for kidnappings and abductions since the fall of Saddam's regime. To my right, I could make out three bridges. On the eastern bank of the farthest bridge was the Iraqi National Museum. If I thought they'd be interested, I would have offered my clients a lesson in recent history. Five months earlier, in July 2003, a twenty-four-year-old British freelance journalist from the Scottish Borders was shot dead outside the museum. He wasn't wearing body armour nor was he accompanied by a trained security adviser. Iraq was the first and last war he ever covered.

The view from the Jumhuriya Bridge with its catalogue of brutality focused my mind for what lay ahead: Yafa Street, the final and most treacherous leg of our short journey. Yafa Street dead-ends into the Green Zone, but like many features in Baghdad, it wasn't designed that way. Before the war, it ran east from the Tigris into a heart-shaped series of overpasses that pumped traffic into the four corners of the capital. But the American-led CPA, in its infinite wisdom, located the Green Zone smack in the middle of this critical artery. Rather than move in all directions, traffic travelling east on Yafa Street was forced to divert north-west along the perimeter of the Green Zone.

The results were as dangerous as they were inconvenient. The re-route around the roughly ten-square-kilometre Green Zone triggered bumper-to-bumper traffic jams at all hours, including early morning. One of the worst things you can do in a hostile environment is remain stationary in a vehicle or get caught up in dense traffic where it's nearly impossible to manoeuvre away from an incident. Driving on any stretch of Yafa Street was hazardous. But the riskiest portion was where the Green Zone cut through it; a traffic choke point which I couldn't avoid. It was the drop-off point for my clients.

As we headed onto Yafa Street, I felt like we were driving into the jaws of a crocodile. So far, CNN had got away with their runs to and from the Green Zone. But the more times they did it, the greater the chances of something happening. It's the law of averages.

As traffic inevitably slowed to a crawl, I searched for potential exits; places where we could jump the kerb and turn around on the pavement in the event of an IED or vehicle-borne bombing. I kept a close watch as we passed the primary vehicle checkpoint for the Green Zone: Assassin's Gate. The name was appropriate. Insurgents had attacked it numerous times.

A few hundred yards further east was my clients' final destination: the checkpoint for the Iraqi Convention Centre where the CPA held its pressers. Unlike Assassin's Gate, the Convention Centre checkpoint sat a couple of hundred yards off the road and could only be approached on foot. I could see from the vehicle that a queue had already formed. It wouldn't take much for an insurgent to wade into the line and open up with an automatic rifle or detonate a suicide vest. Obviously, hanging around there longer than necessary was not a good idea. So you can imagine how stunned I was to see other members of the media standing near the side of the road outside the checkpoint. It was unclear whether they were waiting for colleagues or killing time ahead of the presser. Either way, they were endangering themselves unnecessarily.

Our driver pulled up at the base of the traffic choke point to let us out. I asked him to keep the engine running and turn the vehicle around while I escorted the clients through the checkpoint and to the Convention Centre inside the Green Zone. Both my clients got out of the vehicle without their body armour and helmets.

'What are you doing?' I asked.

'Going inside,' said the male producer.

'Not without your body armour and helmets,' I said.

He looked at me as if I'd just said something completely preposterous. 'We don't need body armour in the Green Zone,' he said.

I reminded him that the Green Zone had suffered numerous rocket attacks, some of them fatal. I also pointed out that there was no guarantee that our vehicle would be the one to collect them after the presser.

'Better to have all your kit with you than be stranded without it,' I said.

The female producer listened to me and grabbed her body armour. The male producer walked away from the vehicle empty-handed.

The Convention Centre checkpoint resembled much of the Green Zone's perimeter: a collection of razor wire, blast walls, sandbags and heavily armed soldiers. Head on, it gave the sense of being a highly secured area, which was misleading to say the least. The checkpoint was flanked on one side by a car park and on the other by some disused buildings. Insurgents could lie up in either area for hours or even days waiting to strike.

The Americans guarding the checkpoint didn't seem switched on to that or other possible attack scenarios. I got the sense they were very blasé about security, perhaps because they hadn't experienced an incident in a while. I kept our vehicle in line of sight as I walked my clients through the queue. If something did happen, the first thing the Yanks would do was shut the gates, leaving everyone outside to fend for themselves. I didn't want to be searching for our vehicle in the middle of a panicked mob. After a few cursory searches and flashes of their media credentials, my clients cleared the checkpoint and headed on to the Convention Centre. The morning was looking up. I had delivered the producers safely to their destination. Now all I had to do was get myself and the driver back to the hotel in one piece.

As I walked the few hundred yards to our vehicle, I noticed how well it blended with the rest of the traffic. It was very low profile for Baghdad, which meant insurgents would be less likely to single it out. That's the key to operating successfully as a security adviser in Iraq or practically any other hostile environment; remain as inconspicuous as possible. Driving an unremarkable vehicle, concealing weapons, wearing body armour underneath clothing – all these things help. But external trappings are only part of it. Maintaining a low profile also extends to conduct. It's imperative to behave respectfully towards the local population; try not to offend people, observe local customs whenever possible and always remember to act like a guest and not a conqueror.

The driver had pulled up on the pavement about twenty yards east of the base of the traffic choke point. The short distance from myself to the vehicle stretched out before me like an ocean of chaos. Horns were beeping from all directions as frustrated drivers inched their cars and trucks through the log jam.

Suddenly, the normal traffic sounds were drowned out by revving engines and screeching tyres. I looked to my right and saw a convoy of four white 4x4s thundering out of the Green Zone. It was a commercial security detail. Men were hanging out the windows, brandishing weapons and screaming at the top of their lungs, 'Get the fuck out of the way!'

Terrified pedestrians ran for cover while drivers tried in vain to manoeuvre themselves out of the path of the convoy. From the way they were acting, waving weapons, screaming aggressively, ramming vehicles aside, the men in the 4x4s appeared as if they were escaping an enemy attack. I had been switched on to potential hazards from the moment I'd left the Palestine and I couldn't see anything in the vicinity that would warrant that kind of stance.

I would learn soon enough that the security detail didn't need a reason for their actions. Without warning, one of the men in the convoy swung round and aimed his rifle directly at me.

CHAPTER 15

I looked at the security adviser pointing his weapon at me and shook my head in disgust. I thought my biggest worry on this assignment would be insurgents. It turned out the first people to target me in Iraq were members of my own profession.

Two Iraqis standing next to me had witnessed the entire episode. They glanced over as if to say, 'We're all in this together.' Good thing they didn't realize what I did for a living. The look of hatred on their faces was unmistakable.

I was embarrassed that those 'advisers' in the convoy had the same job title as me. The worst part was I knew there were more like them in Iraq.

I had got a preview the day before in the lobbies of the Sheraton and Palestine hotels. Walking into the complex was like lifting the curtain on a freak show. The place was crawling with security advisers looking after media and civilian contractors. One of the first details I encountered, sadly, was a British Close Protection team escorting a client off an elevator. I stared at them slack-jawed as they strutted past. There were six advisers in all: two ahead of the client and four backing him. Every member of the team was wearing body armour over their clothing and carrying a range of different weapons in full view; from AKs and submachine guns, down to back-up pistols in waist holsters. Never had I seen such an unnecessary, over-the-top display of firepower in a hotel lobby – or anywhere else for that matter.

I'm sure those lads were well intentioned. They probably

thought their overt stance would intimidate would-be attackers and keep them at bay. Maybe in a Hollywood movie, but in the real world of hostile environments the worst thing you can do is draw attention to yourself and your client unnecessarily. A security team that advertises its capabilities is asking to be attacked. It's not a matter of if they'll get hit, but when.

As bad as those Brits were, the American security details I saw were even worse. Not only did they wear body armour on top of their clothing and flash weapons for all to see but many of them were obviously on steroids, wore sunglasses indoors (a habit which really hacks me off) and had pistols and knives strapped to their legs.

I was stunned by the sheer number of cowboys, Walter Mittys and posers I saw just in the Sheraton/Palestine complex alone. Less than a year earlier, most lads on The Circuit had the skills and knowledge to behave professionally in a hostile environment. But the aftermath of the Iraq invasion had opened the floodgates to The Circuit, changing it beyond recognition.

The Circuit's transformation may have started with 11 September but it kicked into high gear in April 2003, with the announcement of the $18.4 billion reconstruction fund to help get Iraq up and running again after years of war and economic sanctions. Administered by the US government, the fund awarded contracts worth billions of dollars to rebuild Iraq's infrastructure and construct new public services such as hospitals and schools.

The main recipients of these multi-billion-dollar contracts were commercial firms staffed by civilian experts in engineering and other fields; civvies who needed looking after in 'post-conflict' Iraq. That's where The Circuit came in. The coalition had always planned to use commercial security companies to look after reconstruction projects, but the role of CSCs was meant to be limited. Even the most astute industry insider couldn't have predicted that commercial security personnel would[11] eventually represent the second largest foreign armed force in Iraq[12] behind the US military.

It all came down to the US-led coalition's handling of post-invasion Iraq. You can debate endlessly about whether the US and Britain should have gone to war in the first place but few would disagree that the follow-up was a disaster. From the US military's failure to adopt a less intimidating stance towards Iraq's civilians, to the incredibly ill-considered decision to disband the country's armed forces, the coalition's post-invasion strategy in Iraq will go down as one of the most notorious screw-ups in modern military history.

In a situation like Iraq where the military is left chasing the error, the number of troops needed to secure the ground rises substantially. I estimate the US alone would have needed to commit at least 50,000 additional troops to sort out its portion of Iraq. But President George W. Bush and his administration had sold the public on a war with few casualties and a quick resolution. For political reasons, US leaders – and British for that matter – wanted to maintain the illusion that Iraq could be secured with no additional commitment of resources. The Circuit helped them achieve that.

As Iraq descended into chaos, the troops on the ground became stretched to the limit fighting a growing insurgency. Rather than deploy more soldiers, the US and UK governments responded by outsourcing more military jobs to the private sector in order to free up the troops they had in theatre. Military tasks such as guarding coalition compounds, embassies, diplo-

---

11 CSCs often use the term 'post-conflict' to describe post-invasion Iraq and Afghanistan. The term suggests a stable environment that is secure. In my view, 'post-invasion' is a far more accurate term.

12 According to a report from the US Government Accountability Office there were 48,000 commercial security personnel working in Iraq as of June 2006. As of May 2007, the Pentagon estimated there were 126,000 commercial security personnel working in Iraq. (Source: *New York Times* 19 May 2007, 'Contractor Deaths in Iraq Soar to Record' by John M. Broder & James Risen.).

matic staff, running supply convoys and training Iraqi police all shifted to The Circuit.

Outsourced military jobs were only the half of it. As Iraq became a more dangerous place to do business the security needs of civilian contractors hired to rebuild the country became ever greater. The more the insurgency gained traction, the more reconstruction funds were diverted into the pockets of CSCs.

The biggest loser in all of this was the Iraqi people. Far from improving, their daily lives degenerated into a struggle for survival. But the coalition troops on the ground also picked up a big part of the tab by suffering enormously due to the lack of proper military reinforcements.

Meanwhile, The Circuit never had it so good; CSCs were eating up a bigger and bigger slice of the reconstruction fund while picking up more and more outsourced military jobs. Niche tasks like looking after media were also booming. In short, the debacle in Iraq had turned into a twenty-first-century gold-rush. In 2003, the collective annual revenue of British CSCs alone totalled approximately £320 million. By 2004, annual revenues had exploded to more than £1.8 billion.[13]

All those new security contracts funding the boom required people to staff them, and it wasn't long before demand for advisers trained in hostile environments quickly overwhelmed supply. Standards, as I'd already seen for myself, had gone into freefall. It didn't help matters that CSCs aren't regulated, so there was no legal requirement for due diligence when hiring advisers. Even a military background, though the norm, was no longer a hard and fast requirement. I was meeting lads in Iraq who'd worked as bouncers before joining The Circuit!

That's not to say everyone was playing at it. I saw plenty of advisers in Iraq maintaining a low profile and conducting them-

13 'Corporate Mercenaries: The Threat of Private Military and Security Companies'; War on Want, 2006.

selves with the utmost professionalism. But in my heart of hearts, I knew it didn't matter how well I or anyone else did their job; skilled or incompetent, we'd all be lumped together.

It was a distressing state of affairs, not least because it made operating in Iraq that much more hazardous. I wondered how many enemies were made when that American security detail blasted out of the Green Zone. How many Iraqi civilians turned against the coalition as a result?

As much as I was concerned for the state of British CSCs, two weeks operating in and around Baghdad confirmed in my mind at least that US firms were the worse of the two. There seemed to be little difference between the way American soldiers and American security teams operated in hostile environments. I had an idea the mistakes of the US military were being carried over into the commercial world. My first assignment north of Baghdad would confirm it.

CHAPTER 16

After a few weeks of looking after CNN in and around Baghdad, I was asked by Senior International Correspondent Nic Robertson to accompany him and his crew on a US military embed north of the capital. It may sound redundant for a journalist to bring a security adviser on an assignment where they'll be surrounded by uniformed troops. But soldiers have enough to do without the added burden of looking after the media. Being embedded with a military unit in a hostile environment is one of the most dangerous assignments a journalist can accept. Soldiers are targeted all the time, so anyone with them is a target too. A trained security adviser using proactive skills can assess the operational environment for an embedded news team, i.e. mode of transportation, accommodation, etc., and make an early call as to whether a story can be got safely.

I said yes to Nic's request without hesitation. I had been assigned to him previously in the West Bank and admired his work tremendously. He wasn't afraid to tackle controversial topics and report the facts in full, even if it upset some viewers. I also found Nic very easy to work with; he doesn't smoke, never drinks on the job and keeps himself in great shape. It is much easier looking after an alert, hard-working, disciplined correspondent than one whose physical and mental state has deteriorated through drinking, smoking and lack of exercise.

I was also very intrigued by the main focus of Nic's embed. He was profiling Lieutenant Colonel Nathan Sassaman, at the time, a rising star in the US military. Sassaman had been written about extensively in the US media and had gained notoriety for, among other things, wrapping an entire Iraqi village in barbed wire to flush out insurgents.[14]

Sassaman had recently been assigned the task of crushing militant activity in Samarra, a city located in the heart of the Sunni triangle. Stretching from Ramadi in the south-west to Saddam Hussein's home town of Tikrit in the north to Baghdad in the south-east, the Sunni triangle had become the epicentre of armed Sunni opposition to the US-led coalition.

One of the most hazardous aspects of the embed was actually getting there. The only road connecting Baghdad to Samarra was a main supply route for coalition forces where IEDs and more elaborate roadside ambushes were commonplace. We needed a minimum of two 4x4s for the journey: one for Nic and his crew and another to serve as a lookout and backup vehicle in case the client's broke down or became disabled in an ambush.

Samarra is only sixty-five miles from Baghdad, but I insisted on departing before nine to ensure we had plenty of daylight for our trip. There were several checkpoints along the way which would slow us down. Also, one insurgent attack could stretch our modest drive into an epic journey.

Our small convoy left the Palestine with Nic, his crew and a local driver in the lead vehicle and me and a local driver in the other. Once we cleared the traffic of central Baghdad, the road began flowing like a river after a heavy rain. I hoped it would continue that way. It wasn't to be. About twenty miles north of the Iraqi capital, traffic started to slow. The cars ahead of us weren't stopping, but it was obvious something was causing them to proceed cautiously. I figured either we were approaching a very slow-moving, heavily guarded convoy that wouldn't allow anyone to pass, or someone had got hit by insurgents. It

14 Dexter Filkins, 'Tough New Tactics by U.S. Tighten Grip on Iraq Towns', *New York Times*, 7 Dec. 2003.

turned out to be the latter. A US military and civilian logistical convoy had been attacked. The convoy's trucks were riddled with bullet holes and the cabs were splattered with blood. We missed the incident by approximately twenty minutes.

No one had to tell us what had happened. From the wreckage, it looked as if the insurgents had followed a classic ambush pattern. First, they paralysed the convoy by blowing one of the lead vehicles off the road with an IED. They then launched a follow-up attack with small-arms fire. I didn't spot any Iraqi civilian vehicles in the remains. By that point, Iraqis and most foreigners in Iraq knew that driving too close to a military convoy was a double peril: they could either find themselves caught up in an insurgent attack or the convoy could mistake them for militants and open fire.

The casualities had been evacuated by the time we drove past and US soldiers along with Iraqi police were doing their utmost to secure the area as quickly as possible. They didn't want to give the insurgents another opportunity to strike by remaining stationary for too long.

As was standard procedure, we maintained a healthy distance between ourselves and other convoys for the rest of the trip, reaching the outskirts of Samarra around noon local time. It was a crystal-clear day and I could see the city's skyline in the distance; a series of low-level rooftops crowned by the magnificent dome of a grand mosque.

Sassaman's camp was located in a small, flat hamlet on the edge of the city. As we pulled off the main highway, I asked Yasir, my local driver, to move ahead of Nic's vehicle. There was a checkpoint and I wanted to get there first in case the troops manning it were trigger-happy. There had already been numerous incidents involving nervous US soldiers firing on innocent civilians at checkpoints. I was relieved to see Iraqi police were in charge of the checkpoint. I used the opportunity to have Yasir double-check our directions to the base. He rolled down the window and spoke with the police who pointed us towards an abandoned school complex up the road.

Given the volatile nature of the area, I expected the base to meet the highest possible security standards. But as soon as the perimeter came into view, my alarm bells started ringing. Though the complex was ringed with twelve-foot-high, reinforced concrete blast walls – an excellent defensive measure – all of the sentry towers we drove past were unmanned. At twenty feet high, the towers were the only way for the soldiers inside to see over the blast walls. Leaving them empty effectively blinded the entire base to what was happening on their doorstep.

After a standard vehicle search, including the once-over by dogs trained to sniff for explosives, we were cleared through the main gates of the base. Once inside, I started looking for potential security weaknesses. The base was laid out in a quadrangle centred on a helipad big enough to accommodate two Chinook helicopters. To the front of the quadrangle was the base headquarters, a rectangular one-storey building surrounded by small outbuildings and a parking area for armoured vehicles; on the far side of the quadrangle stood a sixty-foot-high rusting water tower. One look at the water tower and the words 'reference point' flashed though my mind; insurgents could use it as a guide to help them fire mortars at the base more accurately.

We had just started unloading our gear when Lt Colonel Sassaman and his Direct Commander (his boss) walked out of the headquarters building. As soon as the Commander laid eyes on the big TV camera, he gave Sassaman a dirty look. I got the feeling the two men didn't get on well. Perhaps the Commander didn't approve of Sassaman's media exposure.

Before the embed, Nic had given me several recent articles on Sassaman. They all painted a picture of someone who was larger than life. The hype surrounding him reached back as far as officer training school, where Sassaman had distinguished himself as an accomplished sportsman, particularly in American football. Seeing the man in the flesh, he certainly looked the part; almost six feet tall with broad shoulders and close-cropped hair, he was in very good shape for a man in his forties with all the confidence an officer of his rank should possess.

Having seen his Direct Commander off, Sassaman walked over to greet us. After a brief introduction, he told us he had to meet with a group of elders from Samarra. He apologized for not being able to stand and talk longer and extended an invitation to Nic and the crew to join him on a patrol later that afternoon. He then handed us over to one of his junior officers to show us to our quarters.

As Sassaman headed off, I wondered whether all the good press he'd received would come back to bite him in the arse. I had read about his meetings with tribal elders, which sounded like a good way to win people over. Perhaps the meetings would have been more successful, however, had Sassaman's other policies been more complementary.

To be fair, Sassaman's task was Sisyphean. He had a battalion of men (roughly 800 soldiers) to secure 466 square miles of the most volatile territory in Iraq. He tackled his mission with a two-pronged approach: during the day, he'd engage the locals in constructive dialogue. By night, he'd conduct door-to-door raids on homes to root out militants. Some would call that strategy 'carrot and stick'. To me, it's more like Jekyll and Hyde. What's the point of courting local leaders in broad daylight if you're going to terrorize the people they represent after the sun goes down?

Scaring the locals appeared to be just one of Sassaman's mistakes. Many people, me included, would consider some of his tactics humiliating. An example of this involved the small Sunni village of Abu Hisham where one of his junior officers was killed in an RPG attack. The day after the attack, Sassaman ordered his troops to surround the village with razor wire and issue ID cards – written in English only – to all men between the ages of seventeen and sixty-five. The men were then forced to queue at checkpoints and show their ID cards when coming and going from their own homes.

It was as if Sassaman had ripped a page right out of the Israeli Defence Force's playbook (one of the junior officers at the base later told me that he had received training from the IDF). I had seen for myself how Israel's tactics only hardened Hamas's resolve. Sassaman may have managed to capture a few insurgents in Abu Hisham, but at what cost? In my view, he'd sacrificed a long-term solution to short-term insecurities.

The junior officer showed us to our accommodation, an old classroom which we'd be sharing with a handful of troops. When we got there, a group of soldiers were sitting around cleaning their weapons. They had rolled out the welcome mat for CNN, putting up extra bunk beds in anticipation of our arrival. Unfortunately, their hospitality didn't seem to extend to our Iraqi drivers. The soldiers glared at them like the enemy.

I stared at the soldiers until they went back to cleaning their weapons. While Nic and his crew got their kit together for the patrol, I took Yasir and the other driver outside. I let them know how angry I was about the cold reception they'd received and told them to let me know if anyone at the base gave them a hard time. Yasir said not to worry; he was used to being treated that way by Americans. I'd worked with Yasir fairly consistently by that point. He was a cracking young lad; reliable, intelligent, hard-working. He had taken a driving job with CNN to fund his education. I reminded him that we were there together as a team and all of us – British, American and Iraqi – deserved to be treated well by our hosts.

Around 1.30 p.m., we left our quarters for the pre-patrol briefing – a meeting to get all the soldiers and any press tagging along up to speed. During the briefing, I learned that there was only room for Nic and his cameraman to accompany the troops. I would have to stay behind. After listening to the

Officer in Charge, however, I was fine with the arrangement. The patrol had been well thought out so I was happy to let my clients go.

With Nic and his shooter away for a few hours, I took the opportunity to conduct a more thorough security audit of the base, starting with where we'd be sleeping. Directly opposite our accommodation was a fenced-off patch of ground approximately fifty yards in diameter which the Americans used as a holding area for Iraqis they'd picked up on patrol and detained. There were a few dozen detainees of various ages milling around inside the barbed wire. Some of the younger ones were huddled together in groups. One detainee looked like he was well into his seventies. He was on his own, barefoot and shivering under a blanket. There was a two-litre plastic water bottle on the ground next to him. He must have been there a while because it was practically overflowing with urine.

It was a very disturbing sight but what troubled me even more were the security implications of the set-up. From what I could see, the detainees were left completely to their own devices in the holding area. No one was guarding or observing them to try and determine which ones were behaving like insurgents (i.e. the ones liaising with others) and which ones were acting like innocent bystanders (the old man).

Even more worrying was that a portaloo had been positioned inside the holding area right next to the barbed wire fencing. It would have taken nothing for the detainees to kick over the portaloo, bring down the barbed wire, run over the top and escape the compound. If they were really savvy, they would stop at the nearest outbuilding – which happened to be ours – grab whatever weapons they could and shoot their way out of the base. They certainly wouldn't have to worry about guards firing on them from the unmanned sentry towers I'd seen.

I soon discovered that the holding of detainees was the final stage in a very flawed process. During my audit, I watched a foot patrol return to base with several new detainees in tow.

They were blindfolded and their hands were tied behind their backs. The soldiers ordered the men to squat outside the blast walls of the main headquarters. I then watched, slack-jawed, as the soldiers removed all the blindfolds and started questioning the detainees one by one, out in the open.

I took a photo because I knew if I told my mates, no one would believe me. These were suspected insurgents and there they were with a ringside seat to every vital activity taking place inside the base. An insurgent could gather loads of information from that location: how many soldiers were stationed in the camp, what types of weapons they carried, how many armoured vehicles were in use versus soft-skinned, what time of day patrols left and returned, locations within the camp like the HQ building, cookhouse, accommodation buildings, etc., not to mention where those locations stood in relation to the rusting water tower.

The US soldiers appeared oblivious to all of this, so much so that a group of commanders stood at the foot of the detainee line discussing their exploits in vivid detail. I listened to them bang on about patrols past, present and future over fat cigars and huge mugs of coffee bearing the unit's insignia. If any of the detainees understood English – which was very likely – they were in a wonderful position to eavesdrop and gather even more intelligence.

The base's handling of detainees was riddled with errors from start to finish, but there was an easy way to put it all right. I saw several buildings in the camp that were structurally sound but missing windows and doors. I thought with some dark hessian screening, those buildings could be converted into holding cells. The detainees could then be taken to the buildings blindfolded. Once inside, the blindfolds could come off and the administration process could happen without the detainees ever seeing the camp's inner workings.

My audit complete, I decided to take my findings to the man in charge, Sassaman. In my experience, officers usually don't react well to unsolicited, constructive criticism, especially when it comes from a civilian and a foreigner at that. But keeping my mouth shut would have exposed my clients and me to unnecessary danger. A base camp is supposed to be a defended position where soldiers can rest, recuperate and train between operations. As far as I was concerned, security wise, this camp was an absolute shambles. It was a wonder anyone could sleep there. I knew I couldn't.

As soon as Nic returned from his patrol, I pulled him aside and got him up to speed. He agreed that I should have a word with Sassaman as soon as possible. Later that evening, Sassaman consented to see me at Nic's request. I caught Sassaman between tasks. He had just completed a report on his day's activities and was about to bury his head in his operational order for an evening patrol. He greeted me cordially and asked if I wouldn't mind speaking to a soldier he described as one of his 'better officers'.

I knew I was being passed off but I did as Sassaman requested. I went to see the junior officer – he was six foot six and just as wide.

After a quick introduction, I sat down and started listing my concerns. The meeting was as brief as it was frustrating. I asked the officer why there were no guards stationed in the sentry towers.

'Fuck it, man,' he said. 'We're trying to entice these fuckers over the wall so we can take them on!'

When I told him about the potential for the detainees to kick over the portaloo in the holding area and escape, I got a similar response.

'Fuck it, man, we want them to come at us so we can take them on!'

That seemed to be his answer for everything. If he was one of Sassaman's 'better officers', the Americans didn't have a hope in hell of securing Samarra. Although he was three times bigger than me, I told the officer I didn't agree with his tactics or his attitude and that I would raise my concerns directly with his Commanding Officer.

'Fuck it, man, do what you want. We're here to kill Iraqis,' he said.

I left the officer and went straight back to Sassaman.

'I think you sent me to the wrong man,' I said.

'Why?' Sassaman asked.

By that point I'd lost patience. I didn't have time to tiptoe around personalities or worry about offending people.

'You seriously need to listen to what I've got to say. You've got problems,' I said.

Sassaman paused and looked me in the eye. 'OK, Bob. Please give me twenty minutes.'

I returned to Sassaman's office to find him flanked by his 2 I/C (second in command) and Sergeant Major. I wasn't sure if he'd gathered them there to listen to me or lock me up. Maybe both.

Again, I began with the guard towers. 'Why aren't they manned?' I asked.

Sassaman explained that he didn't have the troops to spare; if his soldiers weren't on patrol they were resting up for the next one.

I pointed out that while I sympathized with his manpower issues, it was imperative that he and his troops live in a secure environment. If soldiers don't feel secure when they rest, their performance on the ground will eventually suffer.

To my surprise Sassaman and his officers agreed with me.

I then asked Sassaman if insurgents had fired mortar rounds at his base.

'Three times,' he said, adding that the strikes had been very accurate.

'Why do you think that is?' I asked.

'I'm not sure,' said Sassaman.

'Do you think it has something to do with the sixty-foot water tower in the middle of your camp?' I asked.

Sassaman and his officers looked at each other and then at me.

'It's a brilliant reference point,' I explained.

'Shit,' said the Sergeant Major. 'We didn't think of that.'

'You may want to dismantle the water tower, especially as it's not in use,' I said.

The Sergeant Major pulled out a pen and paper and started taking notes.

Next, I listed the problems I'd observed regarding their handling of Iraqi detainees. I gave them my idea for converting the unused outbuildings into processing and holding areas. I also suggested that in the meantime they removed the portaloo from the holding area and posted sentries outside the barbed wire to observe for signs of suspicious activity.

When I finished, Sassaman and his officers looked at me as if I'd just unravelled the secrets of the pyramids. I was starting to understand why the Americans assumed such an aggressive stance all the time. Living and working in a state of perpetual insecurity without the proper skills to limit the risks is enough to drive even the most controlled character into a frenzied state. Maintaining a cool head whilst operating in an insurgent-rich environment requires proper training, pre-deployment. It certainly didn't appear as if Sassaman had received it. And if a highly competent, committed officer assigned to one of the most dangerous areas of Iraq hadn't got it, then it was doubtful anyone else in the US military had. That meant that the ex-US soldiers feeding American CSCs were in the same boat – only worse: they didn't have a professional army to bail them out if they got in the shit.

Sassaman and his officers were very gracious. They all thanked me for sharing my concerns and suggestions. Later, the Sergeant Major came to see me privately. He thanked me again and told me he'd taken on board all that I'd said and that it was indeed appreciated. He wasn't bullshitting; that same night hessian screening was wrapped around the detainee holding area and the portaloo was removed. Had I known they would act on my advice so swiftly, I would have asked them to give an extra blanket and a pair of shoes to the shivering old man.

CHAPTER 17

By February 2004 I was rounding into the final stretch of a two-month assignment with CNN Baghdad. My first post-invasion trip to Iraq had been marked by both high and low points. At the pinnacle was the time I'd spent looking after Nic Robertson and his crew as they filmed their documentary. Thanks to Nic, I was exposed to an incredible cross section of players in Iraq's unfolding drama. In addition to Lt Colonel Nathan Sassaman, Nic interviewed a highly articulate Shiite widow seeking compensation from the US military for mistakenly bombing her house into oblivion; an outspoken Iraqi police major who wasn't afraid to stand up to insurgents or his American mentors; and the heir to Iraq's throne, Sharif Ali bin Hussein – a man with the potential to unite Iraq's historically warring factions but whose constitutional monarchy movement lacked American backing.

As a fly on the wall during most of the documentary's filming, I was able to form my own opinions of what was really happening in Iraq and, more importantly, where the situation was headed. My views didn't at all reflect the optimistic scenarios touted by the White House and Downing Street at the time. Neither did Nic's documentary, which fearlessly broke ranks with the buoyant reporting of most major American news outlets.

The Iraq war was nearing its first anniversary and the country was tipping into a downward spiral. For CNN, covering the nation's descent into chaos had gone from impartial to personal.

While I was looking after Nic in Kurdistan, a CNN convoy was ambushed on the outskirts of Baghdad. A British cameraman was wounded and two Iraqi CNN employees were killed in the attack including Yasir, the bright young driver who'd taken the job with CNN to pay for his education. I was gutted when I heard the news.

The hazards for security advisers operating in Iraq were falling into a pecking order. Top of the list was running convoys for the military. A close second was driving clients around Baghdad.

Road congestion in the Iraqi capital, as I'd learned during that first run to the Green Zone, was a huge security issue. Get stuck in traffic or take a wrong turn and you could be escorting your client home in a body bag. That's why, even before I left for Baghdad, I started learning the road systems. By the end of my first week, I practically knew my way around blindfolded. No road could be deemed safe, but some were definitely more dangerous than others. At the start of 2004, the worst was the twelve-kilometre stretch of highway leading from the Green Zone to Baghdad International Airport. As an MSR for the US military, the airport road was a hornets' nest of insurgent activity. It wasn't uncommon for multiple attacks to happen there in a single day.

With flying fast becoming the preferred mode of transport in and out of Baghdad, driving on the airport road was unavoidable. My fellow advisers and I would make several runs a week to drop off and collect CNN staffers. There were also occasions when the story required a trip to and from the airport – stories like the plight of Baka Ali Hussein.

After Nic wrapped filming on his documentary, I was assigned to look after Brent Sadler, a highly experienced CNN Middle East correspondent. One of the stories Brent was working on was an update of a report he'd filed right after the US-led invasion. Brent's original report focused on Baka Ali Hussein, a four-year-old Iraqi boy who'd been accidentally shot in the head by US troops. Though he survived the attack, the bullet wedged into the base of Hussein's skull affecting his ability to walk and speak. The only hope for the wee lad was a specialist operation which he couldn't get in Baghdad.

Brent's first report on Baka Ali Hussein was heart-wrenching; the kind of human interest story that normally gets a response from viewers – and it did. After the story aired, Greek authorities offered to fly Hussein to Athens for medical treatment. Seven months later, the young boy was on the mend and ready to return to his family. The Greek Ambassador to Iraq invited Brent to accompany him to the airport to film the homecoming.

Since we'd be travelling on the airport road, I insisted on the same two-vehicle convoy configuration I'd used for Nic's trip to Samarra; Brent and his cameraman would travel in the lead vehicle while I would ride in the backing vehicle with an Iraqi driver.

Our first stop was an area I knew well: the al-Mansoor district where the Greek Ambassador kept his residence. Favoured by foreign diplomats and wealthy Iraqis such as Sharif Ali bin Hussein, al-Mansoor was a target-rich environment for insurgents and kidnappers looking to score big ransoms.

Despite all that I'd seen in Iraq, I thought surely security at the ambassador's residence would be airtight. Not so. We drove right into the compound without being stopped or searched. Imagine if we'd been suicide bombers. We parked up and an armed man – a westerner – walked over. He was tall, clean shaven and carried himself like a Rupert.

I dismounted my vehicle and introduced myself.

'What are you doing?' he asked. His accent was English, public school.

I explained that we were with CNN and had been invited to accompany the ambassador to the airport. The man said he'd been expecting us and that we would be joining the ambassador's convoy.

'Where are you from?' he asked.

'Scotland.'

He laughed. 'I meant what's your background?'

'I served in the British Army.'

'What unit?'

'I had twenty years in Hereford,' I replied. It was not a cryptic response. Anyone with a military background would know I was referring to the Regiment.

'What about you?' I asked.

'I was a Captain in the Royal Logistic Corps,' he said.

I was right. He was a Rupert. What I couldn't understand though was why he was working Close Protection for a senior diplomat. The Royal Logistic Corps teaches great skills for moving large numbers of men, materials and equipment around a war zone but it has no bearing whatsoever on CP work. A better military background for a team leader in Close Protection is ex-Special Forces or ex-Royal Military Police trained in CP (the Royal Military Police have always had good liaison with the SAS on the subject of Close Protection).

'How did you get into CP work?' I asked.

'The company I work for prefers my kind of background,' he said. 'All my men are ex-Royal Logistic Corps.'

'That's all well and good but what do you know about Close Protection?' I asked.

'We've all read up on it. We know what we're doing,' he assured me.

I had never heard of an adviser's CP training consisting solely of 'reading up' on the subject. What seemed even more shocking to me, though, was that his client, an ambassador, hadn't been given a top-of-the-line team. Of all the individuals requiring Close Protection in Iraq, you'd think diplomats would be assigned only the most experienced advisers.

The way in which the CP team approached their task struck me as extremely laid back, to put it mildly. Not only did they allow us to drive right up to the ambassador's residence without so much as flashing a credential, but the armoured vehicles for the ambassador's convoy were sitting empty on the street twenty minutes before our scheduled departure.

'Where are your men?' I asked the Rupert.

'Out back having a brew and cigarette,' he said.

Those vehicles should have been manned well in advance of the ambassador's departure. A CP team needs to be at the ready at least thirty minutes before a client undertakes a journey in a hostile environment. The Logistic Corps lads should have been in their vehicles ensuring they were serviceable and observing the area for signs of possible surveillance.

Twenty minutes later the ambassador emerged from his residence and climbed into his vehicle, a large blue 4x4 with a big Greek flag stuck on the back window. Why his CP team would want to advertise the ambassador's identity was a mystery to me. When I looked at that sticker, I didn't see a flag. I saw a target. Had the ambassador been my client, I would have insisted the flag be removed.

The convoy consisted of six vehicles including ours. Once the ambassador was in position, I slipped our 4x4s behind his backing vehicle. That put Brent's vehicle in position 4 and mine in position 5.

The convoy cleared al-Mansoor without a problem and headed towards the airport road. Everything was going like clockwork as we turned onto a slip road connecting to a flyover. Then it all went pear-shaped. Vehicle 1, containing members of the ambassador's security detail, missed the turn-off for the flyover and continued down the slip road. At first I thought they'd done it intentionally. I waited for someone to radio with news that the trip to the airport had been aborted.

The radios were silent.

Then, to my utter amazement, vehicle 2 – the ambassador's

vehicle – took the flyover straight onto the airport road, while vehicle 3, his backing vehicle, missed the turn-off. The ambassador was driving on the airport road unaccompanied! I radioed ahead to Brent's vehicle and instructed the driver to follow the ambassador and told them I'd be right behind.

As my vehicle turned onto the flyover I looked in the rear view mirror to see if vehicle 6 was on the ball. It wasn't. Vehicle 6 missed the turn-off as well and continued right on down the slip road. It was The Circuit's version of a comedy of errors; the Greek Ambassador was driving on the most dangerous road in all of Iraq and his CP team was nowhere to be found.

My Iraqi driver burst out laughing – and I must admit, so did I, though my amusement was mixed with embarrassment over the fact that the CP team was British.

It was a farcical situation but my giggle was short lived. When we got within a mile of the airport, traffic on the highway slowed; a US military patrol had been hit by an IED and soldiers were working furiously to clear the road. The attack reminded me of the drive to Samarra; I scanned the area to see if the insurgents who'd detonated the IED were waiting to launch a follow-up attack with small-arms fire. The US military patrol's misfortune turned out to be a lucky break for the Royal Logistic lads. It gave them a chance to catch up with their client.

When we got to the airport, the Rupert in charge of the ambassador's CP team pulled me aside.

'All these fucking roads in Baghdad look alike,' he said, searching my face for some sort of confirmation that this was a legitimate reason for his blunder.

He wasn't a bad lad, but there was no excusing his actions. You don't lose your client in a hostile environment.

'Don't you and your men use spotted maps?' I asked.

'What's a spotted map?' asked the Rupert.

Spotted maps are a basic tool of the CP trade. They mark locations using an encrypted system. In my opinion, they are an indispensable navigation tool in any environment, especially if you have to give your location out over unsecured communications lines. They also eliminate the need to memorize foreign street names. Spotted maps aside, at the very least the team should have done a dry run ahead of time.

'Didn't you recce the route before taking your client out?' I asked.

'We don't have time for recces,' said the Rupert.

That was no kind of answer. You make the time.

The airport was well secured so I was fine with staying off to one side and letting Brent and his crew get on with it.

While they were filming, I had a word with another member of the ambassador's CP team, a lad in his late thirties. He'd been on The Circuit less than a month. When I asked him what he did before taking up CP work, he told me he'd been working in Manchester as a social worker for the past nine years after retiring from the Royal Logistic Corps.

The ambassador's CP team were well meaning, but neither their military nor civilian backgrounds had prepared them to look after a diplomat in a hostile environment or indeed any other environment. Ultimately, I didn't blame them for accepting the assignment. At that point in time, The Circuit was paying advisers in Iraq on average between £300 and £500 per day; an eye-popping sum for most ex-military lads, Ruperts included. The fault in my opinion lay firmly with the team's managers back in the UK. They were the ones responsible for ensuring that the advisers dispatched to Iraq had the backgrounds and skills to execute, amongst other things, a competent vehicle move. Instead, they sent a team who lost their client on the most dangerous road in the country.

It was another sad day for The Circuit in Iraq. For Baka Ali Hussein, however, things were looking up. As I watched him leave the aircraft, it was obvious the wee boy had been through hell; his head was shaved and there was a huge scar across his skull. One of his eyes was slightly askew as a result of his injuries. But he was a strong little character. He was full of energy as he walked completely unaided off the aircraft and into the terminal where members of his family and the Greek ambassador were waiting to greet him.

It was a very emotional scene. Hussein hugged and kissed the ambassador and Brent, whom he thanked again and again. The boy's family couldn't stop crying and expressing their gratitude. In a city of despair, it was nice to see people crying tears of joy for a change.

It was the only happy ending I would ever see in Baghdad.

CHAPTER 18

'We'll be landing in Kabul, inshahallah, at ten-thirty local time,' said the air hostess. I braced myself for a nail-biting journey. Even if I were religious, the Arabic for 'God willing' isn't what I want to hear right before take-off.

It was April 2004 and I'd signed on for another turn with AKE looking after CNN's Nic Robertson while he filmed a documentary – this time in Afghanistan. I'd met up with Nic and his crew in Islamabad for the short flight to Kabul. Not having been to Afghanistan I was very excited about the assignment. Getting there was another matter.

You'd think, given the miles I've flown in my adult life, that I'd be as comfortable on an aeroplane as I am in my own home. Not so. When I was a nineteen-year-old soldier in the RAF Regiment Parachute Squadron, a C-130 on a routine maintenance flight crashed in a wood six hundred yards from me. I still remember, clear as day, the huge fireball shooting up from the treetops and the overwhelming smell of aviation fuel. I ran to the site to try and help, but electrical explosions were erupting everywhere and I couldn't get near the centre of the crash. All I could see was the broken tail fin, pieces of fuselage and body parts strewn across the woods.

Though I went on to make hundreds of parachute jumps when I was in the military, I never forgot the horror of that C-130 crash. To this day I have to summon all my courage before boarding a plane, even in good conditions – which are rare when flying into Kabul, especially the final part. Kabul sits in a bowl surrounded by mountain ranges and the currents flowing over them can toss an aeroplane like a child in a bouncy castle.

The first twenty minutes of our flight were smooth. Then the plane started shaking violently. With every jolt my fingers gouged the armrests. I practically clawed through to the seat frame when I looked out the window; the wings of our aircraft appeared to be inches from the snowy peaks of the southern Hindu Kush Mountains.

I tried to take my mind off the flight by focusing on the landscape beneath us. It was utterly wild; a hostile environment in every sense. Inevitably, my mind wandered to what would happen if the plane crashed. I always fly with my GPS, Silva compass and satellite phone on me just in case. Perhaps I'm paranoid but I decided long ago that if a plane drops out of the sky with me in it, I'm not going to stick around and starve waiting to be rescued. Perhaps I was overly influenced by the story of the Argentinian rugby team who crashed in the Andes in the 1970s, and survived by eating their dead mates.

The mountains receded and we made our final descent into Kabul. I breathed a sigh of relief as the plane touched down, not realizing that the most chaotic portion of the flight was about to begin. As soon as the wheels bounced on the tarmac, most of the passengers jumped up from their seats and started pulling down their belongings from the overhead compartments. During taxi, there was a near punch-up as a group of men jostled for first position at the aircraft's main exit. It was a good introduction to a country where there are no rules and only the strongest survive.

I had many reasons for taking an assignment in Afghanistan. A few of my mates on The Circuit had been there before me and I found their stories about the country and its people fascinating. I couldn't turn down the opportunity to see it all for myself. Wanderlust aside, I also had a burning professional interest in the country. I was very disturbed by what was happening to The

Circuit in Iraq and I wanted to see if the slide in standards had spread elsewhere. I was also curious about Afghanistan's general security situation – an interest which fit perfectly with Nic's documentary.

Nic was an old Afghan hand, having first reported on the Taliban in 1996 when they took Kabul. Afghanistan had fallen off the media's radar in the wake of the Iraq war and Nic felt it was high time for a look in. He wanted to 'take the pulse' of Afghanistan to determine if the US-led coalition was making any headway towards securing the country. Nic reasoned that if the coalition was succeeding in Afghanistan, they'd have a blueprint to follow for Iraq. Conversely, if things weren't going so well and the coalition was blowing it in Afghanistan, Iraq could go the same way.

As for specific stories, Nic was adamant about two. First, he wanted to land an embed with US troops operating in southern Afghanistan. Secondly, he wanted to report on the coalition's efforts to rein in Afghanistan's opium production.

As I stepped off the aircraft, the first thing that struck me was how war-torn Kabul Airport looked. This was 2004, nearly two and half years after the American-led invasion, and the debris of battles long since past still littered the place. Rusting Russian-made tanks, helicopters and other armour lay everywhere. Men in face shields and protective clothing were busy clearing land-mines from the side of the runway. It amazed me that commercial flights were allowed to land whilst this was going on.

Inside the terminal, we were met by a CNN 'fixer' I'll call Hamid. Fixers are retained by the media to help out in foreign countries. Usually a national or someone from a neighbouring country, they're jacks of all trades who translate, set up interviews, find hotels, gather information on stories and get you and your kit past customs officials without getting bogged down in searches and paperwork.

A good fixer is worth his weight in gold and I'd heard from

advisers who'd worked with CNN Kabul previously that Hamid was one of the best: hard-working, efficient and a qualified medical doctor to boot.

Hamid hugged Nic and gave me a deceptively strong handshake. Though the man was built like a bull, his manicured beard gave him an almost gentle appearance (I later found out that many men in Hamid's family had represented Afghanistan in wrestling competitions).

Hamid asked for our passports and luggage tags and handed them off to an associate. 'The cars are waiting,' he said.

'What about our kit?' I asked.

'Don't worry,' he said. 'My brother is the security commander here. Everything will be at our hotel by lunchtime.'

Hamid was already living up to his reputation.

Outside the terminal, two Toyota Hilux Surfs were waiting for us with the engines running. The Hilux is very popular in Afghanistan and therefore quite low profile. Once we were all in, the drivers initiated the central locks and opened the windows no more than an inch; wide enough for ventilation but sufficiently narrow to prevent anyone from tossing a hand grenade inside.

The advisers who'd come before me had taught CNN's local hires well. That's the thing about standards on The Circuit. When they're high, each successive adviser on a job benefits from the groundwork laid before them. When standards are low, it's the opposite; you're either starting from scratch or worse – cleaning up a mess someone else has left behind.

As we turned onto the main road, I quickly realized that the battle scars at Kabul Airport were superficial wounds compared with the rest of the city. Many of the buildings we passed were nothing more than crumbling shells, yet many were still inhabited. We drove past an old bombed-out apartment block that was missing entire sections of exterior walls. I saw women and children living inside, completely exposed to the elements. Some families were on the top floors. One wrong step and they could easily fall to their deaths. It was disgraceful to see people living that way.

An equally outrageous situation was waiting just a few miles up the road, at the Masood roundabout, one of Kabul's busiest. Just ahead of it was a pedestrian crossing; women in burkas were hovering at either end, trying to cross without being run over. Watching them step out and jump back, I felt incredibly sorry for them. It never dawned on me until that moment that burkas allow no peripheral vision. They're horrible garments that no human being should be forced to wear.

We had no choice but to follow the rest of the traffic from the roundabout onto a congested offshoot. It wasn't the quickest route to our hotel, but as Hamid explained, it was the only one available to us. The road leading directly to our hotel was a no-go zone. Just like Baghdad, the Yanks had located key buildings including the US Embassy and the International Security Assistance Force's (ISAF) headquarters along one of Kabul's most critical traffic arteries and sealed it from unauthorized vehicles (i.e. all locals).

At the first opportunity, our drivers turned off the main road and onto a series of backstreets. I use the term 'street' loosely because they were nothing more than muddy tracks cutting through slums. I couldn't believe the appalling conditions people were living in; rubbish was strewn everywhere. There were no proper sewers, just miles of ditches filled with raw sewage. I saw human waste flowing directly out the sides of buildings and into areas where children were playing or rummaging through piles of debris. And the dust! Dust and exhaust fumes were inescapable. I blew my nose and looked at the tissue; it was black. I've been to some shitholes in my time, but Kabul will take some beating.

Our hotel, the Kabul Inn, had served as CNN's Bureau in 2001 before being converted into a full-time guest house. When we arrived, I was pleased to see that it was set in a walled compound surrounded on three sides by NGO houses with decent security. It was also set back from the main road so it would take one hell of a car bomb to make a serious dent in the place. It was another example of how the advisers who'd come before me had made my job much easier.

Inside the gated courtyard there was a lovely, quiet garden, another plus from a security standpoint. I didn't want my clients sleeping and working in a watering hole hosting international piss-ups every night. Best of all, our rooms were in the back of the main building, the safest possible location.

Once I knew we could sleep soundly at night, I got stuck into securing our daytime movements around Kabul and points beyond. My first order of business was weapons. In Baghdad I was slotted into an ongoing assignment for which weapons had already been procured. CNN didn't maintain a full-time bureau in Kabul, so on this job I'd have to find my own.

As long as you have money, it's always possible to get a hold of weapons in a hostile environment. The trick is to buy wisely. There are lots of things to consider in a country like Afghanistan where at the time there were no regulatory standards. A weapon's origin for one; in Afghanistan, the majority of weapons on offer are either made in Pakistan or Russia and eastern Europe. A Russian/ eastern European-made weapon costs between 500 and 900 US dollars depending on condition and type. Pakistani-made weapons only cost between 300 and 500 US dollars. The price difference is substantial but when you consider that your life can depend on what you buy, you're taking a big chance if you opt for the bargain version. The Russian AK, for example, is the most copied weapon in the world. It's very easy to use compared to its American-made counterpart, the M16. I've seen children strip down an AK, clean it, reassemble and fire in a matter of minutes – sadly. AKs are always in demand and imitations can vary considerably in quality. As a general rule, you can't go wrong with a Russian-made AK47 assault rifle in excellent condition.

Fortunately, Hamid was able to get me a Russian-made 'Kalakov' – an AK47 with a folding butt and shorter barrel. It was an ideal vehicle weapon. He also got the seller to throw in plenty of ammo and magazines.

While Hamid was working on my AK, I'd got in touch with a mate of mine working in Kabul about a pistol. He was able to find me a European-made Sig Sauer 9 mm with European-made ammo and good magazines. As always with new weapons, I found a patch of wasteland where I could test-fire them from various distances and zero the sights to my eye.

I spent the first few days in Kabul accompanying Nic and his crew on shoots with NGOs, United Nations and Afghan Government officials. Many of Nic's interviews focused on the drugs story, specifically the US-led coalition's efforts to eradicate poppy cultivation and stem the flow of opium from Afghanistan (poppies produce opium which is then chemically refined into heroin). It was a sensitive topic as the coalition's eradication programme was proving far less effective than the Taliban's.

In 1999, Afghanistan produced 75 per cent of the world's opium. The following year, 2000, the Taliban decided the country's drugs trade was un-Islamic. They banned farmers from growing poppies and ordered the destruction of opium stockpiles and heroin laboratories. Those who didn't destroy their crops were jailed or shot.

It may not have been 'democratic' but the draconian incentives were a massive success. By early 2001, the United Nations reported that opium production in Afghanistan had been practically wiped out.

Fast forward to the end of 2001; the Taliban are driven out of power and Afghan farmers are once again free to grow what is by far their most profitable cash crop. Many also seize the opportunity to unearth opium they had hidden from the Taliban. The result: by 2003 Afghanistan had reclaimed its crown as the world's number one opium producer.

Afghanistan's drugs trade was as much a setback for the War on Terror as it was for the War on Drugs. In 2004, Afghanistan's illegal drugs trade was worth an estimated one and a half billion dollars a year. A lot of that money went straight into the pockets of Taliban and al-Qaeda in the form of 'protection taxes' levied on poppy farmers and drugs traffickers.

After a few days of researching the drugs story, Nic got a jump on the other goal he'd set for the trip; landing an embed with US troops operating in Afghanistan's southern Khost province. For this particular embed, Nic needed to apply in person to the US military Public Affairs Officer, who only took requests following regularly scheduled pressers.

At the first opportunity, Nic went to a presser and submitted his name for the Khost embed. The PAO told him there were several journalists waiting for that particular embed and that another journalist from a competing network was ahead of him. Nic was also warned that since it had become far too dangerous to drive from Kabul to Khost, the availability of military flights would also be a deciding factor in whether he got the embed.

It was a frustrating state of affairs. Nic didn't have unlimited time in Afghanistan and he wasn't keen on sitting in Kabul waiting for a phone call that might never come. He wanted to get moving on the drugs story as soon as possible to ensure that he fulfilled at least one of his objectives.

On the way back from the presser, we discussed options for covering the coalition's poppy eradication programmes. At the time, most of the media were focusing their coverage on Jalalabad, the capital of Nangarhar province in eastern Afghanistan. Jalalabad had several things going for it including easy access from Kabul and a population that was relatively hospitable to westerners.

But Nic didn't want to go where the rest of the press corps had been. He wanted to go to Helmund, Afghanistan's biggest opium-producing province representing a third of the country's output. Reporting from Helmund had its challenges. It was more difficult to get to than Jalalabad and far more hostile. Taliban elements were reportedly very active there. But if you wanted to get the real story on Afghanistan's drugs trade, Helmund was the place to go.

By the time we arrived at the Kabul Inn Nic had made up his mind. We were going to Helmund.

CHAPTER 19

While I got stuck into the security details of our trip, Nic worked swiftly putting everything in place editorially. He enlisted the help of the country's counter-narcotics police who assigned two officers to accompany us; first to Kandahar for interviews with counter-narcotics officials and then to Helmund, where they'd arranged for CNN to film the destruction of poppy fields.

The counter-narcotics police were eager to show the world that they were making progress eradicating poppy cultivation, so when it came to assessing the trip's security, they pushed the party line. They told Nic he'd be perfectly safe as long as they were with him. Their optimistic spin was also cultural; I was learning fast that Afghans are very proud and very macho. They never say something is too dangerous or too scary to undertake. The most they were willing to concede was that Kandahar and Helmund weren't as safe as Kabul.

I wanted more detail than that – much more. Unlike Iraq, I wasn't operating as part of a team of security advisers who could convene at the end of each day, compare notes and hone the available intelligence of the operations area. On this assignment, I was working alone. It was my responsibility to make sure Nic got his story safely. If he or his crew got hurt, it would be on my head and no one else's.

As with most assignments, I began by consulting the available, published intelligence on the areas we'd be operating in. I was spoilt for choice when it came to the quantity of security reports available. The US military, ISAF and the UN all compiled them for distribution to the press and international community. The problem was these reports were, in my view, extremely political, short on useful details and highly sanitized. There was tremendous pressure at the time to promote the idea that Afghanistan's security was improving. The political leaders who'd sent money and troops to the country had to maintain the perception back home that the resources they'd committed weren't being squandered.

The locals had a very different opinion of the situation. CNN's fixer, Hamid, had contacts all over Afghanistan and what he was hearing was a far cry from the rosy picture being painted by the international community. Another useful source was a security report compiled by ANSO, the Afghan NGO Security Organization. The intelligence in the ANSO reports was more reliable than ISAF's or the coalition's because it was gathered from Afghan NGO employees working around the country. I also found the BBC website extremely beneficial. The BBC employs 'stringers' (part-time, local reporters) all over Afghanistan and their analysis is usually spot on.

A thorough reading of all the material confirmed what I had suspected all along: Afghanistan's security situation had been in steady decline since 2001.

Having completed my background research, I mapped the route we'd travel to Helmund, compiling a list of the possible dangers we could encounter along the way.

The trip would take us from Kabul to Kandahar city, where we'd overnight, down to Lashkar Gah in Helmund province for two days of filming and then back to Kabul. The five-day trip would require us to travel through six Afghan provinces, each with its own internal problems of warlords, anti-western sentiment, insurgents and banditry. Of all the provinces, however, Helmund was far and away the most troubling. Hamid's contacts had told him that the Taliban had successfully regrouped there and that al-Qaeda elements were gaining influence as well.

On the plus side, we had a paved road to travel, the A1, all the way to Helmund province (at which point we'd have to revert to dirt tracks and desert roads). Reconstructed with Japanese aid money, the A1 forms a giant 'U' running from eastern Afghanistan, down south and due west to the Iranian border. The highway is a commercial lifeline for the country and a point of pride for the international community. Due to its political symbolism and the fact that it runs through so many spheres of influence, warlords tend to keep their hands off the A1 lest they invite a military response from ISAF or a tit-for-tat hit and run from a neighbouring warlord.

In the minus column, the A1 was a magnet for insurgent attacks and all sorts of troublemaking by gangs of thieves. Hamid learned that bandits and insurgents had been luring vehicles off the A1 and into ambushes or minefields by setting up fake detours. Unfortunately, simply ignoring the detour signs wasn't an option because not all of them were a bluff. Drainage on the highway wasn't great and a lot of the culverts that ran under it weren't able to cope with the amount of water running off the mountains. When flash floods hit, which happened frequently during the spring thaw, parts of the road would just wash away.

We would have to assess the detours individually as we encountered them. But in terms of proactive measures, there was plenty we could do to minimize the threat of attack. First, we needed to assemble an armed convoy; one that would be imposing enough to ward off troublemakers but not so imposing as to attract unwanted attention. I decided five vehicles was a must; low-profile Toyota 4x4s that could respond well to difficult road conditions (which we would definitely encounter once we turned off the A1). We couldn't use armoured vehicles because at the time they weren't available in Afghanistan. (Today, I wouldn't dream of driving around Afghanistan in anything less than a B6/7 armoured vehicle.) Armoured vehicles also have disadvantages; they can get bogged down in sand, limiting your options when evading a road attack, and they're more likely to trigger an anti-tank mine should you be unfortunate enough to drive over one.

I asked Hamid to find us five reliable local drivers and a dozen Afghan guards from different ethnic backgrounds. I insisted upon using a mix because we'd be moving through areas controlled by different and often quarrelling Afghan tribes. Better to be an equal opportunity offender than appear to be taking sides.

To some, twelve guards may sound like overkill. But if our convoy was ambushed we had to have the ability to extricate ourselves. We would be travelling alone without the benefit of military support or the ability to call it in. My experience in the Regiment had taught me that the side with the heaviest and most accurate firepower keeps the opposition's heads down. Only then do you have a chance to pull back from a bad situation.

When it came to arming our convoy, I wanted nine of the guards to carry AK47s and three of them to have RPDs, Russian-made, belt-fed light machine guns. The mix of weapons was optimal given our circumstances. If we were attacked, in a static situation I could split the guards into three groups, each having the accuracy of three rifles supported by the fire-power of a light machine gun.

As for myself, I'd have my AK in a black canvas bag as a car weapon and my 9 mm hidden around my waist. I also planned to 'arm' myself with two cameras; a pocket-sized Cannon digital and a professional Cannon with a 400 mm lens. Photography is a passion of mine but, leisure pursuits aside, both cameras serve a practical purpose in the field. The professional or 'big' camera as I call it is an excellent cover. If I don't want to stick out as 'the security guy' I can pass myself off as a journalist with a 400 mm lens in my hand. The titchy little camera also has its uses; taking someone's picture can be a great ice-breaker.

Once I'd sorted the convoy details, I drafted daily timetables for our movements, bearing in mind that Nic needed some flexibility to film his stories. The first leg of our trip, Kabul to Kandahar, would take approximately eight hours. I wanted us to leave before first light. At the time, Kabul was reasonably benign, from a security standpoint, with only odd targeting of coalition, government and local military personnel (these attacks would step up considerably over the coming years). In my mind, driving in or near Kabul in the dark hours of early morning was preferable to travelling through the less secure areas around Kandahar after sunset.

At three-thirty the morning of our trip, everyone assembled in the grounds of the Kabul Inn. Our party consisted of me, Nic and his crew, Hamid, twelve Afghan guards, five Afghan drivers and two Afghan counter-narcotics officers. I thanked everyone for showing up on time before launching into a brief lecture on the importance of staying awake during our journey. I couldn't emphasize enough that every set of eyes needed to be open, alert and aware. I couldn't afford to have even one of the guards waking up from a nap in the middle of a firefight, fumbling around for his weapon. My stay-alert policy extended to Nic and his crew as well. One of the biggest problems I've encountered working with the media is getting them to stay awake during journeys. More than one war correspondent has confessed to me that they'd always regarded driving in hostile environments as an opportunity to catch up on their sleep.

After my lecture, I found out which guards and drivers had mechanics experience and distributed them evenly among the vehicles. Next, I assigned each vehicle a specific position and task in the convoy. The 'order of march' as it's known is designed to provide maximum protection to the clients. The first or recce vehicle would travel one to two minutes ahead of everyone else[15] to keep an eye out for possible hazards. The

15 The exact lead time is ultimately dictated by line of sight, communication and terrain.

second vehicle in the convoy would act as front protection for the third vehicle, where the clients, Nic and his crew, would ride. I positioned myself in the fourth or backing vehicle. That way, if Nic's vehicle became disabled in any way, I could cross deck him and his crew directly into mine. The fifth and last vehicle in the convoy would secure us from the rear; the guards could provide early warning if we were attacked from behind and put down fast, accurate fire if we got pinned down.

We left the Kabul Inn at 4 a.m., just as the first signs of traffic were starting to appear. As soon as we were on the road I did a mobile radio check with each vehicle in our convoy; the first of many I would perform every fifteen minutes whilst in transit. It was essential we maintain good communications at all times, the nightmare scenario being that you're attacked and you can't talk to the rest of your team. My vigilance did have a down side; the Afghan guards took my frequent comms checks as an invitation to chatter amongst themselves. I constantly had to ask them to stop tying up our radios with casual banter in case there was something important to get across.

In addition to keeping in contact with everyone, I also initiated procedures for establishing where we were at all times during our trip. Using a handheld GPS, I recorded a latitude and longitude reading of our position – the first of many readings I would take during our journey down to Helmund. I planned to identify the readings or 'way points' by assigning each a landmark name, for example 'mosque', 'culvert' or 'cross roads'. It's much easier to assess your exact location using way points than by referencing a large-scale map. I also planned to take hourly lat and long readings with my satellite phone and send an SMS message with the coordinates back to AKE's ops room in the UK. It's not that I was expecting anyone to come quickly if anything bad happened, but if it did, at least AKE would have a starting point to come and search for us.

Traffic grew heavier as we approached the outskirts of Kabul; trucks, cars and men on bicycles going to work clogged the road. Kabul is surrounded by tiny hamlets and many of the people who live there prefer to travel to the capital at inconvenient hours to avoid being ambushed by bandits.

Around 5 a.m., daylight broke, revealing a diverse, breathtaking landscape. I was mesmerized by the scenery. It was my first trip outside Kabul and the contrast with the capital couldn't have been more striking. Working in Kabul with its open sewers, overcrowding and relentless dust was like working inside a Hoover bag. The countryside, by comparison, was a revelation; every twenty miles the scenery changed; giant red rock formations punching through the earth; pure white peaks sitting atop jagged black mountains; lush green valleys tumbling from foothills speckled with rocks and shrubs.

I wanted nothing more than to pull over and start taking pictures. The pristine mountains were especially enticing; no roads, no ski lifts, just untouched nature begging to be explored. Tempting as these sights were, I knew seeing them on foot was a non-starter. Afghanistan's countryside and even some of its urban areas are littered with millions of anti-personnel mines which kill or maim up to a dozen people a day. You'd think given the carnage the international community would step up its de-mining efforts.[16] Sadly, it all boils down to money; it costs less than fifty US dollars to lay a landmine and up to five hundred to clear just one. Cruel maths indeed.

It was still very early in the morning but the road was getting busier by the minute. Most of the traffic was commercial; large trucks hauling wood or animals to Kabul or carrying consumer goods from Pakistan. Many of the trucks we passed were ornately decorated with brightly coloured, intricate designs and rows of long, brass chains placed as talismans to ward off evil spirits (every bit helps when driving on lawless roads). For the drivers, these trucks are their pride and joy and they spend

16 The brave men who risk their lives on a daily basis decommissioning mines are also frequently targeted by insurgents.

hours embellishing them. Somehow, I couldn't see the drivers of UK haulage trucks doing the same to their vehicles.

About an hour and a half into our journey we experienced our first problem; a tyre puncture on the second vehicle. As I've said, the last thing you want is to be immobile on a road in a hostile environment, so every minute counts. There's no AA in Afghanistan, which is why I canvassed the guards and drivers about mechanics experience prior to our departure. It was essential that each vehicle in the convoy have at least one self-taught mechanic who could improvise a patch or fix an engine if need be.

I was very proud to see all the guards covering each other as we pulled to the side of the road. The tyre was changed in seven minutes flat and we were back on our way. All things being equal, the Afghans in our convoy could have given a Formula 1 team a run for their money.

As we crossed into the second province of our journey, we were greeted by another of Afghanistan's exotic, visual delights; a Kutchi family wandering the countryside. The Kutchi are a nomadic and semi-nomadic people who for centuries have traversed Afghanistan as they make their way from India through Pakistan and into Iran. They travel from valley to valley, grazing their cattle, goats, camels and woolly dogs as big as ponies. The wealthier tribesmen use large trucks to transport their animals but the poor do all their moving on foot. The Kutchi are low in Afghanistan's pecking order and are rarely seen in populated areas. When you do spot them though, they are difficult to miss. Instead of burkas, Kutchi women wear brightly coloured dresses with bursts of orange, red, pink, yellow and blue. Delighted as I was to be seeing an authentic Kutchi family, my heart sank at the sight of women and children wandering the landscape, apparently unconcerned that they might be walking through a heavily mined area.

We were making excellent time, clearing two provinces in two hours. As we crossed into Ghazni, the third province of our journey, we came across a small built-up area with a petrol station. I radioed to the drivers to pull over. I wanted to avoid major towns as much as possible and the small hamlet provided an excellent opportunity to refuel and blast the sand out of the engines.

The dust that accumulates inside vehicles is incredible in Afghanistan and if you don't clean under the bonnet you're asking for trouble. That's why every petrol station in the country is equipped with generators to power high-pressure air hoses for pumping up tyres and blasting engine filters.

While the drivers tended their vehicles and the guards stretched their legs, I had a look around. The first thing that struck me was the faces of the locals at the petrol station. They appeared far more ferocious than the average Afghan on the street in Kabul. In the Afghan capital, many of the local men wear western clothing, keep their faces clean shaven and style their hair like westerners. The only thing western about these men was their obvious dislike for them. It was a useful reminder to all of us that we were now well and truly outside the 'security bubble' of the capital.

We settled our bill quickly and got on our way. The hours passed uneventfully, which was absolutely fine by me. It looked as if our schedule would hold until we ran into a suspicious roadblock forty miles north-east of Kandahar city. It was classic ambush territory; a roadblock flanked by two pieces of high, broken ground. We had already encountered several detours along the A1 but in those instances the road had obviously washed away. This one wasn't so straightforward. The road stretched out in a straight line for at least ten miles, most of it level ground with desert scrub on both sides, which is great for observation. Around the roadblock, however, the ground broke, obstructing the view. It was entirely possible that the road had washed away at the only point for ten miles where bandits or insurgents could ambush vehicles. Then again, it could be a trap.

I radioed the drivers to pull over six hundred metres short of the roadblock. I wanted to see how other traffic fared through the detour before attempting it ourselves. After a couple of minutes, a small truck driven by an Afghan approached. The driver turned right at the detour, disappeared into the broken ground and reappeared on the main road three hundred metres beyond.

I still wasn't satisfied it was completely safe. If the detour was an insurgent trap, they'd be waiting for a westerner or those obviously connected to the coalition, like the Afghan National Army (ANA), to drive by. I decided to send the lead vehicle to test the route. I reminded the driver to follow in the truck's tyre marks in case there were mines.

I watched the lead vehicle turn off the highway, drop into a dry river bed and disappear. Three minutes later it reappeared on the other side of the road block. The driver radioed to say everything was fine. Satisfied, I sent the rest of the convoy through at thirty-second intervals, reminding the drivers once again to follow in each other's tracks. The entire exercise put us ten minutes behind schedule; a minor concession for ensuring our safety.

The city of Kandahar exudes a charm that if it were located in almost any other country would be called quaint. Founded by Alexander the Great in the fourth century BC, it's been luring conquerors ever since: Genghis Khan and Tamerlane in the thirteenth century, the British in the nineteenth century, the Soviets and Taliban in the twentieth century, the US and NATO-led ISAF in the twenty-first. There are no tall buildings in the city and many of its 300,000 inhabitants travel by horse and carriage or three-wheeled tricycle taxis powered by small motorbike engines. The air quality is much cleaner than Kabul and the streets, even at rush hour, are sedate by comparison.

Peel away the pleasant exterior, however, and you'll find a place teaming with radical sentiment. Kandahar was the first major Afghan city to fall to the Taliban in the mid-1990s. The movement's spiritual leader, Mullah Mohammed Omar, made his base there until he was ousted from power in 2001. The city has been a hotbed of drugs trafficking and insurgent activity ever since.

Kandahar sits on the edge of the Spin Boldak road, which runs from Kandahar down to Spin Boldak and across the border to the Pakistani city of Quetta. The route from Quetta on up is used by the Taliban and al-Qaeda to run their suicide bombing missions into Kandahar. From Kandahar on down it's used for ferrying drugs into Pakistan.

Kandahar's first defence against drugs-runners and insurgents is the city's gate, which is guarded round the clock by heavily armed Afghan police. As we learned first hand, the show of force is purely cosmetic. When our convoy drove past, the police didn't seem to be the least bit aware of potential suicide bombers. We got through with little more than a wave.

Our first stop in Kandahar was the city's counter-narcotics unit. Located on an unassuming backstreet well away from the city's main roads, it was a single-storey building surrounded by a perimeter wall. The inconspicuous set-up was probably deliberate. The men inside were very unpopular with some very powerful people.

While the drivers and guards kept an eye on the vehicles the two counter-narcotics escorts from Kabul took the rest of us inside. Afghans are very hospitable and the local Commander of the counter-narcotics unit had lunch waiting for us. While we ate, the Commander briefed Nic on the drugs and security situations in Kandahar and Helmund. He spoke in very measured terms. Nic's report could influence the flow of aid money to his unit and the Commander was trying to get the message across that his teams were making progress.

To be fair, though, he didn't just feed Nic a load of lies to justify his unit's existence. He told Nic that his officers' jobs were complicated by the fact that they all lived in the same provinces where they worked. That meant that the agents and their families (and in Afghanistan, an extended family can have hundreds of members) were easy targets for disgruntled drugs lords. Most tellingly, the Commander conceded – off camera – that the corruption spawned by the illegal drugs trade had reached the highest levels of government. There were persistent, though denied, allegations that the Afghan President's brother, Ahmed Wali Karzai, was profiting handsomely from the nation's opium trade, so much so that the locals had nicknamed him the 'King of Kandahar'.

That night I reflected on the first phase of our journey. Experiencing Afghanistan outside the bubble of Kabul was proving to be quite an eye-opener. The country's security was as bad if not worse than I'd imagined. It was difficult to see how the coalition could be making any progress towards eradicating Afghanistan's drugs trade if the President's own brother was being accused of profiting from it. I wondered what surprises awaited us in Helmund.

CHAPTER 20

I walked towards the group of young men not knowing at all what to expect. I could have observed them more safely from a distance but not more effectively; a trade-off which in this case wouldn't be wise. They knew we were there and I had no idea what they thought about that. I needed to even things up; to see for myself how they reacted to a westerner. Judging from the black turbans on their heads, I doubted they'd be thrilled to see me. The best I could hope for would be indifference. I stretched out my hand to greet them. They didn't respond in kind. They just stood there arms at their sides, staring at me, not a hint of a smile amongst them.

I got the sinking feeling that I may have misjudged the situation. Then again, I hadn't imagined anything quite like this in any of my Helmund scenarios. When Nic said he wanted to 'take the pulse' of Afghanistan I thought he was speaking figuratively. I never thought for a second that I'd find myself literally trying to shake hands with the Taliban.

We left Kandahar at 6.30 a.m. for the final drive to Lashkar Gah, Helmund – the most dangerous leg of our five-day journey. The A1 would take us only a third of the way there, leaving us with two equally undesirable options for the rest of the trip. We could either travel dirt tracks infested with Taliban and bandits or drive through the desert and risk running into a minefield. I decided to wait until we reached the end of the A1 before making any final decisions.

The drive through western Kandahar province offered a

sneak preview of what lay ahead in Helmund: poppy fields. We must have passed about half a dozen, all the size of football pitches. In an effort to conceal them, some of the fields had been planted between acres of wheat or other legitimate crops. But the poppies were in full bloom. There was no mistaking the blankets of deep red, pink and rose-tinged white.

When we reached the turn-off for the A1, I radioed the drivers to pull over. There was a small petrol station and it would be our last chance to refuel, blow out the air filters and check the tyres and lubricants before heading onto rough terrain. I had the vehicles serviced in groups of two so we could speed away quickly should trouble strike. We were now on the outer edges of Helmund province, a very dangerous place for westerners.

During the stop I surveyed the landscape to weigh up whether to take our convoy along the dirt roads or through the desert. Decision time had come. The dirt road was prime ambush territory; it dipped into dead ground at regular intervals, creating ideal hiding places for troublemakers. The desert by comparison was far more appealing. I couldn't rule out the possibility of landmines completely but I was fairly confident we'd be OK. Anti-tank and anti-personnel mines are usually planted in areas where people are restricted in their movements, such as bottlenecks. This was a vast, open expanse of desert.

I had made up my mind. I'd take the convoy off track through the desert for the final leg of our journey to Lashkar Gah. I gathered everyone together for a final brief on how we would undertake the drive. My plan was to travel in an extended line. I told the drivers to follow me in a single file into the desert until I stopped and then line up their vehicles side by side with mine in the centre. From that point, all they had to do was maintain a distance of approximately fifty to one hundred metres between vehicles. I'd take care of navigation and look out for signs of landmines.

We travelled on a straight bearing through the desert for

Taliban observing the token eradication of a poppy field outside Lashkar Gah. Afghanistan, 2004.

In Paktia, mixing with Patcha Khan's people during his road closure. I was very aware that I was the only westerner for miles. This picture was taken by my local driver using my 'small camera'. Afghanistan, 2004.

My dress to travel in vehicles around southern and eastern Afghanistan. I'm not trying to be covert, just low profile enough that I won't stick out to those looking to target westerners. Afghanistan, 2004.

This picture was taken right after Patcha Khan had lifted his road closure just for our convoy. The crowd is a mix of Patcha Khan's supporters and truck drivers. Afghanistan, 2004.

A graveyard of Russian armour east of Kabul. Afghanistan, 2004.

Three Afghan women clad in burkas – garments which, in my view, are oppressive and dangerous because they rob women of peripheral vision. Afghanistan, 2004.

A mountain range between Kabul and Kandahar, an example of Afghanistan's diverse landscapes. Afghanistan, 2005.

An Afghan landmine disposal worker hard at work north of Kabul. He and others like him are the unsung heroes of post-Taliban Afghanistan. By co-operating with the international community, these brave men have become prime targets for insurgents. Afghanistan, 2005.

Riyadh's glittering city centre. Saudi Arabia, 2004.

Two traumatized brothers stand outside their bullet-ridden school, located in the neighbourhood where Saudi troops engaged in a heated battle with militants at an al-Qaeda safe house. Many have mistaken the location in this photograph for Baghdad. Riyadh, 2004.

A footbridge over the filthy Kabul River, a health hazard which has yet to be tackled by the international community. Kabul, 2005.

Security on a mosque rooftop. Kabul, 2005.

A US commercial CP team looking after Afghan President Karzai assumes what I view as an overly aggressive stance. This kind of *modus operandi* reflects very poorly on a client. Afghanistan, 2005.

more than two hours. Since the dirt road meandered through the desert, from time to time we'd see vehicles travelling the road to our right. I was encouraged by the flow of traffic as it signalled that no one was being attacked. As we hit the outskirts of Lashkar Gah, the traffic on the road grew heavier. At that point I decided it was safe enough to divert the convoy back onto the regular road and adopt our usual tactic of one vehicle scouting ahead.

Lashkar Gah offered a taste of what life must have been like in Afghanistan hundreds of years ago; dirt tracks cutting through neighbourhoods of ancient-looking mud-brick buildings. The men were hearty and had deeply lined faces, even the young. I couldn't see a woman anywhere.

The city would be frozen in time were it not for the engineered waterways shooting out from the river running through the centre of it. Back in the 1960s, American companies constructed the irrigation canals to aid agricultural development. I wondered how the American engineers would feel if they knew their goodwill project had been hijacked by poppy growers.

The moment we entered the town, I got a very strange feeling in my gut – one that only grew stronger as we pulled up to our hotel. Located next to the Governor's mansion, the hotel was one of several modern-looking two-storey buildings and bungalows built along a tree-lined street. I later found out that the area had also been built by Americans in the 1960s and that the locals refer to it as 'little America'. Despite the name, there were no internationals in sight other than myself and my clients.

Security in the area was dreadful. There was no vehicle checkpoint at the top of the street, no barriers to control traffic and no blast walls surrounding the buildings to protect against vehicle-born bombs.

The situation was no better inside our hotel. The staff gave us a very dry, emotionless reception. The strange feeling I had grew more intense. I couldn't put my finger on it exactly. Was I feeling this way because the security was so abysmal or was it something more? I went around to the rear of the building to check for areas of vulnerability. The hotel backed directly onto the river; a positive from a security standpoint. What I saw on the other side of the river, however, left me speechless: a poppy field in full bloom.

The Governor of Helmund lived right next door. If he were serious about poppy eradication, you'd think he had got around to destroying the field growing in his own backyard. It made me wonder how he really felt about a bunch of foreign journalists checking on his progress.

I assigned a group of guards to keep an eye on our vehicles and the exterior grounds of our hotel, and arranged for food to be taken to them. In the meantime, a group of local counter-narcotics officers and Governor's aides came to the hotel to discuss Nic's story over lunch. The local officials had arranged for CNN to travel the following day to an area thirty kilometres south of Lashkar Gah to film the poppy-eradication programme in progress. After that, the plan was to return to Lashkar Gah city for interviews with the Governor of Helmund province.

It seemed like a lot to pack into one day, especially as Afghans aren't exactly known for their punctuality. I took Nic to one side to remind him that interview or no interview, we needed to leave Lashkar Gah no later than 3 p.m. I didn't want to cross the desert at night. Nic agreed.

After lunch, I went out to the car park to check on the guards and see if they had anything suspicious to report. I found them observing a group of men about one hundred and fifty yards up the river. The men were playing around, wrestling and pushing one another. Most of them were dressed in dark clothing and black turbans. I asked the guards what they thought of the group. They responded without a hint of embarrassment that they were very afraid as they were certain the young men were Taliban. I radioed Hamid to come outside. I wanted his opinion before deciding my next move.

One look at the men and Hamid agreed with the guards. He reminded me that the Taliban were known to operate freely in Lashkar Gah and that we'd have to be careful of them. I knew right then I'd have to meet the Taliban face to face. The men had probably seen us arrive at the hotel. If not, it wouldn't take them long to figure out we were staying there. I couldn't go through the night wondering if they would attack our location. I needed to assess how great a threat they were to us, if any – something I could only do up close.

I doubted the men spoke English, so I'd have to bring Hamid with me to interpret. He wasn't keen on the idea. I didn't want to push him beyond his comfort level but I really had no choice.

I left my pistol in my vehicle and instructed Hamid to do the same. My thinking was if the young men found weapons on us they'd immediately regard us as hostile. We wouldn't be totally at their mercy, though, as our guards could cover us from the car park. I gave my big camera with the 400 mm lens to one of the guards so he could keep track of what was happening at all times. The camera lens is a terrific optic that can ID an individual from two miles away. Before heading down to the river, I grabbed my small camera. I figured if I carried it openly in my hand, it would make us appear even less intimidating.

As we walked, I scanned the riverbank beyond where the group was gathered. I spotted a man who appeared to be unconnected with them, leaning against a 125cc motorbike. The engine was cut and he was watching me and Hamid intently. As soon as the group saw us, they stopped wrestling. The nearer we got, the harder their expressions grew. At close range, they looked younger than I'd thought but no less fierce. I offered my hand in greeting and they refused it. As I withdrew my hand, a shadow of doubt crept over me. Had I got it wrong? Should I have kept my distance?

Hamid broke the silence, introducing us as international

journalists. This appeared to relax the youths slightly. I offered my hand again. A few of them took it this time, but still no smiles.

A short man in his mid-twenties appeared to be the group's leader. He refused to shake my hand and stared right through me. I thought, to hell with this, aimed my camera directly at him and snapped his picture before he could say anything. I showed him the digital image on the viewing screen. The young man's stony expression gave way to a big smile. He thought the picture was great and invited his mates to take a look. I took photos of all of them and before I knew it, they were all relaxed.

After ten minutes or so of playing official photographer, I turned and waved to the guards back at the car park to let them know we were OK. Hamid chatted with the group casually. He found out that all of them lived in Lashkar Gah.

It was getting near prayer time and the group of young men started to disband; some washed in the river while others walked towards the mosque in town. The brief meeting reassured me that though they were Taliban they didn't represent an immediate threat to us. At worst, they were gathering long-term intelligence for future offensives.

As Hamid and I started back to the hotel, the man who'd been observing us from the motorbike walked over to us. He was older than the group we'd just left and though his beard was untrimmed in the fundamentalist Islamic tradition, his turban was grey and blue – definitely not Taliban.

He introduced himself to Hamid in Pashto and then turned to me. 'Hello. How are you?' he said.

Speaking to me in English was definitely calculated on his part. I asked him who he was and what he wanted from us. He told us his name and described himself as 'former Taliban'. What's more, he claimed to have worked as a bodyguard for Mullah Mohammed Omar, the Taliban's spiritual leader who'd gone into hiding.

The man told us he had a lot of information about the

Taliban if we were interested. I told him the person he needed to talk to was the correspondent and that he wasn't available right now. I also told him that we didn't pay for information, so if it was money he was after, he was wasting his time. He said that wasn't the case and he'd wait for us on the riverbank the following day. I told him we'd be there at 7 a.m. He agreed and we shook hands.

Back at the hotel, I told Nic about the man on the motorbike, his claims about his former life in the Taliban and the offer to meet us the following morning with more information. Both Nic and I were suspicious of his motives. Worst case scenario, he was trying to lure us into an ambush, but it was more likely he was working some sort of angle. It wasn't unheard of for Afghans to misrepresent themselves to the international press in an effort to extort money or help. After weighing up the pros and cons, Nic decided a meeting would be worthwhile.

CHAPTER 21

I rose the next morning at five after a terrible night's sleep. I couldn't stop thinking about our circumstances: our hotel's security was non-existent, Taliban were hanging around outside, and Mullah Omar's bodyguard wanted to chat. No wonder my head was buzzing.

Though bleary-eyed, I was still ready to tackle what promised to be a very hectic day. I had to escort Nic and his crew south of Lashkar Gah to film the destruction of a poppy field; then back to the city to interview the Governor of Helmund province, and then move our entire convoy through the desert to Kandahar before nightfall.

Our first order of business, however, was the early morning meeting with an Afghan who claimed to have once guarded the Taliban's spiritual leader. I had a strong feeling the man wasn't lying to us about his past, but I wasn't going to risk Nic's safety, or mine for that matter, on a hunch. I assigned a handful of our guards to keep an eye on the designated meeting area from 6.30 a.m. onwards. If the meeting turned out to be a trap, the man couldn't overpower us alone. He'd need to send at least one accomplice ahead to lay in wait.

At 6.55 a.m., the man turned up alone on his motorbike. I watched him through the long lens of my big camera as he cut the engine, walked down the riverbank and took a seat on some rocks near the grassy embankment. Using the lens, I scanned upstream, across the far side of the river, and along the fields. I couldn't see anyone lingering about or hiding. I told Nic everything looked fine and we could go ahead with the meeting as planned. Before heading out I tucked my pistol into the back of my trouser waistband along with a map of Afghanistan and Pakistan.

The man smiled and greeted us cordially. I introduced Nic, who offered a few pleasantries before getting down to business.

'What did you want to tell us?' Nic asked.

The man said he could tell us exactly where Mullah Omar was hiding. However, in exchange for the information, he wanted one hundred thousand US dollars and a flight to the United States. My initial thought was 'Yes, we can get you a flight . . . to Guantanamo Bay!' I didn't say it out loud of course.

Nic shook his head. 'As Bob told you yesterday, we're journalists and we don't pay for information,' he said.

The man's pleasant attitude dissolved immediately. He said if we weren't willing to pay him, then he had nothing to say.

Nic reiterated firmly that he wouldn't pay for information.

At that point, the man eased up a bit and started discussing general issues. We didn't have time to engage in idle chitchat, so I pulled out my map, unfolded it on the ground and pointed to it.

'There's the border with Pakistan,' I said. 'Now, where's Mullah Omar?'

The man kneeled down. Instead of pointing to the map with his finger or a blade of grass he clenched his fist and slammed it down on Afghanistan. He ended the meeting by saying he'd be willing to come to Kabul at a later date and talk to us – if we paid him. He then bade us farewell, walked back to his motorbike and drove off.

Nic and I later spoke about the meeting at length. We both felt that the man had told us the truth about his past and that he wasn't a Walter Mitty-type character. I doubt he knew exactly where Mullah Omar was hiding but he probably could have told us whether he was in Afghanistan or Pakistan. But the real story in my mind wasn't Mullah Omar's whereabouts; it was that one of his former followers was keen to sell out his old leadership and jump to the winning side. That showed me that the Taliban wasn't a single unified force of hardcore fundamentalists. Like any organization, it had opportunists who supported the movement when it suited them. It made me wonder how many Afghans had latched onto the US-led coalition for convenience.

The morning meeting came to nothing but that hadn't dampened Nic's enthusiasm or mine for the rest of the day's events. Next on our agenda was the poppy eradication shoot.

After breakfast, a group of counter-narcotics officers and Afghan National Police arrived at our hotel to escort us to a poppy field thirty kilometres south of Lashkar Gah. The Afghans were travelling in a convoy of four pickup trucks and kitted out with AKs, RPGs and machine guns. It would have been a good show of force if their weapons hadn't been in such poor condition. One look and I knew there was no way I could entrust our security to that lot. I insisted on taking all of our guards with us.

We left our hotel around 8.15 a.m. with our five-vehicle convoy sandwiched between the Afghan pickups. We were extremely overt, which I found very unnerving. I would have preferred to travel to the location without the police, but this was their operation and their call. I was lucky to have got permission to bring our guards along.

When it came to destroying poppy fields in Helmund, the counter-narcotics officials were spoilt for choice. We must have passed at least three dozen on the way to our shoot. I had read that Afghan poppy farmers had produced 3,600,000 kilograms of opium the previous year, but it wasn't until I saw mile after mile of poppy fields that I fully appreciated the scale of the problem. From where I sat, the government's goal of wiping out 25 per cent of the nation's poppy production by the end of 2004 seemed a pipe-dream.

What little credibility the eradication programme had in my

eyes was lost as soon as we reached the poppy field earmarked for destruction; it was no bigger than a football pitch; insignificant in terms of acreage. The field was dotted with dozens of bearded, turbaned heads bobbing in a sea of pink and white petals. Some of the men had gathered around a tractor hooked up to a plough. The counter-narcotics team told us they were local farmers who'd come out to protest. It was the Afghan version of a sit-in.

In addition to the protestors, there was a small group of men – some wearing black turbans, others white – observing from the edge of the field. I later found out they were drugs traffickers who'd come to make sure that their poppies were left alone. Finally, there was the poor farmer who owned the field, sat on a mound of earth, surrounded by crying children.

Nic and his cameraman got to work quickly conducting interviews with the protestors, the farmer and the counter-narcotics officials. I stuck by them the whole time, carrying my big camera so I'd look like part of the crew. After the interviews, the main event began. The tractor spluttered to life and started rolling. Row after row of poppies disappeared under the blades of the plough as it circled the field. The process was marked by fits and starts; the farmers had flooded the field the night before and the tractor kept getting bogged down in the mud. Each time it got stuck, the protestors would cheer wildly.

The whole exercise was a farce from start to finish. Moreover, the method used, ploughing the plants under, would only intensify Afghanistan's drugs problem. Any amateur gardener can tell you that once poppies are turned over in the ground they spring back the next harvest at double the yield. The farmer who owned the field could look forward to a bumper crop the next year, courtesy of Afghanistan's counter-narcotics programme.

If the farmer was aware of that fact he seemed to take little comfort in it. I observed him from a distance through my camera lens. The eradication programme was supposed to compensate him for his destroyed crops, but he and his children looked as if they'd lost everything. Zooming in on their tear-streaked faces was like looking into a crystal ball; so much for winning over the next generation of Afghans.

I swung my lens over to the drugs traffickers on the edge of the field. They were still observing passively. I wasn't too worried about them. What did concern me was the prospect of lunatic fringe elements screaming in to take on the authorities. The Afghan police weren't exactly battle-ready. Many of them were sitting down drinking tea with their weapons lying on the grass beside them.

It was a strange affair to say the least. The entire exercise had obviously been staged for the press but I still sensed an undercurrent of very real emotions: anger, defiance, hate and resentment. What was the point of destroying the livelihood of a few small farmers when Afghanistan's drugs lords continued to operate without restraint? This charade played out over two more fields; the tractor getting stuck in the mud, the cheering protestors, the distraught farmers, the drugs traffickers drawing their lines in the sand. Tackling Afghanistan's drugs problem field by field was a fool's errand if ever I saw one.

CHAPTER 22

In the Regiment, training and exercises are treated as importantly as operations; you don't fail either. The key to not failing is to plan everything to the letter. When I was Staff Sergeant of the amphibious troop in the Regiment, I was sent on an exercise in the Far East to Borneo Island. The exercise called for me and another member of the troop to parachute into the sea off Borneo with a two-man collapsible canoe, paddle to the mainland, navigate fifteen miles up an estuary, cache the canoe and move in light order to recce an enemy camp.

My planning of this exercise was meticulous. I consulted tidal charts to plot our recce of the camp at low tide allowing plenty of time to get back to the canoe before high tide hit. When we actually did do the exercise, however, my plans fell apart.

We paddled up the estuary but when we reached the cache area, the river was so high we were paddling between the trees. It didn't make sense to me because the water level exceeded any recorded high tides on the charts. Mind you, the exercise was still a success. Instead of caching the canoe, we lived, recced, slept, ate and did everything else we needed to from it. We achieved our aim, not on foot but by paddling everywhere.

When we returned to base, I spoke to a local fisherman about the high-water level. He told me that due to the interaction of certain moon phases with the broken coastline and offlying islands in that region, once every four years for four days they experience what are known as 'king tides'. These tides can rise twenty feet above normal tide levels. The king tide phenomenon was not recorded in the tide tables or charts, so I had no way of knowing they existed when planning the exercise.

That experience in Borneo taught me to vigorously seek out local knowledge whenever possible. Without it, even the most well-planned operation can fail.

Back in Kabul the press corps was buzzing with talk of 'CNN's trip to Helmund'. It was definitely a coup for Nic Robertson. Rather than follow the herd to Jalalabad he ventured into uncharted territory to deliver a hard-hitting report on Afghanistan's drugs trade.

The night after we got back to Kabul there was a party for journalists, UN and NGO staff at the Intercontinental Hotel. Normally I would discourage my clients from attending what I view as a great opportunity for insurgents to take out dozens of westerners in one fell swoop. But Nic wanted to catch up with his colleagues in the press corps to see what had happened in Kabul while he was away. Admittedly, I also wanted to go. I still had virtually no direct contact with other security advisers working in Afghanistan and I was banking there'd be a few at the Intercon looking after clients.

The party was well under way by the time we got there. Dozens of people were crammed into a suite of rooms; pop music was blaring, alcohol was flowing and the air was thick with cigarette smoke. A small group of westerners was passing around a hash pipe. I couldn't believe it. The international community was supposed to be eradicating Afghanistan's drugs trade, not funding it. Few seemed to care either that they were breaking Afghan law by consuming alcohol. I'd never seen some individuals show such a total disregard for the delicate nature of an operating environment.

I spent most of the party in a corner drinking orange juice and talking to some journalists who I knew from Iraq and the West Bank. Like Nic, these were highly professional individuals who'd gone to the party to catch up with their peers, not to get pissed.

At one point, a female producer from Sky News approached me. She wanted to know how we pulled off the Helmund trip and whether I thought her team could do it as well. I asked her if she had a security adviser. The producer pointed to a tall lad in his mid-thirties. A group of people was huddled around him and he seemed to be the life and soul of the party.

'What's his background?' I asked.

'He's an ex-military medic,' said the producer.

I told her he'd be very useful if they got wounded, but it sounded to me like he didn't have the right military background to manage a trip to a place like Helmund. I explained that in the military, it's pretty much 'horses for courses'; a medic does medical work, an infantry man does infantry work, a Close Protection team protects, etc. In order to anticipate and respond effectively to all the security issues a news team encounters – i.e. travelling alone without military support, working among civilian populations, embedding with troops, etc. – an adviser needs to have the proper training. I told her that if her adviser did not have proactive skills, she should look for one who did, such as an ex-SAS lad or someone with a background in covert military surveillance. Ideally, the adviser would blend in with the rest of her team and not stand out. Finally, I recommended she find someone who understood her objectives and could help her get stories. Security advisers are expensive but if they help a news crew get world exclusives, they pay for themselves several times over.

The next morning, Nic turned his attention to the other goal he'd set for himself on this trip; the embed in Khost province. He hadn't heard back yet from the US military Public Affairs Officer but knew he could get the go-ahead at any time. When the call did come, Nic wanted to be as prepared as possible to cover the story.

With that in mind, he asked CNN's local fixer Hamid if he knew of anyone who'd been to Khost recently or could offer some insights on what was really going on there. As usual, Hamid came through with a real winner: an ANA Commander who'd just returned from Khost. The Commander agreed to sit down with us for an informal, background meeting.

The briefing took place around the dinner table and lasted several hours. Nic, his crew and I were in attendance as was Hamid, who acted as translator.

The Commander had just returned from fighting alongside US troops stationed in Khost province. The joint military operation involved stopping Taliban and al-Qaeda militants from coming over the border through Pakistan. The Commander told us the enemy was proving quite formidable and he'd lost a great deal of men that year, even though it was only April. Moreover, insurgent activity wasn't confined to the border. The Taliban and al-Qaeda, he said, had joined forces in Khost and were getting stronger by the day.

When the Commander was asked whether the coalition's reconstruction projects were winning the support of the local population, he laughed. The militants, he said, had a far more effective method of securing loyalty; they threatened to kill anyone who cooperated with the coalition. Working with westerners of any sort, including non-military, wasn't tolerated. The insurgents were offering a bounty of US$25,000 for the head of any westerner caught in Khost province – a king's ransom in a country where the average household income is only three hundred dollars a year.

The background briefing was invaluable in my eyes. Though it was common knowledge that Khost was dangerous, the Commander had given us a more detailed picture of the province's security issues. Moreover, he'd given us specific intelligence that we never would have found in a published source.

*

A few days later, I accompanied Nic to the weekly press conference at the US military base in Kabul. Nic still hadn't heard a word on his embed request and he wanted to meet directly with the PAO to check his status.

I'd been to a few pressers in Kabul by that point and I found them to be a real giggle. A US Army officer would come out and tell a load of rubbish to the media about how well the US and ISAF missions were going and how the reconstruction efforts were right on schedule.

I expected the propaganda. What surprised me, however, was the follow-up by the press corps. Many of the journalists didn't question the official version of events and when someone did ask a hard-hitting question, the press officer would skirt the issue by saying he'd have to 'look into it' and get back to them later. Rarely would the journalists help each other out by asking follow-up questions.

On one occasion in particular the US military just plain lied by providing the press officer in Kabul with a misleading account of an incident. It was announced that a US Ranger had been shot dead in what was described as a 'huge' gun battle with the opposition near the Pakistan border. It was big news in the US because the dead soldier, Pat Tillman, had been an American football star who had turned down a multimillion-dollar sports contract to fight the War on Terror. I remember turning to Nic and saying that the description of a 'huge' battle didn't ring true. If it had indeed been a contact involving dozens of troops, it was unlikely that only one soldier would have died. I smelled a rat. I told Nic I'd bet my mortgage that the lad had been hit by his own side.

Sure enough, an American broadcaster asked whether the soldier was killed by 'friendly fire'. The press officer was adamant that there were no reports to suggest that was the case. Over a month later, the US military finally came clean and admitted that the soldier had indeed been a victim of friendly fire. Poor laddie; he was undoubtedly brave and honourable, turning down a fortune to do what he believed was the right thing. It was disgraceful that his own military did not tell the public about the full circumstances of his death for so long.

At the presser, Nic learned that the PAO he'd left his request with had been replaced while we were in Helmund. The new PAO was a short little major with a squeaky voice and an annoying habit of speaking to people without removing his sunglasses (probably because he didn't want to look anyone in the eye). I disliked him immediately.

The PAO told Nic that his Khost embed was imminent and would more than likely come through within the next forty-eight hours. When it did, the military would fly him and his crew to Camp Solerno, a forward operations base in Khost only a few miles from the Pakistan border. Just like his predecessor, this PAO told Nic that driving to the embed was out of the question.

I had to excuse myself while Nic went over the details with the PAO. I was afraid if I stuck around, I'd compromise Nic's chances of landing the embed. Everything about the PAO wound me up. I don't hide my feelings well and in retrospect it was terrible of me to show my emotions on my face, but for reasons I couldn't understand at the time all I wanted to do was rip the sunglasses of his fat little head and chin him.

Nic was excited after his meeting with the PAO, but his enthusiasm was dampened by the crew limits placed on him. The military aircraft could only accommodate three civilians. A standard news crew is comprised of a correspondent, camera person and producer. Normally, I'd replace the producer. As I've said before, even though embedded journalists are surrounded by soldiers, it's still a very dangerous assignment. But CNN wanted Nic to file live reports from Khost which meant he'd have to take the 'fly away' (satellite) engineer with him. When all was done and dusted, there was simply no room for me.

Later than evening, around 10 p.m. local time, I heard Nic shouting for me from his room. I went to see him immediately. He was going wild.

'What's the matter?' I asked.

Nic told me he had just got a call from the PAO. He had the embed, but there were no flights available to transport him and the crew to the base in Khost. It got worse; the PAO warned Nic that if he didn't present himself at the gates of Camp Solerno by 3.30 p.m. the next day, he'd lose the embed and his name would fall to the back of the queue.

CHAPTER 23

Nic asked me if there was any way we could drive to Khost. Nic is a very proud man and, like me, whatever he's thinking shows on his face. He would never beg me to make the trip but it was crystal clear from his expression that he was desperate to go.

It was extremely unethical in my view for the PAO to warn us against driving to Khost and then leave Nic with no other option for getting to the embed. To me, it seemed like a stitch-up and I wasn't going to stand for it.

Luckily, I'd anticipated just this sort of scenario. The PAO seemed a little bastard and I'd got the feeling that if Nic did get the embed there'd be a sting in the tail somewhere. I'd already approached Hamid and our local drivers with the possibility of driving to Khost. To a man, they were all happy to do the trip with us. I'd built up a lot of goodwill during our journey to Kandahar and Helmund. I'm sure hazard pay also played a role; local wages tripled on assignments outside Kabul due to the increased risks.

'OK,' I said. 'We'll drive. And I'll get you there safely.'

Nic was over the moon. He spent the rest of the night taking care of administrative details which included compiling a manifest for the PAO detailing the names and titles of who would need to overnight at Camp Solerno. The list included all the westerners in our party: Nic, his cameraman, the engineer and me.

While Nic dealt with the Yanks, Hamid and I pulled together the travel plan and security arrangements; no mean feat considering it was Friday night and we were in a Muslim country (it's like trying to get something done on a Sunday night in London).

To get to Camp Solerno we'd have to travel through Kabul province, then south through Lowgar province, then south-east towards Gardez, the capital of Paktia province and then finally through Khost province. Weather permitting, I figured the entire trip would take approximately nine and half hours.

Once again, we needed to leave Kabul no later than 3.30 a.m. On this trip especially, it was crucial we have plenty of daylight to spare at the other end as driving through Khost at night was unthinkable. Nine and a half hours was probably a conservative estimate but I needed to err on the side of caution because the variables of the journey were difficult to gauge. Road conditions, for example, were impossible to predict. We'd be travelling on a series of old, poorly maintained roads, not a sleek new highway like the A1 through Kandahar and Helmund. Terrain was another variable; instead of driving past mountains, this time we'd be driving over them; three mountain ranges in total. We also had to consider who was in charge of the areas we'd be traversing. The roads we'd be travelling were not as critical commercially or militarily as the A1 so the coalition tended not to get involved each time a warlord flexed his muscles and closed one down. The fiefdoms we'd be driving through would be exactly that; territory controlled by individual warlords, each of whom governed according to their own rules, laws and whims.

Warlords and dodgy mountain tracks notwithstanding, we also had the standard security issues to prepare for including insurgents and armed bandits.

For our convoy, I decided to employ the same mix of vehicles that had worked so well on our last trip; five low-profile Toyota 4x4s. The only difference was this time Nic needed to bring the live truck, which I was happy to do.[17] That boosted our convoy

17 If Nic were flying to Khost, the satellite dish would have been broken down into individual boxes and loaded onto the aircraft – hence the term 'fly away'.

to six vehicles. Despite the addition of the extra truck, we still only required twelve Afghan guards. As before, I wanted them drawn from various Afghan tribes: nine armed with AKs and the other three with light machine guns.

The next morning Nic and the crew were awake and ready to go at 3.15 a.m. All the Afghans were on time as well. I told the sleepy group they must have stayed up all night to make sure they weren't late – which got a bit of a laugh.

Bearing in mind, however, that neither I nor anyone else in our convoy had got much rest, I began my brief again by reminding everyone of the importance of staying awake at all times during our journey. I told the group our objective was to get to the gates of Camp Solerno no later than an hour before last light.

Next, I gave them the overnight plan: Nic, the crew and I would spend the night at Camp Solerno while Hamid and the rest of the Afghans in our party would stay at a hotel in Khost town. Even though I wouldn't be joining Nic on his embed, I couldn't stay in Khost town with the rest of our party. With a $25,000 bounty on the head of any westerner, it would pose a risk to me personally and endanger any Afghan seen with me.

I warned the guards who'd come on the Helmund trip that we'd likely encounter far worse conditions this time around, so they should be prepared. As for the new faces, I found out who among them had mechanics experience before assigning them to vehicles.

Finally, I asked each of the guards to show me their weapons. One of the younger guards, a new lad, spoke exceptionally good English. I thought I'd hit the jackpot with him, getting a guard and translator in one – that is, until I asked to see his AK. He told me, in impeccable English, that he didn't have a weapon. When I asked him why, he fell silent and shrugged his shoulders. I had no choice but to tell him he wasn't coming; English or no English, without a weapon, the young guard wasn't a guard, he was a passenger and I had enough of those.

Our six-vehicle convoy headed out one guard down but on time. I positioned the live truck third from front, and Nic and his crew in the fourth vehicle. That way, my clients would still receive the best possible cover if we were attacked.

The streets were very empty and we cleared the city centre in no time. It wasn't until we hit the southern outskirts of Kabul that we started to see activity. The local butchers were out by the side of the road, slaughtering sheep and cattle to sell as fresh meat at the morning markets. It was a hell of a sight. In the headlights I could see a father and son carving up an entire water buffalo with meat cleavers.

At 7 a.m. we stopped at a petrol station to refuel and blast out the engine filters. There was a little market stall attached to the station and a couple of the guards and drivers took the opportunity to chat with the locals and buy some bread to supplement the food supplies we had packed in the vehicles along with water. Afghan bread is thick, flat and very hearty. When it's fresh it's beautiful but once it goes stale (which happens within minutes) you can use it as plasterboard. The bread is never sold in bags but rather hung over metal rods in the open air until it's purchased. You do have to think about how many hands have handled it before it gets to you; bearing in mind that loo roll is not commonly used in Afghanistan. I hadn't eaten in over twelve hours so loo roll or not, I was happy to get stuck in.

Barring a couple of tyre changes, this was our first major stop. I was amazed that despite difficult road conditions we still had all six vehicles moving. We'd been fortunate for sure, but our luck could change at any time. We still had three mountain ranges to cross and hours of hostile terrain ahead of us.

At approximately 9 a.m. we ascended the first major mountain range of our journey along a narrow dirt and gravel track. We wound our way through the foothills past an ever changing landscape which gave way to something I hadn't yet encountered in Afghanistan: trees, one approximately every twenty metres.

One of the Afghans told me that when he was much younger, the hillsides were strewn with thick forest. Afghanistan's deforestation didn't happen as a consequence of development. The trees were chopped down after Kabul's electricity plants were destroyed during the civil war of the 1990s. Even today, the majority of Kabul's homes and buildings are heated with wood-burning stoves.

We continued on up the mountain, reaching the snow line at approximately eight thousand feet. I was concerned as we didn't have snow chains for the vehicles (they weren't available). I'd checked the weather the night before and there was no warning of snowfall for the area. Driving in Afghanistan is bad enough in decent conditions. Now, the local drivers had to navigate icy, inadequate roads in vehicles with very little tread on the tyres.

Even at these altitudes we encountered Kutchi families travelling with their camels and goats. Their brightly coloured clothing stood out against the blanket of white stretching above and below them.

My heart was pounding as we snaked our way around hairpin turns past sheer cliffs, some with one-thousand-foot drops. There were no barriers of any sort to stop us from sliding over the edge and falling into the boulder-strewn valley below. I stayed on top of the drivers, telling them to brake well ahead of the turns and stay in the lowest gear so we didn't go tumbling over the side.

One of our drivers radioed that the top of the mountain pass had a stunning view to the south-east towards the Pakistan border. There was also a police checkpoint. I decided it would be a good place to park up and look over the vehicles to make sure they were in good order for the steep drive back down the mountain.

At the checkpoint, the police cautioned us to be very wary of bandits on the way down. Fortunately, in addition to beautiful views, the mountaintop offered a tremendous vantage point to survey the ground we had to cover. Visibility was outstanding and I could see at least twenty miles in each direction. It was indeed excellent bandit country. Winding roads, broken features, uneven ground; the terrain was tailor-made for ambushes. On a clear day like the one we were having, a bandit could easily mark a potential target such as a heavily loaded lorry and wait patiently for it to pass.

I gathered the drivers, guards and the TV crew together to brief them before we headed back down the mountain. I told them they'd done ever so well staying awake on the first part of our journey and that now, more than ever, everyone needed to remain alert and to keep their wits about them. I reiterated what the police had said about bandits and laid down a strategy for negotiating the terrain ahead.

The plan was as follows: about one hundred metres ahead of any bend, I'd get out of my vehicle along with the Afghan guards positioned at the front of our convoy. The guards would cover me while I peered down the pass to the next level below to see if it was clear; my thinking being that if I was a bandit, I'd ambush a vehicle driving into a bend when it's travelling slowly and is at its most vulnerable.

By the time we got a third of the way down the mountain, we'd performed this operation three times. I was starting to think it would be nothing more than an exercise. Then, on the fourth bend, to my amazement, I spotted a group of bandits waiting below us. There were three men in total, wrapped in blankets, huddled around a brush fire. Each of them was armed with an AK47. I looked over the cliff down to the next road level. Sure enough, there was a large rocky outcrop to the side of the road that hid the group from anyone travelling up the mountain. I was lucky I could see them from above.

We outnumbered the bandits four to one but I wanted to avoid a firefight if possible. The moment you draw your weapon, the danger to your clients increases exponentially. I decided that if our convoy looked large and aggressive, the bandits would think twice before taking us on.

I gathered the drivers and guards together and mapped out a

new strategy: instead of sending the lead vehicle as a scout thirty seconds ahead of the rest of the convoy, we'd all descend together at fifty-metre intervals around the bend and past the bandits. Once I was sure everyone understood exactly what needed to be done, I dispatched the drivers to their vehicles, sent a lat and long reading back to AKE's ops office in the UK and performed a radio check. I also took my vehicle weapon from its bag and laid it across my lap. All of my senses converged to focus on the task at hand. I'm not sure what concerned me more: the prospect of getting into a firefight with three armed Afghans or having our closely grouped vehicles pile into one another and go sliding off the mountain.

As we rounded the bend towards the bandits, my heart skipped a beat. I could see them reaching for their rifles. Both of my hands were on my AK but I had no urge to lift it from my lap and show it to them. As I've said, you never draw your weapon unless it's absolutely necessary.

My restraint paid off. Instead of opening fire, the bandits hid their AKs under their blankets. As our convoy approached, they stood up from the fire to get a closer look. It was apparent at that point that they had no intention of attacking us. They'd probably been waiting for a truck driver travelling alone or at the very least a group they outnumbered. As my vehicle drove past their position I looked each bandit in the eye – not aggressively but confidently to reinforce in their minds that we weren't an easy target. Their eyes were glazed over and swollen. I suspected they were high on drugs.

Eight hours into our journey we entered a narrow valley into Zadran, an area of Paktia province controlled by Patcha Khan, an infamous warlord who runs his fiefdom with an iron fist. American forces knew not to go anywhere near Patcha Khan's territory. Only two weeks before our journey, an American logistical convoy travelling exactly the same route had been attacked and looted by Patcha Khan's forces. They let the

American soldiers go with a warning to tell other internationals not to trespass there again. The empty, bullet-ridden containers with US military markings were still lying in the riverbed as we drove past. At that moment, I realized that we hadn't seen any sign of the coalition for hours.

The valleys of Paktia gave way to the flatlands leading to Khost province. We'd been on the road now for more than nine hours – which I'd originally estimated as our total travel time – and we still hadn't arrived at Camp Solerno.

At the time, Khost province was (and still remains) one of the most fiercely anti-western areas in all of Afghanistan. Ethnically, it is predominantly Pashtoon, which is reflected in the way men dress; long shirts, baggy trousers, flat hats or Pashtoon turbans worn around the head with a long trail of cloth draped to the waist. They keep their beards natural and heavy in the fundamentalist Islamic tradition. In Khost, if you do see a woman, which is rare indeed, they are always covered in a burka.

Eleven and a half hours into our journey we entered the outskirts of Khost town; the last populated area we'd drive past before reaching Camp Solerno some four miles away. The main road through Khost is a bumpy dirt track that skirts along the town's edges rather than passing through the centre. As our convoy lurched along in late-afternoon traffic at ten miles per hour, I felt like we were a million miles from Kabul. Surrounded by flatlands and bordered by a range of mountains to the south-east, Khost town was one of the most inhospitable places I've ever had the misfortune to travel through. The flatlands lent themselves to hit-and-run attacks, which we knew were very frequent. But my biggest concern by far was the mountains; specifically, what lay on the other side of them.

The mountain range marked the border with Pakistan, but not the Pakistan controlled by the government in Islamabad and closely allied with America in the War on Terror. The area of Pakistan neighbouring Khost is Waziristan, part of Pakistan's 'tribal areas': seven autonomous regions that stretch along the

Afghan border. Waziristan is an authority unto itself. Its inhabitants are ethnic Pashtoon and have no allegiance whatsoever to the government in Islamabad. The Pashtoon of Waziristan don't even consider themselves Pakistani. They regard themselves as Afghans.

Waziristan and the rest of the tribal areas are the cradle of the Taliban and the loyalty of the people to its native sons hadn't diminished. When the Americans invaded Afghanistan in 2001, the Taliban in Khost simply walked over the mountains to safety; hence why the Yanks and the ANA were engaged in a joint operation aimed at stopping the Taliban from launching attacks over the border.

At long last, Camp Solerno came into view. At first, it appeared to have decent security including a high perimeter fence and guard towers manned by Afghan soldiers dotted at regular intervals. But it sat on very flat land flanked by high ground on one side; not exactly the best defensive position. I could see how it would be very easy for the Taliban to mortar or rocket the base and get away with it. Vulnerable or not, Camp Solerno was the only friendly patch of territory for over a hundred miles and I welcomed the sight of it. I looked at my watch. It was approaching 3:30 p.m. local time. The trip I had estimated would take nine hours had in fact taken twelve. Good thing we left Kabul on time.

At this point, instinct was telling me to relax and take a deep breath. I was about to deliver my clients and myself to the only place in Khost where westerners could spend the night in relative safety. Experience, however, was telling me to stay alert. We weren't out of the woods yet. I radioed all the drivers to tell them to stay sharp.

Like Iraq, the entrances to military complexes in Afghanistan draw suicide bombers like flies to honey and Camp Solerno was no exception. The entrance to the base had two layers of security: first, a vehicle checkpoint manned by Afghan soldiers followed by a main gate guarded by US soldiers and reinforced with a barrier, guard house and blast walls. As we approached the first checkpoint, one of the tyres on my vehicle blew out. I radioed the rest of the convoy to drop Nic inside the main gate while we got roadworthy. I hadn't travelled this far to have my clients ambushed on the doorstep of their destination.

The Afghan soldiers manning the vehicle checkpoint kept the rest of the traffic at bay while we mended the flat tyre. As usual, our drivers and security guards had us back under way in no time. When we caught up with the rest of the convoy, they were parked up in a holding area just outside the main gate. I didn't see Nic and his crew, so I assumed they were already safely inside the camp.

I got out of my vehicle and walked towards the main gate. As I approached, I saw Nic standing on the other side of the barrier, engaged in what appeared to be a heated exchange with the American Guard Commander. When I reached the barrier, the US guards told me to stop and go no further. I looked at them as if they were joking. They responded by pointing their M16s at me. Mind you, as a fair-skinned, middle-aged Scotsman, I hardly fit the profile of an Afghan suicide bomber. Something was very, very wrong.

Nic walked towards the barrier, his face contorted in disbelief and anger. Trailing alongside him was the Guard Commander, a Sergeant dressed in green combats with an airborne insignia, body armour and army-issue sunglasses strung on a headband.

'I can't believe this,' said Nic. 'They won't let you in.'

'What do you mean?' I asked.

'They won't let you in,' said Nic. 'They're saying the list they got from the PAO back in Kabul doesn't have your name on it.'

'How's that possible?' I asked.

'I don't know what's going on here,' Nic said. 'I phoned the PAO last night with all of our names, yours included. I also emailed him the full manifest before we left this morning.'

Nic was obviously distressed by the situation but there was nothing he could do to fix it. I knew for a fact that he had submitted my name on the original manifest. It wasn't his fault. The PAO in Kabul was the person responsible for making sure Nic's full list was sent to Camp Solerno. Could it have been an innocent mistake? Anything is possible, but my immediate gut feeling was that my name had been left off intentionally.

I looked at the Guard Commander. He didn't look the brightest of the bunch but surely he could figure out I wasn't an al-Qaeda or Taliban operative.

'There's been a mistake here, mate,' I said.

The Guard Commander didn't care. 'Sorry, man, but if your name ain't on the list, you ain't gettin' in.'

So much for being reasonable. I explained to him that it had taken us twelve hours to get there and that driving back to Kabul wasn't an option. I also told him about the US$25,000 bounty on the head of any westerner captured in Khost.

'I feel for you,' said the Guard Commander, 'but it ain't my problem.'

I demanded to see the operations officer, only to be told, 'He's in a meeting'. I persisted and eventually a Captain turned up. I tried appealing to his common sense. Obviously I posed no threat to the base. Moreover, I was British and the last time I checked the Brits were part of the US-led coalition in Afghanistan. The Captain, who also wore a uniform plastered in badges, was apologetic, but he refused to overrule his Guard Commander. They had their procedures, he explained, and if my name wasn't on the list, they weren't authorized to let me in.

There was no use arguing with them. When they looked at me they didn't see a real person, let alone an ally. All they saw was a problem, one which they had no intention of rectifying even it meant sending me into the arms of the enemy.

The sun was setting and I had run out of options. I had to face facts. I had no choice but to spend the night in Khost town with a $25,000 bounty on my head.

CHAPTER 24

I was exhausted and angry. I'd delivered Nic and his crew safely to Camp Solerno only to be denied access myself due to a clerical error. After a gruelling twelve-hour journey negotiating icy mountain roads and armed bandits, I had to switch into overdrive when all I wanted to do was get my head down. That base was the only safe haven for westerners in all of Khost province. Driving back to Kabul with the rest of our group was a non-starter. If bandits didn't get us then the hairpin turns through the mountain passes in the dark surely would. Over-nighting in Khost town was my only option.

Nic was still standing by the main gate, intent on not budging until the Americans pulled their heads out of their arses and let me in. The US soldiers who'd refused me entry made no secret of the fact that they just wanted me to go away. By that point, I was happy to oblige them. I had to get moving if I was going to make Khost town before sundown. I told Nic not to worry and that I'd call him that evening and again in the morning to let him know I was OK.

I headed back to the car park where our Afghan drivers and guards were taking a well-deserved break. When Hamid saw me he asked if I'd forgotten something.

'I haven't forgotten anything,' I told him. 'I'd rather spend the night with you lot then spend one night with the Americans.'

Hamid laughed and translated what I'd said for the guards and drivers, who found it very amusing. He asked me what had happened and I told him about my exchange with the soldiers at the gate.

'Do I look like a suicide bomber?' I asked.

One of the guards who spoke English chimed in. 'Yes, Bob, you do.'

Everyone laughed again. I'd be sleeping in a hornets' nest that night but at least my bunk mates had a sense of humour.

Back in Kabul, Hamid had arranged for the Afghans in our party to overnight at a mothballed hotel in Khost town. I couldn't just show up there with them and hope no one would notice me. I needed to know exactly what we were driving into so I could limit the risks for all of us.

If my presence in Khost town became public knowledge it would endanger me and the rest of the team. Hamid, the drivers and our guards would be labelled traitors for working with a westerner and treated as such. The fact that they were all Afghans wouldn't help them a bit. Afghans vary tremendously in appearance, from their physical features to the way they dress. The people of Khost are ethnic Pashtoon and some of the Afghans on my team were ethnic Tajik and proud ex-Northern Alliance soldiers. The Northern Alliance had been locked in a bloody civil war with the Pashtoon of the south during the 1990s and people had long memories for the atrocities committed on both sides.

I needed Hamid to find out exactly where the hotel was located and who else was staying there. I asked him who his point of contact was. Luckily, it was the hotel's co-owner and caretaker, so we could get the information quickly without having to run our request through a chain of people. I warned Hamid not to mention that there was a westerner with him. If word spread that there was an infidel in town, the scenario would be bleak; first the locals find out, then the police (most of who are corrupt as hell and play both sides) and next thing you know the Taliban and al-Qaeda are assaulting your position.

The caretaker told Hamid that the hotel was completely

empty and that he should look for a four-storey building located in the town centre right next to a police station (a negative in my view).

I asked Hamid how long it would take to get there. He reckoned it would be about a twenty- to thirty-minute drive. We only had forty minutes of daylight remaining. I didn't want to get caught out after sundown but I decided to stay back and send Hamid ahead with two vehicles to collect the keys and recce the hotel. We'd be cutting it close but it was the safest way to proceed.

I instructed Hamid to check each floor of the hotel including the roof to make sure there was absolutely no one else there. When he was certain the place was empty and there was no one hanging around outside asking questions, only then should he call me and I'd go join him.

Thirty minutes later, Hamid rang. Traffic was light and it had taken him only twenty minutes to get to the hotel. He said everything looked fine. The accommodation was very basic; there was no running water or electricity but there were beds to sleep on and padlocks on all the doors and windows for which the caretaker had given him keys. I told him to make sure that there were enough beds on the top floor for all of us and to stock it with enough additional furniture to barricade the stairwells.

With no time to spare, the remainder of our convoy headed into Khost town. The outskirts were sparsely populated with only the odd farmhouse and the setting sun cast a brilliant pink and orange glow over the grassy flatlands. Normally, I'm no fan of driving at dusk in hostile environments, but the low light did make it more difficult for anyone we passed to see inside our vehicle. Luckily, I had dressed in local gear before leaving Kabul that morning: baggy pants, a long khamis and turban. I'd also grown a beard a few weeks before the trip. Mind you, even with the clothes and beard, I'd never pass as an Afghan. But the local dress did break up my outline as we drove along, so at least I didn't stick out to the casual observer.

By the time we reached Khost town, the residents were out in full force, either making their way home or going to evening prayers. The architecture of Khost was standard Afghan: box-like mud and brick structures painted in washed-out colours. Many of the buildings had courtyards surrounded by perimeter walls with brightly decorated wood or metal doors. As with the rest of Afghanistan, open sewers stood in place of nonexistent pavements.

The road we were travelling was bumpy to the extreme and there were no rules to keep drivers in line, other than the threat of ending up in a ditch. I asked my driver to be very cautious. A minor fender-bender could easily blow up into a major incident if I was found out.

Each set of eyes we passed seemed to linger in our direction. Our vehicles may have been low profile but that didn't stop us from being scrutinized by everyone on the street. The fact that we were driving together marked us as a convoy, something which by that time had become an increasingly rare sight in Khost town.

Eighteen months earlier, the streets of Khost had been busy with convoys ferrying western aid workers and their local entourages. They blew into town promising to build proper roads, schools, medical clinics; the usual projects financed by western governments and funnelled through 'non-partisan' NGOs. Our hotel, which now stood empty, had largely catered to international do-gooders travelling from Kabul or over the border from Pakistan. But as soon as the security situation turned sour the aid workers packed their bags, suspended their projects and left town. The handful of aid agencies that did stay were staffed exclusively by locals.

I looked at the faces we drove past wondering what they must think of westerners. First, western militaries drop bombs on their villages to drive out the Taliban. Then western do-gooders leave before delivering on their promises of better living conditions. Destruction and deceit – that's what the west represented to these people. Enticing as a US $25,000 bounty must have been, I'm sure there was more than one person in Khost who would have been happy to deliver the head of a westerner to the Taliban and al-Qaeda free of charge.

The streets were still bustling with end-of-day activity when we reached our hotel; a concrete rectangle surrounded by a courtyard with a perimeter fence. It was smack in the middle of a bazaar. The shops had closed but plenty of people were walking around, drinking small glasses of tea and buying kebabs from street vendors. The smell of charcoal and grilled meat made me realize how hungry I was. I'd only had bread and water that day.

Hamid was waiting for us outside the hotel's gate. As soon as we pulled up, he let us into the walled courtyard. I asked my driver to reverse in, but Hamid had parked his vehicles in nose first. I radioed Hamid and asked him to turn them around. I didn't want to idle on the street for a second longer than necessary but I had to plan ahead. If trouble hit in the middle of the night, I wanted all the vehicles facing the street, ready to scream out at a moment's notice.

Once inside the compound, I waited for Hamid to padlock the gate before dismounting my vehicle. I could just imagine some nosy busybody poking his head inside the courtyard to see who'd come to town.

As soon as my feet hit the ground, my legs stiffened like two lead weights. The journey from the base to the hotel had taken only twenty minutes but the added stress made it feel like twenty hours. I wanted to collapse into bed, but there was still a lot of work to do.

I walked inside the hotel and was immediately overcome by the smell of stagnant air. No one had lived there for several months and it looked as if time had stood still. Every surface including the floors was covered with a thick blanket of fine, talcum-like dust that lay undisturbed except for the freshly made footprints left by Hamid and the guards.

Everyone had assembled on the ground floor to await instructions for the night. I began by splitting the guards into groups and assigning shifts to each for patrolling the interior of the building and the courtyard where we'd parked the vehicles. I didn't need to tell them how crucial it was for those on duty to stay awake; they knew the dangers of our situation. I did assure them, however, that the rotations would allow each man at least four hours of sleep. I urged them to do their best to get some rest. I didn't want to attempt the return journey with a punchy, sleep-deprived team.

I asked Hamid if anyone had approached him when he first arrived. He said no one had stopped him, so he assumed that people thought we were a group of Afghans from Kabul just passing through.

'Where's the caretaker?' I asked.

'I sent him to get food and drinks for us,' said Hamid.

'If he finds out I'm here, will he tell anyone?' I asked.

Hamid smiled. 'Absolutely not,' he said.

Unbeknown to me, Hamid had put something of an insurance policy in place back in Kabul. He'd found out about the hotel through friends of his; friends who knew the caretaker and how to find him. Hamid had warned the caretaker that if anything happened to any of us, his friends knew who to trace it to – and it would be dealt with.

I wanted to get up on the roof while there was still a few minutes of twilight remaining. I needed to know whether we were overlooked, if any buildings buttressed ours and whether an attack could be launched from a neighbouring rooftop.

I grabbed my camera with the 400 mm lens and headed upstairs with Hamid, stopping on each floor to have a look around. It was obvious that the owners had invested a lot of effort into securing the building. The windows of the hotel were metal framed with metal shutters, bars and padlocks. When we reached the top floor, I saw that Hamid had already prepared the furniture to barricade us in. The door opening onto the rooftop was secured in a similar fashion to the hotel's windows: a metal frame with a bar and padlock which Hamid opened with the keys the caretaker had given him. The rooftop was uncluttered except for three old satellite dishes and surrounded by a five-foot-high barrier on all sides. I told Hamid to crouch down and stay level with the barrier to make sure no one saw us walking around.

My primary concern was whether anyone could access our hotel from a neighbouring building. At the back of the hotel, I spied one potential problem: a commercial structure about one hundred yards away that overlooked us. I used the long lens on my camera to look through the windows. It was quiet and no one seemed to have taken notice of us. Next, I checked the front of the hotel. There was a lot of noise and people were still walking around on the streets below. To the right of the hotel was a mosque. It was brightly lit and people were gathered in the courtyard. Between the mosque and our hotel, about eight yards away, was the police station; a bit too close for my comfort level but there was nothing I could do about it. I moved to the other side of the hotel; all was quiet.

My 360-degree survey left me satisfied that it would be difficult for anyone to gain access to our rooftop without a very long ladder. I asked Hamid if he'd spotted any potential hazards and he said no. Hamid wasn't a security man, but as an Afghan he had a greater sensitivity than me to any anomalies on the streets.

While we were on the roof, the caretaker had returned with dinner, which he'd laid out on plastic sheets at the end of the corridor on the top floor. By the time we finished our recce, the guards and drivers had gathered on two old, dusty sofas and were tucking into mutton kebabs, rice, bread and soft drinks.

The caretaker didn't notice me when I walked in. I doubted I could keep my identity concealed for long so I broke the ice by making a casual remark. The sound of English spoken in an undoubtedly western accent immediately caught his attention.

He looked up at me. We were both taken aback; the caretaker's face was heavily scarred and he had only one eye, which was as wide as a saucer. I'm sure the last person he expected to see in his hotel was a westerner.

I shook his hand and asked him how he was. The caretaker bowed his head and gave the typical Muslim response – 'alhamdulilah' (praise be to God) – very friendly given the circumstances. I thanked him for the food and for allowing us to stay at his hotel. I also complimented him on how well he'd secured the premises, which seemed to please him greatly.

The caretaker asked me where I was from.

'Scotland,' I said.

A big smile spread across his mangled face. 'Braveheart!' he said.

I wondered if Mel Gibson had any idea that his portrayal of William Wallace had won over fans as far afield as Khost.

A bit more small talk and I asked the caretaker the question I really needed answered: had he told anyone he had guests staying at his hotel? He assured me he hadn't, adding that there were many bad people in town and it was in his interests as well that no one know we were there.

After dinner the guards on duty broke off to their stations while the rest got their heads down. Luckily, the caretaker had his own place right next door to the hotel and he'd graciously offered the use of his home to the vehicle guards so they could take turns sleeping and have access to running water for Muslim ablutions. That meant the rest of us could barricade ourselves in on the top floor for the rest of the night. We'd keep in touch with the vehicle guards via radio.

Before going quiet for the evening, I grabbed two guards for one last patrol of the rooftop. The lights at street level were very bright and we couldn't see any activity. It was completely dead except for the strange sight of a mixed-breed dog that someone had shaved and covered in different coloured paints and slogans written in Arabic script. I asked the guards if they could figure out what was written on the dog but they were as baffled as I was. The dog walked past our hotel several times. By the third turn I asked the guards jokingly if it was an al-Qaeda decoy meant to flush us out.

After a couple of hours on the rooftop, I decided to move the guards inside and station them on the central corridor. We bolted, chained and locked the rooftop door behind us and barricaded it with furniture. As an extra precaution, we also jammed table legs against it to prevent anyone from battering it down.

I carried on with the corridor guards for another hour before leaving them to get some sleep. If we survived the night, we'd still be facing a long and treacherous journey back to Kabul and I'd need my wits about me.

I lay down on my bed with my compact AK across my chest and tried to get some sleep. It was a struggle. Each squeak of the floors or creak of the ceilings startled me to attention. I felt extremely vulnerable. If we were attacked, we had only ourselves to rely on. The American military was only four miles away, but they may as well have been four hundred.

I was still seething over the way the Yanks had thrown me to the wolves but I can't say I was surprised by their actions. A mate of mine working in Iraq had also had the door slammed in his face by the American military during a crisis. He was escorting his client, a US civilian, when their convoy was attacked by insurgents. My mate and the rest of his CP team tried to get the client to the safe haven of an American military base only to be turned away. He showed the guards passports and corporate ID cards but they wouldn't let his client in.[18]

I got out of bed twice during the night to make sure the

18 I went on to see the same thing again in 2006 when riots broke out in the streets of the Afghan capital. The first thing the US military did was lock down their bases and not let anyone in; no US civilians, no journalists, no civilians from allied nations and certainly no friendly Afghans. Everyone was turned away at the gates, even British Embassy officials.

guards on duty were awake. They were. All of them knew as well as I did that the likelihood of an incident was high. By 4.30 a.m., we'd all passed a restless night but one that was thankfully behind us. I'd told the lads we'd leave the hotel by 5 a.m. sharp. I wanted to be out with the first casual flow of vehicles on the road. Better to blend in with the local traffic than leave too early and look like we were sneaking out of town.

Before we left, I thanked the men for their vigilance during the night and reminded them of the importance of staying alert while we were on the road. There was still dangerous ground to cover and everyone had to be switched on. I also promised them that when we got to Kabul, safely, I'd take them all out to dinner. My presence had greatly endangered everyone and I was grateful to them for sticking by me. It was literally the very least I could do.

I had one last item of business to take care of before getting under way. I gave Hamid one hundred US dollars to give to the caretaker. I don't believe you can ever buy security; after all, what's one hundred dollars compared with twenty-five thousand? The tip was my way of saying thanks for being such a gracious and discreet host.

Our convoy pulled out of the hotel compound and joined the early morning traffic. We meandered our way out of Khost town and continued on a north-west bearing. I've never been so glad to put a patch of land behind me.

That night in Kabul, a group of exhausted Afghans and one red-eyed Scotsman sat down to dinner in one of the capital's finest Afghan restaurants. We dined on mutton, chicken, dumplings and rice with sultanas. Afterwards, I was happy to pick up the tab.[19]

---

19 And I didn't expense it.

CHAPTER 25

Terrorist organizations need two things to thrive: a breeding ground and a training ground. During winter and spring of 2004, I visited the two principal training grounds for Islamic insurgents: Iraq and Afghanistan. In the summer of that year, I had the opportunity to see the world's foremost jihadist breeding ground: Saudi Arabia.

When Nic Robertson rang to see if I'd be interested in looking after him and his team (via AKE) for a documentary they were shooting in Saudi Arabia, I told him to count me in. I'd been there once before with the Regiment during the first Gulf War but my experience of the country had been confined to air bases and the desert. I'd been itching to return to Saudi Arabia ever since the 11 September attacks. The majority of the 11 September hijackers were Saudi, and the country was and, in my opinion, remains the premier hub for al-Qaeda financing and recruitment. Seeing the real Saudi was crucial for advancing my understanding of the al-Qaeda threat.

The working title of Nic's documentary was *Kingdom on the Brink*, which couldn't have been more appropriate. In the months leading up to our trip Saudi Arabia had been rife with al-Qaeda activity. In May of that year, al-Qaeda militants attacked two oil installations and a foreign workers' compound in the eastern city of Khobar. During a twenty-five-hour rampage, al-Qaeda militants rounded up fifty people, killing twenty-two. The militants reportedly focused their fury on Christian hostages, allowing Muslims to go free. In June of that year, al-Qaeda militants abducted Paul M. Johnson, a US helicopter engineer working in Saudi for the American defence contractor Lockheed Martin. In exchange for Johnson's life, the kidnappers demanded that the Saudi Government release prisoners arrested for links with radical groups. When their demands weren't met, they beheaded Johnson. Pictures of the execution were posted on an Islamic website.

Of all the horrific incidents in Saudi that year, the one which perhaps resonated most with Nic and his crew was the killing and wounding of two members of their own profession. In June 2004 two BBC journalists were fired on by militants while filming in Suweidi, a known al-Qaeda neighborhood in Riyadh, the Saudi capital. Cameraman Simon Cumbers was killed. Correspondent Frank Gardner survived the attack but was left paralysed by his injuries.

Before the BBC incident, many journalists regarded Saudi as a soft environment compared to Afghanistan and Iraq. In truth, Saudi is perhaps more dangerous because the risks involved in operating there are hidden beneath a benign exterior and are therefore more difficult to recognize. Sadly, it took a tragedy like the BBC shootings to goad western media organizations into providing security for journalists operating in Saudi. It was a sobering reminder that the country was indeed a hostile environment; one full of Islamic militants who regard all westerners – journalists, oil workers or otherwise – as legitimate targets.

Nic had a large crew in tow for this project including a cameraman and two producers; one from CNN headquarters in Atlanta and a young Arab producer educated in England with numerous Middle East contacts. It was a big group to look after, especially as I'd be operating on my own again. Moreover, I couldn't arm myself during any portion of the trip. You can't carry weapons in Saudi so the security I provided would have to be entirely proactive.

The assignment also introduced a variable I hadn't yet

encountered on The Circuit: a 'minder' who would accompany us at all times during our trip. Minders are government officials who ensure that the host country is portrayed in a positive light. In other words, they try to keep journalists from getting too close to the truth. I had reason to believe, however, that Saudi minders might be playing both sides. The BBC lads were with a government minder when they were attacked. The minder got away without a scratch and there was speculation at the time amongst the international media that he may have helped orchestrate the incident.[20]

Our minder was waiting for us as soon as we stepped off the plane in Riyadh. A smiling, rotund man with a moustache and Saudi headdress, he looked jovial and not the least bit threatening. Then again, appearances can be deceiving. The minder had prearranged transport to our hotel. On the drive over, we passed dozens of international compounds, all of which looked very vulnerable to attack. It was little wonder al-Qaeda had been busy that year. As we turned from the main highway into our hotel complex, it appeared as if the authorities had taken steps to enhance security. The hotel was surrounded by police vehicles as well as hotel guards. The extra measures did little, however, to reassure me. It was still possible for militants to hit the hotel with a truck bomb or send fifty angry men through the security cordon and spray the place with gunfire.

My clients and I were assigned to a block of rooms at the end of a corridor on the fourth floor. I was well pleased. If the hotel was attacked in the middle of the night, I didn't want to be wandering from floor to floor, rounding up Nic and his crew to get them to safety.

While my clients sorted their gear, I performed a security audit of the complex. The hotel was a soaring glass structure with a sky bridge leading directly to a shopping mall; beautiful

---

20 Frank Gardner reportedly came to accept that the minder assigned to him and Simon Cumbers by the Saudi Ministry of Information was not complicit in the attack.

to look at but not optimal from a security standpoint. I took a quick walk through the mall to get my bearings. From the coffee bars to the burger joints, it was exactly like the ones I'd visited in the United States, with two exceptions: first, the women were covered from head to toe in black veils. Secondly, there were the police. Along with the regular uniformed officers there were Mutaween – religious police who enforce Saudi Arabia's hard-core Wahhabist tenets, such as strict dress codes.

During my rounds I bumped into an ex-Marine looking after a Sky News team at the same hotel. I was heartened to see that other networks were taking the security situation in Saudi seriously. Hopefully, the BBC incident would remain an isolated one.

Later that afternoon, Nic and his crew sat down with the minder to discuss what they hoped to accomplish during their stay. Nic explained, with the utmost diplomacy, that in the light of recent events in the Kingdom, it would be useful to examine the tensions between Saudi Arabia's religious and progressive elements. He wanted to visit several regions of the Kingdom in order to profile a cross section of Saudi society: a wealthy prince, an architect, a lawyer, a businesswoman, a young person and a reformed radical.

What Nic didn't tell the minder was that he was also hoping to interview a person with intimate knowledge of al-Qaeda; namely, Osama bin Laden's brother-in-law.

The first character Nic profiled was Prince Al Waleed bin Talal, one of the wealthiest men in the Kingdom, not to mention the world. We accompanied the Prince on his private jet from Riyadh to Jeddah and back. The aircraft was decked out with every possible luxury, from a shower to a private bedroom. The Prince also had a 'chase' jet that followed him everywhere, in case his primary jet broke down. I'd seen some filthy rich people on The Circuit, including royalty, but none who could afford to have a backup jet trail them wherever they went. I imagined the Prince's conspicuous consumption, along with that of the rest of the Saudi royals, was breeding a tremendous amount of contempt among the Kingdom's less privileged inhabitants.

We got a first-hand look at the fallout from that simmering anger as soon as we arrived back in Riyadh. It was 11 p.m. local time. While driving to our hotel, one of Nic's contacts rang to say a battle had broken out between Saudi police and Islamic militants in the King Fahd district of the city. Luckily, our minder had left us for the night, so we could divert there immediately.

We could see tracer rounds criss-crossing the sky as we neared the incident area. Two rings of Saudi police had surrounded the house where the militants were holed up. We managed to drive past the outer cordon of Saudi security approximately three blocks from the fighting. Nic and the crew stayed with the vehicles while I grabbed a small DV camera to recce the area. I wanted to see if it was possible to get past the inner cordon and film.

Obviously the Saudi authorities didn't want journalists getting too close so I had to work quickly. I managed to reach the edge of the inner cordon; the police were firing sporadically into a wide area. The shooting was very indiscriminate and far too dangerous to observe up close, so I decided to keep myself and the crew behind the two cordons.

After a while our government minder caught up with us. Rather than send us back to our hotel, he very kindly got permission for CNN to film the outer cordon police checkpoints. He even arranged for Nic to interview a Police Commander. Nic did live shots through the night, updating the story with each new detail coming out of the Saudi Interior Ministry. The next morning, while the majority of the press stationed at our hotel was waking to news of a shoot-out at an al-Qaeda safe house in Riyadh, Nic was putting the story to bed: two suspected militants were killed in the battle and three wounded; one of the militants blew himself up at the gates of the house in an apparent suicide attack on police. The police recovered a cache of weapons from the house including surface-to-air missiles, RPGs, automatic rifles, grenades, ammo and explosive materials. They also made a grisly discovery in the refrigerator: the head of Paul Johnson, the US engineer who'd been captured and killed by al-Qaeda operatives a month earlier.

Two days after the shoot-out, CNN was granted exclusive permission to interview the Riyadh Police Chief outside the captured safe house. Aside from removing the bodies, the authorities had done little to tidy up before we got there. The building was pocked with bullet holes and blood was smeared on the steps leading up to the front door and on the door itself. Clothing, beds and other furniture were stacked in the courtyard outside. The most disturbing sight was the front gate of the house; a metal door with plastic sheeting that had melted from the heat generated by the blast of the suicide bomber.

While we were filming, residents who'd evacuated the neighbourhood during the battle were returning home. The people were as modest as their houses; middle class and unassuming, a side of Saudi Arabia few outsiders see. Judging from the state of their neighbourhood, the residents had had good reason to flee. The courtyard walls bordering the street and a school building at the end of it were all peppered with bullet holes.

I spoke with some of the residents to see what they could tell me about the incident. One man who lived next door to the safe house said he'd hidden under furniture with his three-year-old daughter for eleven hours, until he was sure that the fighting had stopped.

At the end of the battle-scarred street was a sight common in the Saudi capital: a plastic yellow rubbish bin with the words 'Riyadh the Clean City' written in Arabic and English. Two little boys both under the age of eight were playing near the bin. I asked who they were. They told me they were brothers and pointed to their home; it was four doors down from the al-Qaeda safe house. I photographed them in front of their school at the end of the street. The boys appeared traumatized standing in front of the bullet-riddled building. The location could easily have been mistaken for Baghdad.

CHAPTER 26

My work on The Circuit has put me face to face with some notorious rogues. I always find these encounters remarkable. Meeting infamous figures in the flesh, listening to them being interviewed uncut and unedited, is fascinating. Western governments have a bad habit of personalizing the War on Terror by reducing it to a series of Most Wanted posters. But I've learned over the years that terrorist organizations don't rest on the shoulders of individuals. Take Osama bin Laden out of the equation and al-Qaeda still exists.

By summer 2004, my rogues' gallery included the likes of Yasir Arafat and Sheikh Yassin. Thanks to Nic, I was poised to add a few new faces. Nic wanted to include two so-called 'reformed' Islamic radicals in his documentary on Saudi Arabia. One of the interviewees, a young Saudi who'd been jailed for his beliefs, reformed and released, had been lined up and approved by the minder. The other character Nic wanted to interview would have to be pursued through less overt channels.

If the name Mohammed Jamal Khalifa doesn't ring a bell, his brother-in-law's may – Osama bin Laden. For over a decade, Khalifa lived and worked side by side with bin Laden. The two met at university in 1976. During the 1980s, they joined other jihadists in Afghanistan to fight the Soviet occupation. In 1986, according to Khalifa, the fast friends went their separate ways. Khalifa claimed he fell out with bin Laden over the formation of al-Qaeda. After the 11 September attacks, Khalifa publicly denied having ever been an active member of the organization.

The CIA disagreed. They believed Khalifa had worked as al-Qaeda's money man in the Philippines, setting up front companies to finance operations for the terror group Abu Sayyaf. Throughout the early 1990s, Khalifa did leave quite an incriminating trail. His business cards were found in apartments rented to Ramzi Yousseff, the convicted ringleader of the 1993 World Trade Center bombing. In 1994 Khalifa was detained in California by FBI officials. Bomb-making manuals written in Arabic were among his personal belongings.

Khalifa maintained his innocence throughout, claiming that the companies he started were legitimate Islamic charities. The only time he was jailed was in Saudi Arabia shortly after the 11 September 2001 attacks. After his release, he was barred from leaving the country for several years. He went on to publicly denounce al-Qaeda.

After prison, Khalifa all but disappeared from public view. He opened a fish restaurant outside the Saudi coastal city of Jeddah and rarely gave interviews. His low profile suited the Saudi authorities. Given his background, Khalifa was hardly an ideal poster child for Saudi Arabia's reformed radicals. Requesting an interview with him through the minder was a non-starter. If Nic wanted to get Khalifa on camera, he'd have to do it on the sly.

A few days after the shoot-out at the al-Qaeda safe house in Riyadh, I accompanied Nic and his crew to Jeddah to film some additional pre-approved elements for the documentary. The trip involved switching minders; the one in Riyadh saw us off at the airport and another met us off the plane in Jeddah. The Jeddah minder wasn't nearly as vigilant as his counterpart in Riyadh. He drove us to our hotel, dropped us off and said he'd be back in the morning. It was a golden opportunity. As soon as the minder left, the young CNN producer with the great contacts was on the phone; the interview with Khalifa was Nic's if he wanted it.

The interview was to take place that same night at Khalifa's restaurant approximately an hour's drive from Jeddah. The timing was great from a security standpoint. Driving at night would make it much harder for people on the roads to see into our vehicles and identify us as westerners.

Khalifa's restaurant was full of diners when we arrived. A short and stocky young man introducing himself as Khalifa's son met us at the entrance. He escorted us to a private room in the back and told us his father would be in shortly.

I was very excited by the prospect of meeting Khalifa face to face. I couldn't believe he'd got away with so much. I wondered whether the real man would live up to the infamous image.

Khalifa arrived and greeted us cordially. Like Arafat, he was much smaller in person than I'd imagined. He looked and acted as though he came from a privileged background. His mannerisms were as polished as his neatly trimmed facial hair. But for all his refinement, I could tell the man was hard as nails. Khalifa was no ponce. He reminded me of a gangster, albeit one in a long, white man-dress.

Nic lost no time diving into the interview. It was absorbing from start to finish. Many of Nic's questions focused on Khalifa's impressions of bin Laden. The answers confirmed my beliefs about the role of individuals in terrorist organizations. Khalifa described bin Laden as a charismatic individual who easily won over people. 'Many people really love Osama,' he said. Far from a terrorist mastermind, Khalifa claimed bin Laden 'cannot organize anything', and that during the years they lived together it was Khalifa, not bin Laden, who arranged everything from prayer times to picnics. Off camera, Khalifa commented that the al-Qaeda leader was nothing more than a figurehead. As he put it, the west had turned bin Laden into 'the Nike stripe' of terrorism.

In addition to bin Laden, Nic pressed Khalifa over allegations about his involvement in al-Qaeda. Khalifa said he was 'very confident' that the allegations couldn't be proven. To this day I wonder what made him so self-assured because he looked to me to be guilty as hell. To underscore his innocence, Khalifa threw in a personal appeal to bin Laden. 'Please come out,' he said to the camera. 'Tell those people to stop. You are the one who can tell that, and you are the one who can stop it.' Cagey character.

After the interview Khalifa invited us to dine in one of the restaurant's private rooms. The fish was out of this world. Perhaps if he'd stuck with the restaurant business Khalifa would have got away with his wicked past. In 2007, however, it caught up with him. Khalifa died in a violent attack on a gem mine he owned in Madagascar. According to published reports, some twenty-odd men stormed Khalifa's guest house; he was shot twice, stabbed and hacked with an axe. When I read about it, I wondered whether it was simply a case of a business deal gone bad, a revenge attack by al-Qaeda, or perhaps even the CIA.

Back in Riyadh, Nic caught up with the other reformed radical he wanted to interview, a young man by the name of Abdullah al Otaibi. Abdullah had spent ten years in a Saudi jail for his radical Islamic thinking. Middle class and sheltered, his background had little in common with that of the worldly, wealthy Khalifa. Yet both men were seduced by extremist ideas.

Abdullah gave his interview to CNN in Arabic. More than once, he openly criticized Saudi clerics whom he blamed for pushing moderate Muslims like himself towards extremism. It all sounded a bit too rehearsed in my view. If the Saudis could convince the world that al-Qaeda had come about solely because of extremist interpretations of the Koran, then all they had to do was root out the bad clerics and problem solved. If only it were that easy. During his interview, Abdullah mentioned that during his radical years he'd lived with a group of fellow jihadists in Suweidi, the al-Qaeda neighbourhood where the BBC crew had been attacked. Nic was very keen to film Abdullah in his old stomping ground and to record a stand-up where the BBC incident had taken place.

As much as I wanted to accommodate Nic, filming in Suweidi

presented a huge security problem. Nic and I usually get on very well. But we can have strong words when he wants to achieve something which I view as too dangerous. This was one of those occasions. Nic insisted he needed the Suweidi elements for his documentary. I appreciated his desire to be thorough with his reporting, but there was absolutely no way I was going to stand back and allow the crew to film on streets crawling with al-Qaeda. For a while, we were at loggerheads on how to proceed.

After mulling it over, I presented Nic with a compromise. I proposed that rather than have the whole crew go charging into Suweidi cold, Abdullah and I first recce the neighbourhood by car. If Abdullah were driving, I could film him with a hand-held DV camera talking about his old house and other relevant landmarks as we drove past them. I could also covertly film the area where the BBC crew had been ambushed. If I determined afterwards that it was too dangerous for the crew to go, at the very least, Nic would have b-roll for his story.

Fortunately, Nic agreed with the plan. I promised him that if there was any way for him to film inside Suweidi safely, I'd make it happen. Much to my surprise, the minder was also in favour of Abdullah and me going to Suweidi alone. Frankly, I was happy to leave him behind. Our minder had been helpful but I still didn't trust him.

The next morning, following a quick brief, Abdullah and I were off. As we drove, I thought about what to ask him on camera once we got to Suweidi. There were so many questions he'd avoided when Nic interviewed him. Abdullah wouldn't say, for example, why extremist ideas had appealed to him in the first place. He didn't criticize the Saudi royal family, nor did he express any frustration with living in a monarchy that barred people like him from having a voice in politics. The most Abdullah offered were vague references about how he'd been convinced that being religious was 'better' for him.

By that point, however, I didn't need an explanation from

Abdullah. The fifteen-minute drive from our hotel to the edge of Suweidi illustrated perfectly why so many young Saudi men were embracing jihadist ideals. The centre of the Saudi capital is a collection of beautiful skyscrapers and air-conditioned shopping malls housing every luxury under the sun. It's the epicentre of the country's 'haves'. Push out from the centre of Riyadh and you see how many 'have-nots' populate the Kingdom. There are middle-class neighbourhoods, nondescript, modest places like the King Fahd district where the shoot-out at the al-Qaeda safe house took place. Go a little further and you find neighbourhoods like Suweidi, areas which by Saudi standards are deprived.

I knew from my previous work on The Circuit that not all Gulf Arabs were obscenely wealthy. I didn't realize, however, what a huge middle class existed in Saudi Arabia. The country is full of young men like Abdullah who could never afford a private jet, let alone two. I imagined even elite Saudis like Khalifa must have felt inadequate compared to the likes of Prince Al Waleed bin Talal.

While we were driving, Abdullah started chatting with me – in English. I was somewhat taken back because I'd assumed when he gave his interview in Arabic that his English was limited. In fact, it was quite good. For instance, he asked me where I was from.

'Scotland,' I said.

'Braveheart!' he exclaimed. 'You know what it's like to be oppressed.'

It was obvious he was drawing a parallel with his own experience. That comment convinced me that it wasn't religion that had driven Abdullah, and others like him, towards extremism. It was resentment and anger; resentment toward a royal family that hoarded and squandered the country's wealth and anger toward the western nations that enabled them to get away with it.

I could have kicked myself for not having the camera rolling.

Inside Suweidi, Abdullah followed my driving instructions to the letter; slowing down when we passed significant landmarks but never stopping. On camera, he talked more about Suweidi's current troubles than his own chequered past. He pointed out at least four areas where incidents had recently taken place, from gun battles to helicopter attacks. My heart sank as he pointed to where the BBC crew had been shot. Poor lads. It's difficult for any journalist, including those with experience in hostile environments, to balance reporting needs with security needs. The two are often at odds and when presented with one or the other, ambitious journalists will usually cross their fingers, go for the story and hope they get away with it. The BBC crew had made the mistake of filming on the streets of Suweidi for nearly half an hour. Militants can organize and stage an attack within minutes. Sadly, the BBC lads didn't have a security adviser around to remind them of this.

Our entire recce took approximately fifty minutes door to door. When we returned to the hotel, I told Nic he could film in Suweidi, as long as he stayed inside the vehicle and kept mobile – which he did. In the end, we were both well pleased: Nic because he'd got the story and me because he'd got it safely.

CHAPTER 27

The year 2004 was shaping up to be great for me professionally. Working with the media was a ball, especially Nic Robertson. I'd seen Nic through some of the most hazardous areas of Afghanistan, Iraq and even Saudi Arabia. From a security standpoint, all of these assignments were successful; partly because we were lucky, but mostly because Nic let me get on with my job.

By autumn 2004, my work for that year had come full circle. AKE asked me to return to Baghdad to look after CNN. I wasn't expecting a carbon copy of my first trip. The insurgency had gained tremendous momentum in the months I'd been away and the operational environment had grown far more treacherous. Hardly a day passed when I didn't hear about a security adviser getting hit in Iraq.

The worsening security situation was apparent as soon as I landed. The AKE convoy waiting to collect me from Baghdad International Airport had been upgraded from soft-skinned to very good-spec, low-profile armoured 4x4s. After a quick brief, including an update of the latest insurgent incidents, I was handed my weapons and kit and off we went to the Palestine hotel. I noted a marked increase in the number of foreign security details driving up and down the airport road. We must have passed at least half a dozen, all of them very overt, from their choice of vehicles to the visibility of weapons and body armour. No wonder security advisers were getting hit practically every day. The one advantage for us, though, was that the conspicuous teams would draw attention away from us.

By the time we reached the Palestine, the AKE lads had caught me up on what was going on with CNN. The network still had a large presence in Baghdad and there were several correspondents and crews operating out of the bureau. Most of the journalists were working within the security guidelines established by AKE, but some insisted on operating unilaterally.

Journalists are competitive; even when they work for the same network they can guard their stories jealously. A minority of CNN staffers were sneaking off without taking advisers or letting anyone know where they were going. It was complete insanity. Not only were they putting themselves at risk by travelling alone, if they went missing, no one would have a clue where to start looking for them.

Even inside the Palestine, this small group of CNN staffers was refusing to maintain any semblance of cohesion with the rest of their team. Rather than sleep on one of two designated floors, they'd scattered themselves throughout the hotel. If the Palestine were attacked, the AKE team would be running all over the place trying to do a head count and get everyone to safety.

The clients also had a major transport issue. I was told that in addition to the two new armoured 4x4s, CNN was still using an armoured BMW 5 series that had been brought in from Amman purely as an interim measure until the 4x4s arrived. The BMW was very old and had broken down on no fewer than three occasions with CNN staff riding inside.

Finally, the AKE lads were contending with a new development that had cropped up during my absence: Iraqi security advisers. CNN had taken on several of them, the argument being that they were more low profile, and much cheaper than western advisers. When it comes to operating low profile, I'm the preacher and the choir. But that wasn't enough in my opinion to overcome the disadvantages of using local security. The Iraqi advisers had limited options outside their home market and would therefore be much more likely to cave in to the client on important issues. Working in their own backyards also exposed the Iraqi advisers to blackmail, extortion and death threats from insurgents.

When I asked what was going on with respect to addressing these issues, the lads told me that they'd all been brought to the attention of the Baghdad Bureau Chief but he hadn't sorted the issues to date. They told me I was welcome to try with him.

Of all the issues brewing at the bureau the one that topped my priority list was the BMW. A vehicle failure in a hostile environment can cost a client their life. At the first opportunity, I went to see it for myself. From a few yards away the car didn't appear armoured, which made it very low profile. But that was the only thing it had going for it. The vehicle was close to thirty years old and had been armoured without upgrading the chassis or engine. No wonder it was breaking down. It's like a person who piles on loads of weight; eventually things start to give out. It was time to either blow up the BMW ourselves or shift it back to Amman. Using it operationally in Baghdad was a disaster waiting to happen.

I went to see the bureau chief immediately. The bureau was located in the Palestine's former swimming pool changing rooms; a large open space with no natural light (sandbags had been piled up outside the only window). It was sectioned off by rows of tables holding computer terminals, editing and viewing equipment. The bureau chief's area was in the centre of the room.

When I saw the bureau chief, I recognized him immediately. It was the same young man I'd escorted to the presser in the Green Zone on my first trip to Baghdad – the one who refused to wear his body armour. I couldn't get through to him back then so it was little wonder my fellow advisers were having difficulty with him now.

I walked over and reintroduced myself to him. His complexion was very pale and pasty – a bad sign. It suggested he probably rarely left the hotel. A bureau chief's main job is to send correspondents and crews out to cover stories. Having worked with the media for a while, I'd learned that the best bureau chiefs get out on the ground whenever possible.[21] Like a military ops officer in a hostile environment, a bureau chief should understand what is safely achievable and what is not. The best way to gain this understanding is through first-hand experience.

I listed my concerns about the BMW to the bureau chief and asked him why, given its history of mechanical failure, it hadn't been replaced with a more reliable vehicle. Before answering me, the bureau chief looked around to see who was listening to our conversation. He told me the car's problems had been fixed and that there was no money in his budget to buy another one.

'Can't you send a memo to Atlanta [CNN Headquarters] explaining that due to the number of crews in situ you require another armoured vehicle?' I asked.

The question really got his back up. He told me it would be him who'd decide which issues to take up with Atlanta – not me. His tone was very defensive. The fact that the conversation was happening within earshot of his staff probably wasn't helping matters. I asked him to take a walk with me around the Palestine's gardens so we could chat privately.

Once outside, I tried to put his mind at ease by telling him that my intention was to help him; not to hinder him or undercut his authority. I explained that sometimes it pays to have a fresh set of eyes on a situation to see where things may be falling down. I then listed my concerns: the BMW, the staff being split all over the hotel, crews taking off unilaterally and the local security advisers.

The bureau chief agreed with certain points, such as consolidating the CNN staff on two floors and making sure no one left

21 The CNN Jerusalem Bureau Chief during my tour there in 2002 was an excellent example of a proactive manager; he was always on the ground. He knew the story inside out and the dangers of covering it.

the hotel without taking an adviser and letting someone know exactly where they were going. He did not agree with me on the issue of local security. The BMW was also a major sticking point; he refused to replace it, arguing that all the mechanical problems had been sorted.

I told him that the vehicle was almost thirty years old and no amount of servicing would make it roadworthy.

He didn't agree.

A few days later I was assigned to look after CNN correspondent Diana Muriel. Thoroughly feminine with a refined demeanour, Diana didn't fit the typical image of a scruffy, weatherbeaten war reporter but her track record spoke for itself; she'd covered riots in Northern Ireland, spent three months in Afghanistan in 2002 and survived a two-month desert embed with the British military during the 2003 Iraq invasion.

Diana was working on a story featuring a local medicine man using traditional practices to treat people for common ailments. Iraq's medical system had once been the envy of the Arab world. Diana's report would show just how badly it had broken down.

The shoot was to take place in Baghdad's Khadamiya district, a forty-minute drive from the Palestine. During the pre-shoot briefing, Diana expressed her reservations about travelling across town. She was wise to be cautious. A dozen journalists had already been abducted in Iraq that year, including an Italian who was killed by his captors. With her pale skin, blue eyes and blonde hair, Diana was a tempting target for kidnappers and insurgents. Thankfully, she was savvy enough to realize that she wasn't going to blend in with the locals just by throwing a scarf over her head.

I assured Diana that if things looked dangerous, we'd turn around and come straight back to the hotel – provided our car was up to the task. The only vehicle available for the shoot was the crappy BMW. I didn't hide my concerns from Diana; she had a right to know all the potential risks involved with getting her story. Before we left the Palestine, I asked the bureau chief again about the BMW's servicing. He was adamant that the vehicle was fine. I still didn't believe it, so I asked our driver to kick over the engine and do a few laps around the car park of the Palestine before we left. I had him keep the engine running while Diana and her shooter loaded their gear into the car.

It was late morning and, as usual, Baghdad's roads were extremely congested. The weather was hot and humid and the BMW's fan laboured like an old man with emphysema to keep us moderately cool. I knew the car's engine would be struggling as well. Somehow, the car made it to Khadamiya without breaking down. I didn't want to risk having it not start up again, so I asked the driver to keep the engine running throughout the shoot.

The doctor's office was located down a narrow passage in the centre of Khadamiya's old town. It was a small surgery with just enough room for the doctor's kit and a patient to sit upright in a chair. During the shoot, two American helicopters flew over us low and fast. The locals disappeared into their houses immediately. One woman was kind enough to beckon us in to take cover with her. I thanked the woman but declined her offer. The people in the neighbourhood were genuinely nice but I knew word of our presence would eventually filter up the street, possibly to the wrong people. The longer we stayed the more vulnerable we became. It was a very worthwhile story and I was happy to continue as long as Diana and her shooter kept things moving. She wrapped the shoot quickly, nailing her stand-up in one take.

The engine was still running when we got back to the car. We all piled inside and headed back towards the Palestine. It looked like we'd complete the assignment without a hitch, and then the car's history caught up with us. It was mid-afternoon, around 3 p.m. local time. We were crawling down a five-lane highway in bumper-to-bumper traffic when the BMW died.

There was no sputtering or lurching – the engine just cut out, full stop.

Our driver steered the vehicle onto the shoulder of the highway. 'It's happening again! It's happening again!' he said.

I asked the driver to get out and check under the bonnet (if Diana or I were to leave the vehicle, we'd instantly draw attention). While the driver tried in vain to fix the engine, I called the AKE operations desk at the bureau for backup. The lad on the desk was fuming that the vehicle had broken down – again. Two minutes later he rang back to say that one of CNN's local fixers was in the vicinity and would divert to our location to collect us.

I saw the fixer heading towards us in the opposite direction down the highway. When he drew parallel with our position, he pulled over and waved. The fixer was a welcome sight but I still had to get everyone across ten lanes of Baghdad traffic in full view of everyone. To make matters worse, the driver refused to leave the vehicle. I told him there was no way we could cross the highway without being seen. Everyone would know he was working with westerners, which could mark him a target.

The driver understood but refused to abandon the BMW, afraid that if he did, he'd be fired. I told him that was rubbish and CNN would never do that, but nothing I said would convince him. It did occur to me to simply set the BMW on fire (I carry a flare in my kit just for that sort of situation), but short of chinning the driver and throwing him over my shoulder – which wasn't an option – there was nothing I could do to get him to come with us.

I couldn't be skipping across the road several times; everything, people and gear, had to be cross-decked to the fixer's vehicle in one go. Fortunately, Diana was wearing her head scarf and all of us were wearing body armour underneath our clothes. We were as low profile as we could possibly get. I grabbed my car weapon, an AK, but kept it in its canvas bag with the zip open for easy access. We moved in a close-knit group; the crew in front, followed by Diana and me at their backs. Traffic was moving slowly and many of the drivers on the road were able to figure out our situation. The majority were hospitable; a couple of lorry drivers pulled up, leaving gaps for us to cross. But the friendly drivers weren't my concern. I was worried about the ones in the background, the insurgents and opportunists waiting to abduct a westerner. It took less than thirty seconds for all of us to cross the ten lanes and jump into the fixer's vehicle. As we pulled away, I looked back at the driver; he was leaning over the open bonnet and talking on his phone.

When we got to the bureau I was relieved to learn that our driver had managed to restart the BMW and was en route to the Palestine. I asked the AKE ops desk to let me know when he arrived safely. I then went to have a word with the bureau chief. I found him sitting at his desk.

'Can we talk?' I asked.

He looked up at me and started rocking back and forth in his chair. 'Why, Bob? Are you going to pick on me again?'

I was trying very hard to maintain a sense of diplomacy. I asked the bureau chief if I could have a word with him privately. Away from the prying eyes and ears of the rest of the bureau, I told him in no uncertain terms that enough was enough, and if he didn't stand up to be counted and get a proper armoured vehicle in to replace the BMW then we were going to have some serious issues.

He continued to insist that the BMW had been serviced and it shouldn't have broken down.

'Grow up,' I said.

I told him no matter how many times the BMW was serviced, it was too old and worn out to use operationally. By this point, I got the feeling he wanted out of the conversation. He told me he would see what he could do about getting a replacement vehicle.

I felt enormously frustrated. I'd never had a real problem with a client before – strained relations occasionally – but never a situation where I was unable to do my job properly. I can't force a client to follow my advice. But if I'm out on the ground with them, I have a duty to maintain the highest possible security standards. I can't allow a dangerous situation to fester simply to appease a client. Doing so would be unprofessional and that's just not on.

CHAPTER 28

A week after the BMW incident, Diana Muriel asked if I'd join her on a military embed in Sadr City, a highly volatile, poor Shiite neighbourhood of Baghdad. I'd been there several times during my first trip to Iraq, but by September 2004 the area had become far too dangerous for western media to visit unilaterally.

Sadr City was an insurgent's haven for several reasons. A rabbit warren of densely packed buildings and narrow streets, the layout was ideal for guerrilla warfare. It was a natural base of support for the Mehdi Army, a heavily armed Shiite militia created by the firebrand cleric Muqtada al Sadr (Sadr City was named after his father). The Mehdi Army had been very active in Iraq that year, engaging coalition forces in a series of intense street battles. In Sadr City, the militia was proving to be quite a nuisance, hitting the Yanks regularly with rockets, IEDs and small-arms fire.

It was early morning when we arrived at the US military base on the central eastern outskirts of Sadr City. Diana checked in with the Public Affairs Officer to get our schedule for the next twenty-four hours. She was told we'd be joining two patrols; one that afternoon in the southern part of Sadr City and an evening patrol penetrating deep into the city centre.

Diana used the down time before our first patrol to shoot some general b-roll for her stories. The cameraman was getting pictures of APCs and tanks when insurgents fired a mortar round at the base. The rocket landed on a parked fuel truck which burst into flames. If that weren't enough, the fire spread to three other fuel trucks. I don't know what the Americans were thinking parking them side-by-side. No one was hurt in the attack but it was one hell of a bonfire.

Less visually engaging but of much more interest to me was the sight of a coalition sniper team dismounting a helicopter. I was full of envy when I saw .50 sniper rifles over their shoulders. I'd tested a variant of those weapons when I headed up the Regiment's anti-terrorist sniper team. They're very powerful; with the right bullet a sniper can smash an engine block from two kilometres away. I wondered where the lads were going. Wherever it was, the team was sure to be a huge asset to their deploying unit.

The first patrol of the embed was meant to be little more than a public relations excursion to showcase a US military reconstruction project in the south of Sadr City, an area perceived by the Americans to be softer than the city centre. Around 2 p.m. local time, we set off in a convoy of eight armoured Humvees. As we drove, the Americans staggered their vehicles at regular intervals to ensure that if one got hit by an IED the rest wouldn't get caught up in the explosion. We wound our way through dusty, tapered streets past loads of locals, many of whom were young and unemployed. Their expressions were hard and unwelcoming.

Our first stop was a forward operations base where Diana was invited to interview the commander in charge of the reconstruction project: a damaged water pumping station the US military was repairing. After the interview the Humvees escorted us to the station to film the fruits of the Yanks' labour. When we reached the pumping station, the Humvees parked up in tactical defensive mode; a circular formation for mutual support. We dismounted our vehicles along with a small foot patrol while the rest of the soldiers stayed with the convoy.

I took note of the locals gathered on the streets around us. They seemed friendly enough, though their attitude may have been influenced by the heavy US military presence. Either way,

I was fairly certain they were looking forward to running water regardless of who was providing it.

The pumping station was housed in a one-storey building. The cameraman got a few shots of the exterior before we all headed inside with the foot patrol. The station still wasn't up and running and there were no engineers on site doing repair works; just an old Iraqi man keeping watch over an idle pump. The patrol was shaping up to be a real snooze. Then we heard gunfire. It was very close – right outside the building. It began with AK fire, presumably from insurgents. A few seconds later the Americans responded with small-arms fire and the heavy thud of a .50 heavy machine gun.

The foot patrol that had escorted us inside the pumping station appeared at a loss as to how to respond. They just stood there, slack-jawed, looking at one another. I told the sergeant in charge that we needed to get the CNN crew back to the Humvees. I asked him to radio the soldiers outside and let them know we were coming out and needed cover. In seconds, we were out of the building and into the Humvees. When the shooting stopped, I asked our military hosts for a quick overview of what had happened. Apparently, a car carrying four men had fired on the convoy with AKs and the convoy responded to the threat. All four insurgents were killed in the contact.

We had only been at the pumping station a few minutes, but in a densely populated area like Sadr City that's all it takes for an incident to happen. I bet as soon as we pulled up to the station a tout was on his way to inform the insurgents that a target was in situ. If the militants were Mehdi Army, which I believe they were, they would definitely possess the organizational skills to mount an impromptu attack. As we drove back to the main base I told Diana that the contact was an example of how the Americans were failing to dominate the ground. Had the Americans been winning the war for Sadr City, the touts would have come running to them, not the Mehdi Army.

*

Early that evening, we attended a detailed briefing by the colonel in charge of the night patrol. He explained that we'd be going deep within Sadr City with a large armoured convoy of approximately thirty vehicles backed by helicopter gunships. The purpose of the patrol was to flush out members of the Mehdi Army and engage them.

The main patrol wouldn't get under way until after midnight. In the meantime, we were to deploy early with a small group of Bradley Fighting Vehicles to a forward operations base and wait while the convoy assembled. The armour was coming from locations all around Baghdad, so we were warned that we'd be spending up to five hours at the FOB.

After the brief, I asked the colonel how many OPs they had (covert observation points stationed further out from the FOB).

'None,' he told me.

I thought that was a huge mistake both operationally and strategically. There are half a million people crammed into Sadr City and the potential for collateral damage on any patrol is high. OPs can engage the enemy more accurately than troops operating as part of a large armoured convoy and limit the likelihood of civilian casualties. If you want to keep the local population on side, best to not hit them accidentally.

About an hour before last light, we linked up with a column of four Bradleys and drove to the FOB: a small, two-storey local council complex approximately two miles west of north central Sadr City. I felt very insecure about the location. There was a group of small houses and shops thirty yards across the road from where we'd parked. It would take nothing for an insurgent in one of the shops to lob a grenade at the Bradleys while people were mounting and dismounting.

Our military hosts quickly ushered us inside the building. Within ten minutes, insurgents were firing on our position. The Americans responded with a thunderous volley of gunfire. It was around 8 p.m. local time. We weren't scheduled to mount up with the rest of the convoy until 2 a.m.

As soon as the shooting started Diana was on the phone filing live reports. They must have sounded quite exciting with mortars, RPGs and small-arms fire blasting away in the background. While Diana was between 'phoners' I took a walk upstairs to get a better view on the situation. When I got to the first floor, I was delighted to discover the .50 sniper team I'd seen earlier that day. Not only where they keeping the enemy at bay, but they looked like they were having a ball doing it. They asked me who I was. When I told them I was with CNN, they asked me not to film them. I told them not to worry as we'd respect their anonymity.

I asked them if they were having fun. One of the lads said if they hadn't been there, the insurgents would have overrun the location. I didn't doubt it. For the rest of the evening, a smile spread across my face each time I'd hear the thud of a .50 round leaving the barrel of a rifle. It was tremendously reassuring knowing that those lads were up there working in support of the Yanks.

While we waited for the convoy to assemble, I spoke with some of the soldiers who'd accompanied us in the Bradleys. I was particularly interested in talking with the patrol medic. I wanted to get his opinion on QuikClot, a granular substance that stops massive haemorrhaging. QuikClot was still relatively new, but AKE supplied it in all its medical packs. I'd heard a lot of pros and cons about using it, but never from a frontline medic.

The medic swore by it. He'd used QuikClot on many occasions and in his view it was the best way to stop massive blood loss, the main cause of battlefield deaths. The down side was that in a theatre of war it's not always possible to get a wounded soldier to a medical facility immediately and QuikClot isn't supposed to be left in a wound over a long period of time. The young medic told me that some of the surgeons in the military hospitals thought that if QuikClot is left in a wound too long it can cause limb loss. But as far as the medic was concerned, when the choice was between possible limb loss in the long term and the loss of a life on the ground, he'd apply QuikClot every time.[22]

I later learned that the young medic was up for a bravery award. Apparently, he'd scrambled up to a rooftop to treat a wounded soldier whilst under fire. Though I'd seen some horrendously stupid decision-making during embeds with the US military, I had no doubt that at ground level there were some outstanding young soldiers like that medic doing exceptional deeds.

By 1.45 a.m. the entire convoy had assembled and was ready to depart the FOB. The colonel in command invited Diana, her cameraman and me to ride with him in his Bradley. The colonel rode up front while we piled into the back with two other soldiers. It was a very tight squeeze. The air con wasn't working and it was sweltering inside. I braced myself for a very long, very uncomfortable night.

We were all given headsets to speak with one another and to listen to the colonel commanding the convoy. Unfortunately, the colonel could control which conversation we could and could not hear. But he couldn't edit what we could see. The back of the Bradley was kitted out with a computer screen that allowed us to see what was going on outside and the clarity of the image captured by the night vision camera was outstanding.

The convoy must have looked like a giant armoured crocodile snaking its way towards the centre of Sadr City. It was slow going. Each time we encountered an IED everything would grind to a halt. Five IEDs exploded, causing damage to the convoy but no injuries. On a few occasions, the patrol spotted command wires in advance. Command wires link an IED at one end to the insurgent initiating it at the other. Several times we heard the colonel instruct his gunners to fire at wires and sever them. He told the gunners to make sure their rounds didn't hit

22 I'd go on to borrow that young lad's line when explaining the pros and cons of QuickClot during hostile environment training courses.

civilians or surrounding buildings. Good for him. One of the command wires we encountered led to a mosque. The gunners observed it for several minutes before firing to make sure they were spot on. Had they missed, it would have inflamed local sensibilities.

The helicopter gunships backing the convoy were less discriminating. On the computer screen we could see missiles firing into what the colonel told us were suspected IED locations situated at a major crossroads in the city. I saw two of the gunships fire four missiles each; they landed in a beaten zone measuring between 600 and 800 metres in length and a couple of hundred metres in width; not exactly pinpoint accuracy.

As the hours dragged on, the IEDs became the least of my worries. The heat inside the Bradley had grown unbearable, especially when we were static. I felt like I couldn't get enough air. The fact that we were packed in like sardines with helmets and heavy body armour didn't help. I've wrestled with claustrophobia since I suffered a bad drowning situation during a diving exercise in the Regiment. I'll sail along fine for years at a time, and then Bam! something happens that takes me back to the moment when my lungs filled with water.

It took every ounce of willpower I had not to hit the door lever of the Bradley and run wild into the streets of Sadr City. I stayed in control by focusing on the activity unfolding on the monitor. It also helped that there was a large cool box opposite me with chunks of ice which I kept piling onto the back of my neck.

About four hours into the patrol an IED exploded forward of our vehicle. We could hear and feel the blast from our position in the back of the Bradley so it must have been a big one. At that point, the patrol had achieved absolutely nothing apart from shooting a few wires and whacking missiles into 'possible IED locations'. It looked like the big armoured crocodile wasn't going to draw the Mehdi Army into a fight. The colonel called it a night.

CHAPTER 29

Our embed in Sadr City lasted thirty-six, non-stop hours. When we got back to the Palestine, I took a long, cool shower and fell into bed. Later that afternoon, I went to the bureau to check in with the rest of the AKE team. I found Diana hard at work on yet another story. She'd barely got any sleep before being thrown right back into the mix.

I was making my way to the AKE desk when the bureau chief called me over. As usual, he was sitting in his chair, rocking back and forth.

'You need to take Diana back to Sadr City,' he said.

'Why?' I asked

'She needs to shoot a stand-up for another story,' he said. I searched his face. He seemed completely unaware of the fact that his request was incredibly dangerous.

What the bureau chief wanted was one thing. What Diana wanted was another. If she needed to shoot a stand-up, then I wanted to help her do it – safely.

'Going to Sadr City is out of the question. But if you like, I could take Diana to an area where you can see Sadr City in the background,' I said.

The bureau chief's face tightened. 'So you're telling me you won't do it?' he asked.

'I'm saying it would be absolute madness to drive unilaterally into Sadr City and do a stand-up,' I said.

At that point, Diana jumped into the conversation. She told

the bureau chief she wasn't prepared to drive into Sadr City either, and that my suggestion was a good alternative.

I guess having his correspondent side with the security adviser was the final straw for the bureau chief. He stormed off.

Later that evening, I met with Diana and her cameraman. We all agreed to search for a suitable stand-up location the following morning. I put both armoured 4x4s on reserve for the assignment as the bureau chief still hadn't binned the BMW.

The next morning, before heading out, I briefed our drivers, Diana and the cameraman to make sure we were all on the same page. I explained that our main objective was to find a suitable stand-up location and shoot it in as little time as possible. I wanted to limit our exposure on the ground. With that in mind, I asked Diana and her cameraman to work out what they wanted to do before leaving the Palestine; there'd be no rehashing the stand-up whilst operational.

One of CNN's Iraqi fixers had suggested a location just over a canal running east to west on the southern edge of Sadr city. When we got there, Diana and the cameraman said it would work. I asked them to stay inside their vehicle and review their stand-up notes one more time while I had a look around outside. I immediately spotted a possible drama. Across the road from our location I saw a man crouched down on his knees holding an RPG. After thirty seconds he stood up, ducked into a side street and then walked back out again. He didn't take any notice of us which indicated that he was waiting for a specific target.

Not long after, he was joined by a tall, skinny man wearing a long black leather coat. The man in leather noticed us straight away. He beckoned me over with his hand. I shook my head to indicate that I wouldn't leave my position. The man in leather started walking towards me. I moved ten metres away from our armoured vehicles to meet him. I wanted to keep him away from my clients in case he wanted to make trouble.

'Who are you?' he asked.

I immediately detected something familiar in his accent.

'Journalists,' I said. 'We'll be done here in two minutes.'

'You're Scottish, aren't you?' he said. This time the accent was unmistakable. The man looked Iraqi, but he was definitely a Geordie.

'Yes,' I said. 'Are you a Geordie?'

'Yes,' he said, smiling.

'What are you doing here?' I asked.

'I'm in the Mehdi Army.'

I figured as much. There had been plenty of media reports about British nationals travelling to Iraq to fight alongside the insurgents. But I never thought I'd actually meet one of them.

'What's wrong with the Toon Army?' I said, referring to supporters of Newcastle United football team.

He laughed, but the light-hearted moment was brief. 'You've got twenty minutes,' he said, pointing to his watch.

'Why twenty minutes? I asked.

'Because in twenty minutes time, every day on the button, an American patrol comes past and today they're getting it,' he said and turned to walk away.

I called after him. 'What if the patrol was British?'

He looked back over his shoulder. 'That's why I'm in Baghdad and not Basra.'

I checked my watch to mark the time. Extra incentives aside, I'd never intended to be on the ground anywhere near twenty minutes. I got Diana and her cameraman out of the vehicle. I didn't tell them about the situation with the Geordie and the insurgent with the RPG. I wanted them to concentrate fully on their stand-up, shoot it and get out of there. As for the American patrol, if I could have alerted them I would have but it was impossible. I didn't have their radio frequencies, I had no idea which direction they'd be coming from, and if I did try to wave them down they'd probably think I was an insurgent and drive over me.

Diana did her stand-up in one take and we were off. In total, we'd spent less than ten minutes on the ground. As we were driving back over the canal I heard the double thump of an explosive being detonated. I wondered whether it was the insurgent's RPG slamming into an American military vehicle.

Back at the bureau, we heard that an American patrol had been attacked by insurgents south of Sadr City. Thankfully there were no casualties.

That night I sat on my bed thinking about all that had transpired on this assignment. The Geordie was the clearest signal yet that journalists could no longer operate unilaterally in Baghdad safely.

I decided to call it a day in Iraq. The situation had become too unpredictable and volatile to provide my media clients with proactive security. Even if I switched to working outsourced military jobs, like looking after diplomats, I'd still face the same problems. Driving around in an armoured vehicle all tooled up with your fingers crossed hoping you don't get whacked is not security; it's just playing at it.

Some of the experienced members of the press corps were also thinking about not returning to Iraq. The risk/reward of going around the streets had tipped against them and they weren't willing to endanger life and limb just to stand on a hotel rooftop and repeat parrot fashion what their 'sources' had told them.

The competition between news networks is cut-throat and no one wants to be the first to leave Iraq. As it stands, however, the majority of journalists reporting from Baghdad rarely leave their bureaus, except to go on military embeds. The network hierarchies need to ask themselves whether it's really worth it to put their employees in jeopardy just for the sake of having a minaret in the background of a live shot.

There are wider, more disturbing ramifications to this practice; the western media presence in Iraq feeds the perception that internationals can operate there within a reasonable margin of safety. They can't, nor have they been able to in my opinion since the end of 2004.

In all probability, the insurgents know exactly where all the major international news networks are stationed in Baghdad. For a long time now, most of the news coming out of the Iraqi capital has been negative and worked in favour of the militants. They've had little reason to specifically target news bureaus. But there will come a day when insurgents will take issue with someone's reporting – and when that happens, I have no doubt they'll take out a media location.

If I were to sit down with the major network news heads, I'd advise them all to pull their operations back to Amman, Jordan, and only launch journalists into Baghdad for specific stories. I applaud the network brave enough to lead the way.

PART THREE

BUST & BEYOND

CHAPTER 30

I've often been asked why I never wrote a book about my time in the SAS. The main reason I haven't is out of respect for the lads still in the Regiment. I strongly believe that active SAS soldiers don't deserve retired Regiment lads discussing former exploits in detail because many of the skills that made operations successful in the past are still in use today. Some will argue that's rubbish; the Regiment has moved on since my time. In some respects, I agree. The men in the Regiment today are far better soldiers than I was; in part because as Britain has evolved so too have SAS recruits. I believe the type of man who joins the Regiment improves about every decade and a half. If that weren't the case then the Regiment would be in danger of standing still, which would be disastrous. I'm glad I did selection in the 1970s because I wouldn't have a hope in hell of passing today.

My SAS instructors taught me terrific skills, which I improved on as did others like me. We then passed those skills on to the next generation, who enhanced them further. Each era makes its contributions, but the foundations of SAS soldiering have changed very little throughout the years. Therefore, if I were to write a book giving details of how we performed operations during my time, I truly believe it would compromise Regiment lads today by robbing them of some very effective tools.

So while I'd never pen a detailed memoir about my military career, for the benefit of readers of this book I will offer a brief overview of my worst encounter with bad leadership in the

Regiment. I write about it here for two reasons: first, because a lot has been written about this particular subject, and at least one published first-hand account smeared the reputation of a very fine soldier. As someone whose involvement is not widely known, I'd like to have my say to set the record straight. The second reason I'm writing about this episode is to help you understand why I am so uncompromising when it comes to maintaining operational standards on The Circuit. Bad management, be it in the military or the commercial security world, doesn't just cost money, it costs lives.

It was 1991 – the first Gulf War. The Regiment had deployed three of its four squadrons to the Gulf, including B Squadron where I'd been assigned to upper management. I was thirty-six years old at the time; ancient by Regiment standards. But I was still in excellent physical condition and my knowledge of operations was valued – or so I thought.

The American-led campaign had come up against a major glitch. Then, as now, the US military was overly dependent on technology to execute its battle plans. Weather conditions at the start of the war were terrible and the satellites the Yanks relied on to target enemy positions were being blinded by rain and cloud cover. Technology wasn't enough to win the war. To achieve its aims, America and its allies needed 'eyes on the ground'.

That's where the Regiment came in. The 'headshed' of B Squadron (the OC or Officer Commanding and his Sergeant Major) assigned me to lead an eight-man patrol on an operation behind enemy lines. Our mission: observe the MSR between Jordan and Baghdad for troop movements, vehicles, weapons and other relevant military activity.

The sergeant major handed me a list of lads assigned to my patrol. As patrol leader, I was, in effect, the manager. It was my job to make sure the patrol as a unit had a good cross reference of skills so the individual members could mutually support each other whilst operational.

As I'd been out of B Squadron for about four years doing other tasks, I went to the lads named on the list to get a rundown of their abilities. One of them, Vince, was exactly the kind of soldier I needed; a big, strong, fit lad, Vince was a middle ranker with bags of operational experience. He had the background and character to be an absolute asset to the patrol. I put him at the top of my keep list.

Three of the lads assigned to the patrol, however, were straight off selection and had never been on operations with the Regiment. As great as they were, the new recruits hadn't had time to bed in and learn their core skills: communications, medical, linguistics and demolitions. Given the nature of the mission – operating deep behind enemy lines in a very small team – this was not a job for new boys. It required skilled, veteran troopers.

I canvassed B Squadron to compile an alternative list of lads whom I felt would make a highly effective team. I took the revised list to the headshed. I thought the headshed would be on board with the suggested changes. Hardly. When I presented the alternative list to them, they were infuriated. I explained that I needed experienced troopers with complementary skills to achieve the task but they weren't interested in hearing it. I was told the original list was final and that was it.

I was absolutely shocked. Dismissing a logical argument out of hand was not in keeping with Regimental thinking at all as far as I was concerned. I'd been in the SAS since the age of twenty and never before had I come across such a negative and frankly illogical response.

I couldn't bury my head in the sand to pacify the headshed. There was no way I was going on the ground when I felt strongly that the patrol was a disaster in the making. I hadn't done it before and I wasn't going to do it now. There was a whole squadron to mix and match. It was a dangerous mission and if the patrol lacked comprehensive strength, it would put everyone at risk. I had to get the headshed to agree with the changes.

I explained again that I had compiled the new list for tactical reasons in order to achieve a successful patrol. They still didn't want to hear it. As far as the headshed were concerned the original names were fine and my arguments, solid as they were, counted for nothing. Perhaps they didn't want a strong character questioning their authority. Or perhaps they'd become so mentally committed to their original plan that they couldn't conceive of altering it. I remember thinking they were just out of their depth.

Later that evening I learned from a mate that the OC was planning to send me to the United Arab Emirates to lead the Close Protection team for the British Ambassador. Not only did the OC want me off the patrol, he wanted me out of the war.

The next day I was officially replaced as patrol leader. I was gutted. The Regiment lads meant everything to me. Despite my clash with the headshed, I was still a senior NCO. I couldn't just stand by and let them go forward with what I believed was a fundamentally flawed patrol. I went and had a quiet word with the new patrol leader. I told him my concerns regarding the skills mix, and about my run-in with the headshed. For the sake of the lads, I urged him to go back and convince the headshed to rework the patrol. The new patrol leader thanked me for my input but said he didn't see a problem. He told me not to worry and that he had everything under control.

Later that day, I was dismayed to learn that after their initial deployment into Iraq by helicopter, the patrol planned to operate on foot, rather than take vehicles. I went back to the patrol leader and to some of the lads and told them I thought this was madness. I reminded them that during the Second World War, the founders of the SAS had learned the devastat-

You're never far from poverty in Kabul. A mother and two children begging on a street corner. Afghanistan, 2006.

Instructing a diplomatic CP team on a live fire drill. I'm second from left. Afghanistan, 2006.

top left Yasir Arafat holds his first meeting following the ten-day siege of his compound. Ramallah, 2002. *top right* Me with Yasir Arafat following Operation Defensive Shield. Ramallah, 2002.
middle left Me with Hamas leader Sheikh Ahmed Yassin, the father of Palestinian suicide bombing. Gaza City, 2002. *middle right* The man claiming to be an ex-bodyguard of Taliban spiritual leader Mullah Omar. I took this picture covertly whilst observing him through my 'big camera' prior to our arranged meeting on the banks of the Helmund River. Lashkar Gah, 2004.
bottom The group of young Taliban I approached by the banks of the Helmund River. Lashkar Gah, 2004.

top Afghan warlord Patcha Khan of Zadran addressing his tribal elders. He had just closed a critical commercial route through his fiefdom. Paktia province, 2004.
middle left Me with Osama bin Laden's brother-in-law, Mohammed Khalifa. This photograph was taken following CNN's interview with him at his restaurant. Saudi Arabia, 2004. *middle right* My private meeting with Patcha Khan at his 'safe house' in the dark side of Kabul. Qadeer, my good friend and interpreter for almost four years, is pictured to the far left. Kabul, 2006.
bottom left Abdul Rashid Ghazi, the radical cleric from Islamabad's infamous Red Mosque. I took this picture prior to CNN's interview with him. Weeks later, Ghazi and scores of others were killed when Pakistani troops stormed the mosque. Islamabad, 2007.
bottom right Me with Mullah Zaeef, former Taliban Ambassador to Pakistan, following CNN's interview with him. Kabul, 2007.

Looking for Taliban in an area of Quetta populated by Afghan refugees. Pakistan, 2007.

A Talib (student) from a *madrasah* in Quetta. Pakistan, 2007.

A Kutchi family travelling between mountain ranges. Afghanistan, 2007.

A Blackhawk helicopter coming to collect my clients and me from a US base in Kunar province. Afghanistan, 2007.

Mountain ranges surrounding the Afghan capital. Kabul, 2007.

A US military defensive position in eastern Afghanistan close to the Pakistani tribal area of Waziristan. Afghanistan, 2007.

Tribal elders in Khost province. These men and others like them hold the key to winning local support for Afghanistan's coalition-backed government. Afghanistan, 2007.

Another tragic day for coalition forces in Afghanistan. An American flag flies at half-mast to honour a fallen soldier. 2007 proved the deadliest year to date for coalition forces since the fall of the Taliban in 2001. Somewhere in Afghanistan, 2007.

ing consequences of deploying on foot; if you get bumped (attacked), your firepower is limited to what you can carry and you lack the ability to escape and evade quickly. I told them that vehicles would give them heavy, mounted machine guns to respond to an attack plus the option to bomb-burst, regroup and head west for forty kilometres, where they could join up with D Squadron (who were operating in an adjacent corridor).

It's in the spirit of the SAS to stand up and be counted. But as in any organization, Regiment lads will sometimes ignore their better judgement and get on with the job. I'm certain the new recruits felt a lot of pressure to do so. I'd made a strong case, but in the end the lads decided to stick with their plan and operate on foot as a covert patrol.

I was absolutely devastated that no one in a position of authority would listen to reason. But by that point, I had done all that I could.

Two days later, in the wee hours of the morning, a helicopter deposited the patrol into the Iraqi desert. Eighteen hours later, I learned they had run into enemy fire. Apart from the initial contact report, they hadn't been heard from.

In the meantime, I never went to the United Arab Emirates. I unilaterally transferred myself to D Squadron, where the headshed did listen to my suggestions, and I had a great war.

For the patrol, however, the consequences of poor squadron-level leadership were catastrophic: three members of the patrol died, four were captured and one evaded on foot to Syria. In my view, it remains the worst operational patrol in SAS history.

That patrol is now infamously known by its call sign: Bravo Two Zero.

CHAPTER 31

By the end of 2004, my work with the media had taken me to the Palestinian territories, Iraq, Afghanistan and Saudi Arabia. With each trip, I gained a greater understanding of the agendas driving the War on Terror and the role The Circuit plays in them. Looking back, I couldn't believe how much I'd learned since that first trip to the West Bank. Advising journalists from Ramallah to Riyadh had taught me to think for myself and view all media reports with a critical eye. I felt like I'd got an accelerated university education – better even.

As much as I loved working with the media, by the beginning of 2005 it was time for me to move on to something new. It's important for me to vary clients; different jobs require different skills, and I don't want any of mine wasting away.

During an assignment in Kabul in January that year, I met a Close Protection team looking after an embassy in Afghanistan. The contract for the job was held by a British commercial security company, which I'll call KR. Some of the lads working on the CP team had been in the Regiment with me. They told me if I ever wanted to join them, there'd be a position waiting.

During a break at home I got a call from a KR manager in London – a man I'll call Colin. I'd met Colin years before, when he was an officer with the Special Boat Service. He asked if I'd be interested in becoming the co-Operations Manager of the contract in Kabul.

I didn't say yes immediately. At that point, I'd only worked for boutique firms on The Circuit, or on contracts held independently by mates I trusted. I'd always avoided the big players because on balance they had bad word of mouth. I'd heard countless stories about large CSCs flannelling their clients and their staff on the ground. Big firms also had a reputation for being very tight with wages.

By 2005, wages on The Circuit were in freefall and even the most qualified adviser working in a hostile environment couldn't expect fair compensation. The bubble that had lured dozens of new firms and thousands of new advisers and contractors to The Circuit had burst. The decline followed a classic pattern. When the bubble formed in 2003 the demand for security personnel far outstripped supply. CSCs could practically pluck a figure from thin air when bidding for contracts, and advisers on the ground, no matter what their level of experience, could name their price.

Inevitably, supply caught up with demand and the competition for contracts and positions intensified. CSCs began cutting prices to keep their old contracts and win new ones. The tipping point hit around autumn 2004, when reconstruction contracts started scaling back in Iraq (ironically, due to the deteriorating security situation). In less than three years the pendulum had swung from chronic under-supply of firms and advisers to an unsustainable glut.

Faced with declining revenues, many CSCs tried to buoy their profits by slashing the wages of personnel on the ground. All over The Circuit, advisers were being pushed to sign full-time employment contracts with annual salaries. In 2005, an average contract paid around £50,000 a year, and required the adviser to spend six weeks at a time in a hostile environment with only two weeks off in between rotations. That works out to a rate of approximately £170 per day in theatre; a phenomenal drop in pay considering that two years earlier an adviser in a hostile environment could expect to earn between £300 and £500 per day.

Many advisers held their tongues and took the hit, fearing

that if they complained there were ten others lined up to take their jobs.

That said, I believed at the time, and still do, that highly experienced advisers with key skills can and should charge a premium for their services. When I joined The Circuit, I promised myself I'd only work for a certain fee and I'd never slip below that level no matter what the climate. Just because there's an oversupply of advisers doesn't mean they're all qualified. Some jobs demand a certain level of knowledge and experience to be successful. The old adage 'You get what you pay for' is very relevant in the security world.

It was pointless discussing the job any further with Colin until we first agreed on my daily wage. It took a bit of convincing but he finally relented. With that sorted, we moved on to other points; specifically, I wanted to know how KR conducted itself towards its clients and its employees on the ground. Colin assured me that KR was one of the most professional firms on The Circuit. He asked me to come to his office in London for a meeting so I could see that for myself.

When Colin met me at reception, I barely recognized him. Back in the SBS, he had been in very good physical condition. It looked like years of sitting behind a civilian desk had taken its toll. Colin had gone to seed and he stank of cigarette smoke – a habit I find offensive and unproductive. Our meeting dragged on for an hour and a half. It should have finished within forty-five minutes but Colin had to keep excusing himself to go outside for a cigarette.

I knew from my conversations with the Close Protection team in Kabul that KR had held the embassy contract for just over six months and that it covered both CP for the ambassador as well as hostile environment training for the Afghan guards and drivers employed by the embassy. It was a very demanding workload and KR had assigned two teams of six advisers each to work the contract on back-to-back rotations. As co-Operations Manager, I would be in charge of one rotation.

In between Colin's cigarette breaks, I learned that for budget reasons the embassy's Ministry of Foreign Affairs wanted to reduce the number of advisers for each rotation from six men to two. I told Colin that a two-man Close Protection team was the minimum for looking after a client in London and didn't correspond at all to the level of threat in Kabul. He agreed and said KR was pushing to keep the teams intact but hadn't yet convinced the client.

Convinced or not, I pointed out that you can't have clients dictating the size of a CP team, especially in a hostile environment. Again, Colin agreed and asked if I wouldn't mind pushing the issue directly with the client when I got to Kabul.

Colin then dropped what should have been a bombshell: he informed me that at present the team in Kabul had no weapons but assured me that within the next two to three weeks we'd be receiving top-grade weapons and ammunition. It was a huge red flag. The idea of providing an ambassador in Kabul with unarmed protection is ludicrous. The only reason I didn't walk out of the meeting was that I knew that the lads on the ground had already procured weapons locally.

I should have paid more attention to the warning signs. But I trusted Colin when he said everything would be put right shortly. More fool me.

A week later I touched down in Kabul. My point of contact at the airport was a lad named Joe who'd been with the contract from the beginning. I knew Joe reasonably well and was pleased to be working with him. He had a reputation for being as strong as he is bright. A tall, broad-shouldered, ex-Para in his mid-thirties, Joe's a good heavyweight boxer and a published poet. As soon as I saw Joe's face, I knew something was very wrong. He told me that within three days our six-man team would be slashed to two, leaving only himself and me on the ground.

I told Joe that Colin had assured me that KR London were doing everything at their end to keep our numbers up. Joe said it was too late; the embassy's Ministry of Foreign Affairs had made its decision. The rest of the team were already packing their bags.

During our ride to the hotel, Joe filled me in on some details Colin hadn't mentioned during our meeting. I already knew about KR's failure to provide the team with weapons and ammunition; a situation which Colin had assured me would be remedied within three weeks' time. As it turned out, weapons were just the tip of the iceberg. All of the advisers on the contract had been sent to Kabul armed with nothing but flight tickets and visas; no weapons, no body armour, no helmets, no comms equipment, no medical kit and no armoured vehicles (except for the ambassador's, which was provided directly by his Ministry of Foreign Affairs, not KR). The lads had been trying to make the job work; putting pressure on Colin to send them what they needed and making do in the meantime by scrounging around for bits and pieces from mates attached to other security firms operating in Kabul.

I couldn't believe the embassy had accepted the situation. Given Kabul's declining security situation, the clients did not seem as concerned as they should have been. I suspected they were naïve and didn't know what to look for when it came to CP basics in a hostile environment.

My suspicions were confirmed a day later during my initial meeting with the embassy's home country security manager; I'll call him Mr K. At any embassy, all security issues, including outsourced duties, are coordinated by a manager from the home country. Mr K had taken over his job a week before I arrived in Kabul. He was furious with the service KR had provided. One half of the contract – the provision to train Afghan guards and drivers in security matters – had barely been addressed.

Fortunately, Mr K and I had the same aims: we both wanted the ambassador to have the best possible protection, and the local staff to receive the best possible training. Our immediate priority was the ambassador's CP team; Mr K agreed that a two-man security detail wasn't sufficient. We decided the best course of action would be for me to light a fire under KR London while he took up the matter with his bosses at the Ministry of Foreign Affairs in his home country.

I set about gathering ammunition to present to KR London. I spoke with mates of mine working security details at other embassies around Kabul to get an idea of the size of their CP teams. All of them had more than two advisers and several of the teams were expanding. No one was downsizing.

During these conversations, I also learned of a disturbing new security issue in Kabul. One of the lads told me that his client had been recced several times while travelling around town. My mate was fairly certain that the men doing the surveillance were Pakistani; he'd observed them filming his client from right-hand-drive vehicles (Afghans predominantly use left-hand drive). I asked around to see if anyone else had had similar problems. Several mates of mine confirmed that their clients had been recced in this fashion as well.

It would be difficult enough for a two-man team to suss out obvious threats to a client travelling around Kabul. Picking up forms of covert surveillance would be nearly impossible. We desperately needed to boost our numbers back up to six. It was the only way to adequately fulfil the requirements set forth in the contract. The training of the local staff alone was a full-time job, so that was one adviser spoken for. Looking after the ambassador meanwhile required a minimum of five people: four on the ground with the client and one manning an in-country operations desk to coordinate a response in the event of an incident. Let me be very clear on this point: an operations desk is not dispensable. I hate to think what might have happened if AKE hadn't had a manned ops desk in Baghdad to dispatch a vehicle when the BMW broke down with my clients in it.

I put all of this in several emails to Colin. My blood would boil each time I pressed 'Send'. It was well known at the time that security in Kabul was deteriorating rapidly. To me, it was unforgivable that KR London let the contract go down to two men. If the client wouldn't listen to reason, then as far as I was concerned KR should have binned the whole deal.

Three days after arriving in Kabul, the rest of the team had gone leaving just me and Joe to look after a very active client. Unlike some diplomats, this ambassador was not content to sit inside the four walls of his embassy and take meetings. He wanted to go out and see for himself how his nation's money was being spent in Afghanistan.

One of the first issues I had to address was the ambassador's armoured vehicle. It was very high profile. Just like the Greek Ambassador in Iraq, this ambassador had plastered his national flag on his shiny armoured 4x4. I needed to lower the vehicle's profile starting with the flag. I told the ambassador it would have to go. At first he was reluctant. The ambassador was understandably proud of what his country was doing in Afghanistan and believed his nation and its representatives were well liked. I explained that while many Afghans did appreciate his nation's philanthropy, as far as the insurgents were concerned, there was no difference between his country and the United States; any country working in support of the American-backed Afghan government, whether directly or indirectly, was a target. The ambassador was a reasonable man and a rather likeable character. As long as I explained why I insisted on doing things a certain way, he'd let me get on with my job. He agreed to remove the flag from his vehicle.

Next, Joe and I had to get the ambassador's backing vehicle sorted. The ambassador's 4x4 was a top-of-the-line level B6/7 armoured vehicle. As his only alternative means of transport in the event of a breakdown or incident, the backing vehicle should have provided the same level of protection. All we had for the job was a soft-skinned pickup truck.

Following the ambassador around in a soft-skinned pickup was like wearing a track suit to a black tie event. More than once I was stopped and questioned at a venue where I'd just delivered the ambassador because the guards didn't believe I was part of his CP team.

A few days after launching my email campaign, responses started landing in my inbox; all of them assuring me that everything possible was being done to increase our numbers and get us the equipment we needed. To me, Colin and his bosses back in KR London had failed to grasp the urgency of our situation. The safety of the team and the client alone should have spurred KR to fix all of these problems before I even joined the contract.

The situation raised a number of serious questions in my mind about KR's management. It doesn't matter where a manager is based; London, Washington or Dubai, they must keep tabs on what's happening with their contracts at ground level. It's one thing to sit in a plush London office or an expensive restaurant bluffing a client into signing on the dotted line. Where the manager really earns his money is in the contract's execution.

In my view, the moment KR management in London knew there was a chance the contract could be slashed, they should have taken off their stripy suit jackets, rolled up their shirt-sleeves and got stuck in to safeguard the team and the client, not to mention the company's future in Afghanistan.

I suspected nothing would change without a kick up the arse – or to put it more accurately – up the wallet. In my follow-up emails and phone calls to KR London, I highlighted the financial implications of allowing the embassy's Ministry of Foreign Affairs to dictate the number of advisers assigned to the contract. Obviously, the reduction in manpower represented an immediate loss of revenue to KR, but it had long-term implications as well. If the team went from two advisers to none, KR would lose its presence in Afghanistan entirely. With security contracts tapering off in Iraq, commercial security companies needed to move into other markets. KR had established itself in

Afghanistan with a high-profile client; an excellent springboard for capturing other business in country. To sacrifice that foothold was madness.

A few more rounds of emails and I was still getting nowhere with KR London. My patience was exhausted. I asked Colin to fly to Kabul to sort the situation with the embassy. He suggested, and I agreed, that instead of flying to Afghanistan he travel to the embassy's home country and make his appeal directly to the Ministry of Foreign Affairs.

At long last, I thought, Colin was getting off his arse and doing something.

A few days later I hadn't heard anything from Colin, so I sent an email asking him when he planned to fly out for his meeting. I got an 'Out of Office Reply'. Colin had got on a plane all right, but not for business. He'd just left on a ten-day holiday.

CHAPTER 32

I've always been a fan of direct communication. When given the choice, I'd rather have it out with someone face to face than discuss things over the phone or fly emails back and forth. Some people, on the other hand, will do everything in their power to avoid a direct confrontation.

I wanted nothing more than to fly back to London, grab Colin by the lapels of his suit jacket and ask him why he wasn't getting off his fat arse and providing some duty of care to his clients and the team on the ground. But as much as it would make me feel better, I knew it wouldn't fix things. I had to be realistic about the situation. As far as I could see, Colin had shown no interest in lobbying the client to reinstate the team in full. Moreover, we still didn't have proper weapons, transport or kit and the security situation in Kabul was growing deadlier by the day. While Colin was enjoying himself on holiday, a Canadian diplomatic vehicle was hit by an IED east of Kabul. Things were definitely heating up in the Afghan capital. The longer the situation with the embassy contract was allowed to fester the longer the client's security and that of the team would be compromised.

I decided the best course of action would be to play the corporate email game. As much as I love direct communication, it doesn't leave a record of what is said. I needed proof, in writing, that nothing was being done to fix the problems associated with the contract. It was essential I establish a paper trail.

When he returned from his holiday, I wrote a very stern email to Colin and copied his boss on it. Once again, I loaded my memo with as much ammunition as I could, including the attack on the Canadians, to argue the case for swift action. I told him the ambassador had taken a brief home leave and would be back in Kabul in two days' time, so we had a narrow window in which to act.

Rather than follow up on his previous plan of flying to the embassy's home country to make a direct appeal to the Ministry of Foreign Affairs, Colin sent the following response: 'I am convinced that any expansion of the team has to be driven from your end,' he wrote. 'We will, of course endorse and take any action forward.'

I couldn't believe it. He was trying to put the onus on me.

I kept the paper trail going. I argued that I didn't agree that the expansion of the team should be driven by my end and told him that KR should be advising from London directly to the client's home country – not via Kabul. I told him the issue was a matter of priority and reminded him that the ambassador was due back in country.

'In 2 days time Joe and I "play" at looking after the ambassador whilst the [KR] Ops room remains empty,' I wrote. '. . . Not only are we ultra slim on the ground, but in addition we are still waiting on adequate firearms.'

In closing, I referenced the assurances Colin had given me in London.

'I accepted this job believing that we would be fully backed by [KR] London,' I wrote. 'I'll continue to work as I have been doing with the ambassador, however, the London office must represent and act on the intelligence and information that we are sending you. I've tried to be completely pro active in keeping this side going. If we don't get on track soonest, someone could pay with their life.'

To be honest, I fully expected to get sacked for what I'd written. I'd learned that before I took over the team some good ex-Regiment lads had been let go for being outspoken about KR's handling of the embassy contract.

Perhaps it was because I'd put everything in writing, but finally, after a month and a half of relentless badgering on my part, I was told that the team was going back up to two rotations of six advisers. When I heard the news I didn't know whether to be cross with myself for putting up with a bad situation for so long, or to pat myself on the back for sticking with the job and trying to make it work.

It was great to have got the team reinstated in full. I felt strongly that the ambassador was a man worth fighting for and that he deserved to be well looked after. Still, it was a partial victory. We still did not have adequate weapons systems, a level B6/7 backup vehicle or other essential kit.

I tried not to dwell on the negatives and focused on building the best possible CP team for the ambassador. Just like operations in the Regiment, I wanted to make sure we had the right mix of lads with good core skills that could complement each other. Joe had been outstanding during our six weeks together as a two-man team. If I could have got four more Joes, my job would have been easy.

It wasn't. There was a lot of turnover throughout my time on the contract and finding and keeping qualified advisers was an uphill battle from the word go. It seemed each time I'd get a good lad up to speed, he'd resign over the management of the contract in London. Rarely were the replacements dispatched by London up to the mark, even though by that point there were plenty of qualified advisers available.

During the boom years, many commercial security companies sent unqualified advisers to hostile environments because there weren't enough experienced ones to go around. But after the bubble burst, green advisers continued to slip through; partly, because they were cheap but also because some CSCs had found a way to give any adviser, regardless of background, a veneer of credibility: the SIA accreditation.

The Security Industry Authority or SIA was created in 2003 to regulate the commercial security industry in Great Britain. Though a step in the right direction, the SIA in my view falls down on two major counts; first, it cannot *impose* regulations on CSCs. Secondly, it has no authority over security services rendered abroad. The SIA's remit extends only to England, Scotland and Wales.

The SIA has nothing to do with hostile environments but that hasn't stopped CSCs from using the organization as a marketing tool to win contracts in places like Afghanistan and Iraq. Many CSCs boast to potential clients that its employees are 'SIA accredited'. Some CSCs won't hire advisers unless they've sat an SIA-approved CP course, many of which are operated by the CSC in question. Tuition for these courses typically runs from £2,500 to £3,000; money that comes out of the advisers' pockets, not the companies employing them.

During my time as co-Operations Manager on the KR contract, I had almost two dozen SIA-accredited advisers pass through my team. Some were excellent but a large number had no business working CP in a hostile environment. Many with a military Corps background, the non-infanteers, lacked basic weapons and tactics skills. They had no idea how to handle a pistol; their military backgrounds hadn't prepared them and thanks to the UK handgun ban, neither had their SIA courses. It's crucial a CP adviser be fluent in the use of a pistol because it's the immediate backup weapon in a hostile environment (the first is usually the vehicle weapon). It's one thing to play with a pistol loaded with dummy rounds on an SIA course and quite another to carry one with a live round in the chamber ready to fire.

Negligent discharges (unintended firing of weapons) are plentiful on The Circuit. There have even been cases in which advisers have shot themselves accidentally. Rather than ensure that all advisers are properly trained in the use of firearms, many

CSCs have addressed the problem by instructing advisers not to carry weapons with a chambered round.

In addition to weapons handling, some of the lads sent to me by KR London lacked other core skills, such as medical training; a crucial reactive skill in a hostile environment. Tactical driving experience was another area I found wanting. It takes a tremendous amount of training to bounce a serviceable armoured vehicle safely through Baghdad, Kabul or any other busy hostile environment. In my view, the driver is the most important person in the vehicle inclusive of the client because if the driver gets it wrong, everyone is in the shit. It takes a special person to be a top driver. Every trip, no matter what the distance, is exhausting. The driver's awareness is paramount and a good one provides a verbal running commentary to ensure that everyone in the vehicle sees what he sees.

Tactical driving, weapons handling, medical training; all are basic skills every CP adviser should master before working in a hostile environment. Yet some SIA courses devote only a couple of days to each subject. The bottom line is SIA accreditation may prepare an adviser to look after rich foreigners shopping in Knightsbridge, but it has no bearing whatsoever on hostile environments.

Each time KR London sent me an adviser with an SIA tick in the box but little practical knowledge, it was infuriating. Fortunately, some of the SIA lads did have terrific backgrounds and from time to time I was able to cobble together a strong team. In those instances, I'd try to take our professionalism to the next level by running the team through a series of CP training exercises.

The training programme involved both classroom work and a weekly session on the live-fire ranges outside Kabul. My goal for the team was to achieve an operational standard that exceeded anything any of us had done before commercially.

During our live-fire range sessions, we ran drills based

on every conceivable type of contact we could encounter in Afghanistan; from being fired on whilst mending a punctured tyre to a fully fledged technical ambush in which our vehicles were blown off the road and disabled. Our locally procured weapons and ammo worked well enough for us to put down live fire as if we were in a real contact. Unlike top-grade weapons, however, the local ones frequently jammed. We probably carried out more weapons stoppage drills than any other CP team in Afghanistan.

Our objective each time we hit the ranges was to break contact with the 'enemy' within twelve seconds of initiation. It would take a while with each successive team but we always achieved that.

The range sessions were a ball and the classroom work was equally as interesting. The lads had mixed military backgrounds so everyone brought something new to the table when discussing exercise scenarios.

I encouraged everyone to make suggestions and share their own experiences, especially mistakes they'd seen or made. In the security game, your first mistake can be your last. I've always tried to learn from my errors and, whenever possible, from the mistakes of others. In this respect, records of incidents both written and taped can be invaluable training tools.

So-called 'trophy videos' of CP teams operating in hostile environments had become quite common by 2005. Many show real advisers in real contacts. It disgusts me when people outside The Circuit view these videos for voyeuristic reasons. For security professionals, however, trophy videos can offer life-saving insights.

While I was working the embassy contract in Kabul, a trophy video hit the internet featuring an eight-man CP team travelling in a convoy on Baghdad's infamous airport road. The video, which lasts approximately six and half minutes, recorded the team immediately before, during and after a contact with Iraqi insurgents. It was sent to me along with an unofficial post-operations report written by one of the advisers involved in the incident and a sanitized report released by the company employing the team; Edinburgh Risk Security Management.[23]

I thought it would be useful to watch the Edinburgh Risk video with the rest of my team so we could refer to it during our training exercises. I've viewed the video many times since for training purposes and each time my heart goes out to the lads involved. Tragically, the team committed what I see as a series of mistakes. The video is a shambles from the moment you press 'Play'. Shot by a camera mounted on the dashboard of the third vehicle in an Edinburgh Risk convoy, the video begins with two cars stopped on the road heading towards the airport. The vehicles appear to be isolated on their stretch of highway.

When I first viewed the video I immediately thought, 'Why are three cars sitting on an empty road?' After reading the report, I learned that the US military had closed the road heading to the airport following an IED attack. The Edinburgh Risk lads were on their way to the airport to collect a client. Rather than turn around and go back to Baghdad, the team decided to wait until the road reopened. As I've said already, a basic rule of operating in hostile environments is to never sit idle on an open road; that was the team's *second* mistake.

The *first* mistake happened before the video starts. The video shows and the reports corroborate that the convoy was comprised of three low-profile cars: an armoured Mercedes sandwiched between two soft-skin vehicles. As much as I go on about the virtues of travelling low profile, cars are not the best choice for Baghdad; they seriously limit a team's manoeuvrability. A 4x4 that fits the signature of civilian 4x4s around Baghdad can blend in just as easily and offer enough clearance to bump up on kerbs, jump drainage systems and cross highway medians. Sadly, the Edinburgh Risk lads on the video didn't have that option.

23 As of 13 June 2006 the company began trading under the name Edinburgh International.

A few seconds after the video starts, the convoy is fired on by insurgents. Given their direction of travel, it was a contact right flank. Following the initial burst of gunfire two members of the CP team dismount their vehicles from the right side. *Third* mistake; you never get out on the side of a contact. You get out on the opposite side of the vehicle to give yourself some protection from the line of fire.

Fourth mistake: the team should have immediately responded to the contact with covering fire followed quickly by smoke cover. It took the Edinburgh Risk team around seventeen seconds to respond with their first shot and just over a minute to discharge their first smoke grenade. To the uninitiated, seventeen seconds may not sound like a long time but remember; during live-fire training, my team and I aimed to break contact with the enemy completely within twelve seconds. Anything longer is loitering in my view.

Other novice mistakes come out during the video. There's a lot of shouting; an instinctive reaction during a contact but not an effective means of team communication. About a minute and a half into the incident, the team appears to totally dissolve; the occupants in each vehicle are doing their own thing. An adviser is visible in front of the rear vehicle. He seems to be in shock and is carrying an MP5, a 9 mm submachine gun. A 9 mm is a low-velocity weapon and is not suitable for CP vehicle moves. Primary vehicle weapons should be high velocity so the round can punch into an attacking vehicle. The MP5 is totally ineffective for answering towards the enemy in a situation like the one the Edinburgh Risk lads were in.

At six minutes, twenty-seven seconds, the video ends with the Edinburgh Risk team still no closer to safety. The post-incident reports revealed that one adviser died during the contact and two died shortly after as a result of their injuries. Poor fellas.

Each time I watch that video my stomach turns. I'm sure the Edinburgh Risk team were a great bunch of lads but it was painfully obvious from the video that they had no clue how to respond to a bad situation and more importantly how to avoid one in the first place.

Practically every adviser on The Circuit has seen or at least heard of the Edinburgh Risk trophy video. Outside The Circuit, it's barely known because the public, in general, isn't aware that commercial security advisers die all the time in hostile environments.

How many fatal incidents go unnoticed by the public? No one knows for sure because when an adviser dies on the job in Iraq, Afghanistan or any other hostile environment, commercial security companies aren't required to report it. Even when the adviser in question is a British citizen working for a British CSC there's no provision to register the death with the Foreign and Commonwealth Office. It's outrageous. When a British soldier dies abroad, its headline news; the soldier's remains are returned home in a flag-draped coffin; respect is shown, questions are asked and if mistakes were made people are held accountable and hopefully errors aren't repeated. When an adviser working for a CSC dies in a hostile environment, the body can sit for weeks before it's repatriated. I've known cases of advisers being shipped home, unceremoniously, in wooden crates. There's no public mourning and no public inquiry into whether the death could have been prevented. The entire incident is simply swept under the rug.

It's taken a while, but thankfully the public is starting to ask questions. Two enterprising journalists from the *New York Times* tried to uncover how many security personnel have died in Iraq working on US government contracts.[24] According to their findings, between March 2003 and March 2007 917 security personnel assigned to US government contracts in Iraq were killed and more than 12,000 were wounded or injured on the job. The journalists reckoned that private security personnel were dying in Iraq at a rate of one to every four US soldiers.

---

24 John M. Broder and James Risen, 'Contractor Deaths in Iraq Soar to Record', *New York Times*, 19 May 2007.

What makes these findings even more disturbing is that they pertain only to security personnel working specifically in Iraq on US government contracts. They don't, for example, cover security personnel working in places like Afghanistan on British government contracts. The full picture is impossible to ascertain, but individually, CSCs know exactly how much blood is spilled to boost their bottom lines.

Of all the dirty secrets CSCs have, adviser fatalities in hostile environments is by far the worst. I got an idea of how deep the problem runs in 2006, when I was working in Afghanistan for another British firm. During my assignment, I became acquainted with a logistics manager employed by the same company. Over a brew, we'd talk about the state of the The Circuit. Time and again, we'd revisit the same subject: the lack of duty of care to both clients and advisers on the ground. As a logistics manager, he was privy to company information classed as 'confidential'; information that revealed the true cost of putting poorly trained, poorly supported and poorly equipped security personnel to work in hostile environments.

One day his disgust boiled over. By then, he knew my views well and I guess he needed to unload on someone. He invited me to look through the contents of his laptop. For nearly two hours he showed me file after file of confidential information detailing the company's operations in Iraq: graphs, post-incident reports, memos written by in-country ops managers begging for basic equipment. Most troubling of all were the lists of employees killed and wounded on the job; in less than two years nearly sixty employees had been killed in Iraq.

Many of the deaths involved personnel running military supply convoys. The logistics manager told me each incident was recorded on three reports; one written by the team leader on the ground (if he or she hadn't died), an interim report and a final edited version. The families of the deceased were given the final, sanitized report.

Even more outrageous, the incidents were not disclosed to

employees working similar tasks in Iraq and other hostile environments. That meant if mistakes were made, no one was learning from them. The same fatal errors were destined to be repeated again and again.

The logistics manager thought the whole thing was horrendous. He couldn't understand why the company's managers refused to pull the plug on contracts they knew were killing employees by the dozen.

'Is moving 50,000 plastic chairs really worth dying for?' he asked.

I was seething as well.

Some time later I had the opportunity to look at a financial report produced by a British CSC. The report boasted how the firm had maintained its profits in Iraq despite declining sales. What it failed to mention is whether any employees were killed or maimed keeping those Iraq profits buoyant.

CHAPTER 33

Six months into the Kabul embassy job, KR London was still dragging its heels on getting us basic equipment. By that point, all we had received were three medical packs, none of which was complete. The armoured car, meanwhile, had become a real sticking point. Colin absolutely refused to provide us with a level B6/7 backing vehicle for the ambassador, insisting that the client not KR should pay for it. Equipment costings, including an armoured vehicle, should have been included in KR's original bid for the embassy contract. I can only assume that the company left it out in order to make its bid more competitive.

As an interim measure the embassy agreed to loan us a B/4 armoured 4x4 it used as a floating vehicle. It was a nice gesture but at the end of the day the B/4 wasn't up to scratch. As I said, the ambassador needed a backing vehicle that provided the same level of protection as his primary vehicle. The situation was nearing crisis point, as far as I was concerned. Diplomats were being increasingly targeted in and around Kabul. In addition to the Canadians, staff from another high-profile embassy had suffered two IED attacks. In all three instances, fatalities were avoided, in part due to poor initiation by the bombers but also because the vehicles targeted were top-of-the-line B6/7 armoured.

Equipment wasn't the only issue I was grappling with from my end. KR's mismanagement of the contract also extended to wages. New advisers were being paid less than those already on the team, which seriously undermined morale. In theory I didn't have a problem with different members of the team earning different wages; advisers with more advanced skill sets deserve to make more money. But skills had nothing to do with the wage discrepancies. The most recent hires were the lowest paid regardless of ability. It was ludicrous. The two best advisers on the team were fresh out of the Special Boat Service, had fantastic skills and were a real asset, yet they were making less than everyone because they had the least seniority.

Quite rightly, the ex-SBS lads were very upset when they found this out. They came to see me about it. I told them KR had indeed been useless but that the contract was moving to a new department. I assured them that I'd take up the issue with the new managers.

I was fed up and ready to walk. I didn't want to stick around for another Bravo Two Zero, but I decided to stay with the job for two reasons. First, the ambassador asked me personally if I would continue with the embassy for at least another six months. I gave him my word that I would. Secondly, I'd promised the SBS lads that I'd do my utmost to get them what they deserved.

During my home leave the new managing department asked if I would come into KR London for a meeting. I was sure Colin had slated me to them and I was going to be sacked.

It turned out firing me was not on their agenda. The new London-based Operations Manager, a man I'll call Ken, was full of praise for me. He went on and on about how professional I was and what a great job I was doing. My head was so big afterwards I was surprised I could get out of the building. I didn't shy away from telling Ken about the conflicts I'd had with Colin, from the lack of kit to the armoured car to the wage dramas. Ken apologized and told me not to worry; his division was more 'professional' and had a much better understanding of the team's needs. To underscore his commitment, Ken planned to fly to Kabul in the near future to meet directly with the client and the rest of the team.

When Ken arrived in Afghanistan, I met with him privately

to review again the outstanding issues we'd covered in London. While Ken assured me again that we'd soon be receiving weapons and kit from London, he now insisted that the armoured car would have to be paid for by the client.

At that moment, I knew that nothing had changed. I'd have to continue fighting tooth and nail for even the most basic support from KR London. I told Ken that if KR London wouldn't pay for a proper vehicle, then at the very least they needed to impress upon the embassy's Ministry of Foreign Affairs the urgent need to upgrade the ambassador's backing vehicle to a B6/7. Ken suggested that would be going behind the embassy's back. Rubbish. I had a great working relationship with the embassy. Mr K, the embassy's head of security, and I always discussed how to get the best out of the Ministry of Foreign Affairs and KR. I told Ken as much.

Next, I brought up the issue of pay. Suddenly, Ken didn't see a problem with paying the SBS lads less than everyone else. I told him I disagreed. It made no sense that advisers with few key skills were earning more than the SBS lads whose skills were so superior that they spent their spare time training other members of the team.

Ken still didn't agree. I told him if that was how he felt then he could tell the lads himself.

Ken didn't want to meet with the team as a whole but after a few days of pressing him he finally agreed. Taking a page from his London playbook, he kicked off the meeting with praise, telling the team what a marvellous job they were doing. He also apologized for how unprofessional the previous department had been with its handling of the contract.

This time I didn't wear out my arm patting myself on the back.

When he finally got around to the topic of pay scales, Ken dropped a bombshell: he said the wage discrepancies would soon be sorted because he was putting everyone on a new, lower rate. It got worse; not only did Ken expect the team to work for less money, he expected everyone to work longer rotations with less time off in between. To add insult to injury, Ken also informed us that our insurance packages would be slashed.

Ken told the lads the new terms would be written into new contracts that would nullify any outstanding ones they'd signed with KR, including those that hadn't expired. He also said that 7if anyone didn't like it, they were welcome to leave the job.

I couldn't let Ken go unchallenged. I argued that with the security situation in Kabul declining rapidly, if anything the team should be earning more and our insurance packages should be raised. Ken responded that that wasn't how his division did things; KR was a business and the business climate had changed. Belts were tightening all over The Circuit, he said, and KR had to remain competitive. He tried to ease the blow by telling us KR wasn't singling out Afghanistan; they were dropping wages and insurance packages in Iraq as well. Bastard.

After the meeting I gathered the team together. I told them I'd continue to fight London for what they deserved, but I'd understand if they moved on to other things. If they did decide to jump ship, I asked them to please let me know as early as possible so I'd have sufficient time to get good replacements. I'd put my heart into that team and despite everything I wanted to keep it strong.

Over the next couple of weeks the lads got their new contracts. For me personally, I was able to keep my original rotation schedule but I was smacked with a 12.5 per cent pay cut. The only reason I didn't tell KR to shove their job up their arses was because I didn't want to go back on my promise to the ambassador.

After the pay cuts, keeping the job running smoothly was even more of a struggle. One of the SBS lads resigned in disgust, as did several others. Two of the replacement advisers hired by London didn't have the proper skills for the job and had to be sent back (so much for Ken understanding our 'needs'). Moreover, my constant pleas for basic kit were still being ignored. If all of that wasn't bad enough, I soon learned that Ken was loath to support me when the client wanted to ignore my advice and do something dangerous.

About ten months into the contract, the ambassador had to return to his home country for meetings, leaving his deputy in charge. As soon as the ambassador was airborne the deputy announced that he wanted to go out to dinner at a restaurant in Kabul.

Afghan restaurants catering to locals in Kabul are fine, but restaurants popular with internationals are disasters waiting to happen. They are very soft targets – even those that are surrounded by blast walls and have guards posted outside. The fact is, most restaurant guards aren't paid enough to stand and fight and the blast walls are so frail four men could push them down. A car bomb would rip through them like a hot knife through butter.

Many international restaurants in Kabul also serve alcohol, which, as I've mentioned, is illegal in Afghanistan. It's not uncommon for these establishments to be raided by local police. As the police play both sides and it's very easy for insurgents to get their hands on police uniforms, it's impossible to know which raids are legitimate. So if you have a security detail guarding a client in a restaurant and it's stormed by police, it could result in a blue on blue incident.

The ambassador understood my position on dining in restaurants and respected it. The deputy knew it as well, but it didn't stop him from trying it on.

I asked Mr K if he could set up a meeting between the deputy and me so I could explain the situation. Mr K went to the deputy on my behalf but he refused to meet me; he had cabin fever and he wanted to go out to dinner.

I wrote an email to Ken explaining the problem. I wanted him to back me by persuading the embassy's Ministry of Foreign Affairs to rein in the deputy. We were there to advise the client on security matters and the deputy refused to even let me have my say.

Rather than get in touch with the Ministry of Foreign Affairs, Ken responded that I should give the client what he wanted, otherwise KR could lose the contract.

Of course, I didn't agree. It would be one thing if the deputy could ignore my advice and go to a restaurant alone, but it was far too dangerous for diplomats to go anywhere in Kabul without their CP teams. Caving into the client for fear of losing the contract would put everyone – client and advisers – at risk unnecessarily. It would be completely unprofessional. I wrote back to Ken saying as much. I never got a response.

In the meantime, I persisted asking at my end for a meeting with the deputy and, finally, I wore him down. We had a bit of a confrontation but when I explained he'd not only be endangering himself but also his CP team by dining in restaurants, he agreed not to go.

I was very pleased with the outcome. I'd done my job with complete integrity and KR still had the contract. Whether they deserved to keep it or not was another matter.

Eleven months into the contract I had what would be my final confrontation with KR London. It wasn't over restaurants or weapons or even wages; what pushed me over the edge was body armour. I'd become so fed up with the ongoing lack of support for the team that I went, on my own initiative this time, to KR London for a face-to-face with Ken.

During the meeting I noticed six sets of brand-new body armour in the corner of Ken's office. I asked him what they were doing there. He said they'd been purchased for another job which had fallen through. Body armour was among the basic items the team had been forced to scrounge for because KR hadn't provided any.

I asked Ken to ship the body armour to Kabul as soon as possible. He said he couldn't do it until the client paid for it first. It was the final straw. Ken must have known he had advisers on the ground risking serious injury and death due to lack of proper equipment. But he'd rather let the body armour sit in his office collecting dust than dent his profit margins.

Shortly after that meeting I resigned (but not before badgering Ken into sending the body armour to Kabul). I'd fulfilled my commitment to the ambassador and I was very proud of the fact that he remained alive and unharmed on my watch. But I couldn't take another minute of working for KR. In my resignation letter, I cited the 'catastrophic mismanagement' of the contract and listed all the ways in which KR London had failed to provide a duty of care to its clients and to its employees in Kabul. I also mentioned that I was fully aware that KR was using my CV to woo potential clients, claiming it represented the type of adviser they deploy to hostile environments.

'I'm sure the client would be impressed,' I wrote, 'if this letter of resignation accompanied that CV.'

CHAPTER 34

'He will meet with you but we must leave right now.' Qadeer, my translator, was beaming with pride. He'd been working on my behalf for months to get this meeting. I would have to get a move on. I was soaking wet with sweat from training and my clothes were plastered to my body. There was no way I could meet anyone looking and smelling like I did. If there's one thing I hate it's rushing around catering for fast balls. Then again, when you're summoned by an Afghan warlord 'right now', then *now* it is.

It was November 2006. Getting a face-to-face with the Afghan warlord Patcha Khan had been a goal of mine for some time. In March of that year, shortly after I resigned from the KR job, I accepted an assignment in Afghanistan running a hostile environment training task for Afghan nationals (the programme was paid for by the British Government and contracted out to a British CSC). The training task was fascinating. My 'students' came from all over Afghanistan, including areas controlled by the Taliban. They were constantly feeding me fantastic first-hand information about what was happening in their villages and provinces. Some of it I dismissed as folklore but many of the stories rang very true.

Not surprisingly, the intelligence from my students was far more disturbing than most of the news reports coming out of Afghanistan. Working with journalists had taught me to dig deep to uncover the reality of a situation. Though I hadn't advised the media in over a year, my passion for finding the truth had only strengthened. Hence my desire for a meeting with Patcha Khan; I wanted to get a tribal authority figure's thoughts on Afghanistan's present and future.

I ran to my room, stripped off my training kit and hit the shower. As I washed I mentally prioritized the questions I'd like to ask Patcha Khan. I would be lucky to get even twenty minutes with him. As warlords go, Patcha Khan was a busy one; balancing the family business of ruling Zadran, a district in Afghanistan's Paktia province, with his new job at the time – an elected MP.

Patcha Khan wasn't the only Afghan warlord playing at democracy but the men straddling Afghanistan's stubborn tribal past and its shaky 'democratic' future were an exclusive club. The country's President, Hamid Karzai, wasn't even a member. Karzai has no control over his own province of Kandahar. In fact, he has no authority outside the capital, hence his nickname, 'the Mayor of Kabul'.

I had met Patcha Khan once before briefly back in 2004. I was on my way to Khost province to collect Nic Robertson from an embed. The journey from Kabul required me to travel on a main road through Zadran – Patcha Khan's turf.

Back then, Patcha Khan wasn't part of the Kabul-based central government (I use the term 'central' in the loosest possible sense). Karzai and the Northern Alliance generals he'd appointed to his cabinet regarded Patcha Khan, a southerner, as a dangerous renegade. Karzai went so far as to send one of his lackeys to Zadran to try and overthrow him. Big mistake.

Patcha Khan responded to the attempted coup by showing Karzai exactly who was in charge of Zadran. He shut down the only road linking Khost town near the Pakistan border with the city of Gardez; a critical commercial route for anyone travelling north-west from Pakistan up to Kabul. Coalition forces, having been intimidated by Patcha Khan's militia in the past, weren't prepared to intervene.

The road closure brought the entire area to a standstill. I

learned about it when my convoy encountered hundreds of vehicles stopped in a valley. Scores of drivers and passengers were stuck in the searing heat with nowhere to go. I didn't know how long the closure would last and I wasn't going to stick around and find out. I grabbed my big camera and, posing as a news photographer, bluffed my way past Patcha Khan's guards into a meeting with the man himself. Once inside, I 'interviewed' Patcha Khan about the road closure. I then told him that as a stills photographer I could only report his story on the internet but if he'd let me collect my colleague from Khost there was a possibility the story could appear on international television. Patcha Khan ordered his men to open the road – just for us.

A few days later a group of elders from Zadran persuaded Patcha Khan to reopen the road to the public. They feared that if the stand-off with the central government continued, he would be targeted by American forces.

Patcha Khan proved he wasn't afraid to flex his muscles and anger Karzai, which by default meant he wasn't afraid to anger the Americans. That defiance made him something of an honest broker in my book. He may have gone on to become an elected MP but he didn't owe his legitimacy to Kabul. If things were as bad as I suspected in Afghanistan, he wouldn't spin the situation. Patcha Khan would tell the truth, no matter how politically inconvenient. He was more warrior than politician and he'd shown enormous restraint, in my opinion, by closing the road when the standard response in Afghanistan is to take no prisoners – literally. By joining parliament, he'd also shown that he could bury the hatchet for the good of his country. I was looking forward to speaking with him again.

Qadeer was waiting in our vehicle with the engine running. I climbed in the driver's seat and checked my gear to make sure I hadn't left anything behind; medical bag, comms, local cell phone, city map, spare vehicle keys, 9 mm pistol and an AK47 short. Even though we were in a hurry, I wasn't going to cut corners on the equipment check. Once we left the safety of our secured compound we'd be straight onto one of the most dangerous roads in all of Afghanistan.

The Jalalabad Road is as manic as it is treacherous; a dog-eat-dog free-for-all where armoured 4x4s, creaky old lorries and dilapidated cars fight it out with pedestrians, bicycles and donkey carts. Locals drive their transport on any side of the road they see fit, cutting up other vehicles and pulling across the road without indicating. The sun had just dipped behind the mountains surrounding Kabul as we turned onto the Jalalabad Road. Traffic was heavy and with no streetlights and no wind blowing, the thick Kabul dust hung low in the oncoming headlights, making it difficult to see bicycles, motorbikes and carts. On the plus side, the poor visibility made it more difficult for potential suicide bombers to target us.

Another plus was our vehicle. Unlike KR, my new employers had provided me with a top-of-the-range B6/7 armoured Toyota Hilux. I certainly felt better driving around Kabul, but I still had to remain vigilant. Though the chances of surviving an attack increase exponentially when you upgrade from a B/4 to B6/7, it's still no guarantee. Many people make the mistake of believing that an armoured vehicle will protect them from anything. It won't. No amount of modern armoured materials can. With enough explosives moulded correctly and enough accuracy, a suicide bomber will almost always kill or maim his – or her – intended target.

Suicide bombers had been having a field day on the Jalalabad Road in 2006; blowing up NATO military convoys, targeting government officials, the Afghan military and police, and any vehicle that appeared overtly western. Their preferred methods of attack involved either deploying on foot, jumping in front of a target and detonating a bomb vest, or packing a vehicle full of explosives and driving alongside or directly into a target.

I kept checking in a 360-degree arc for anyone who might be

marking us. In addition to suicide bombers, I was also worried about insurgents deploying a new type of IED: the 'magnetic' explosive device that can stick to any metallic surface in a second. Everything looked clear – a good sign. But we hadn't yet encountered the most treacherous stretch of the road: the Jalalabad Road roundabout. As a major traffic choke point, this particular roundabout is a suicide bomber's playground. Even if you have the skills to recognize a potential bomber closing in on your position, it's almost impossible to escape. The only proactive thing you can do is try and hang back, so if the need arises, you can push through the traffic and get away.

A bottleneck had formed just ahead of the roundabout. I tried to put some distance between our 4x4 and the vehicles in front of us as we merged with the slow-moving traffic. The muscles in my neck tensed as clusters of cars with horns honking closed in around us. I felt like a fish caught in a current. Finally, we reached our turn-off and broke free. I looked at the roundabout in my rear-view mirror and shook the tension from my shoulders.

We continued on towards the Kabul River: a shallow, stinking sludge pool that cuts through the middle of the capital like gangrene on a wounded limb, and headed to our first stop, the Kabul National Stadium. The Taliban once used the stadium as a venue for public executions. When they were ousted, the Afghan people reclaimed it for happier tasks. On any given day, across from the stadium, you can find children playing football or flying kites in large open fields. In the car park, barrow boys sell phone cards, fruits, vegetables or whatever else they can find to scratch out a living.

Children were still playing football outside the stadium in the dark as we pulled into the car park. Qadeer had been told one of Patcha Khan's representatives would be waiting there to escort us to the warlord's home. We would recognize the escort by his vehicle: a red car. We spotted it immediately. The escort, a young man with a trimmed, full beard and dressed in traditional Afghan clothing, was standing beside it. I scanned the other vehicles in the parking area to see if anyone was watching us, waiting to follow. The escort smiled, signalled to us to follow and ducked into his car. As we drove off behind him, I continued to keep an eye on the vehicles in the car park. After a few street turns, I was satisfied we weren't being tailed.

We followed the red car through the south-east of the city and out towards the edge of town. The further we drove, the darker the streets became until the light disappeared entirely. With nothing but the moon and our headlights to illuminate our path, I could barely make out the shadowy figures of armed guards stationed outside houses and compounds. We had entered 'the dark side' of Kabul.

The centre of Kabul has decent amounts of electricity and the businesses and wealthy individuals who live there supplement the frequent power-cuts with expensive fuel-fired generators. The dark side of town is a different story. There are no neon signs advertising goods and services or 'luxury' guest houses lit up like candles. The only light on the dark side is the ambient glow of hurricane lamps peaking out from behind old wooden doors and window frames.

We drove further into the darkness, snaking our way around potholes so deep they could swallow a motorbike. The odd whiff of human excrement wafted through the car vents. It underscored just how little had changed in Afghanistan. Five years on from the US-led invasion and there was still no reliable electricity in the capital and no sewage system. Shit still flowed onto the streets like fifteenth-century London and many homes had no running water. I had seen children working fourteen-hour days hauling buckets of water up steep hills to supply the houses on top.

What exactly had the legions of aid workers bumping through Kabul in their 4x4s been up to all this time, aside from driving up rents and prices of basic goods such as bread and fruit? One fruit vendor told me he couldn't afford to eat what he sells.

Only rich internationals and Afghans lucky enough to work for them earned enough to buy fruit in Kabul. Rather than elevate average Afghans in the capital, foreigners were making them feel inferior. No wonder the locals referred to the international community as 'the Toyota Taliban'.

After fifteen minutes, we found ourselves turning down a side street that was clearly different from the rest of the neighbourhoods we'd driven through. Unlike the guards we'd observed on the fringe of the dark side, the armed security men on this street were alert, professional and very strict in their signalling as to what they wanted us to do. These were Patcha Khan's men and they were in total control.

The guards directed us to a small, secured parking area. In Kabul it's essential that you park in a well-guarded spot; not so much to deter thieves as to ensure that no one plants an explosive device on your vehicle while you're away from it (nevertheless, I always check my vehicle thoroughly if it's been out of my sight, even for a minute).

I was confident that Patcha Khan's men had the street's security pretty well sewn up, so I decided to leave my pistol and AK short in the 4x4. Sometimes you have to make what appear to be counter-intuitive calls in hostile environments – decisions that can profoundly affect your next move. Though I always keep my weapons covert, as we were meeting with a warlord, it was pretty much given that we'd be searched by his bodyguards. There was no point in allowing them to see my weapons and assess my capabilities. It's not that I distrusted Patcha Khan's men, but in Afghanistan today's friend can easily become tomorrow's enemy.

We locked our vehicle and thanked the escort for leading us there. I asked him if he'd waited long at the stadium and he replied, with typical Pashtoon politeness, that he hadn't been waiting long at all. Qadeer and I were then presented to the guards standing outside Patcha Khan's residence. As I'd predicted, they searched us both thoroughly. Qadeer and I were then shown to a large room traditionally furnished with a large, red, ornamental rug and big matching cushions lining the walls. Patcha Khan and one of his constituents, a businessman, were sat at one end of the room. His aide and a group of bodyguards were sat at the other.

As soon as we walked in, Patcha Khan sprang to his feet and greeted us with an outstretched hand and a big smile. A tough character, his deeply lined, heavily moustached face somehow didn't suit a smile. He was dressed nearly the same as he'd been during our first meeting in Zadran – khamis, waistcoat, baggy trousers – only back then he wore a bandolier of ammunition under his waistcoat. I guessed he'd toned down his appearance since becoming an MP. After the usual Muslim greetings, we were invited to take a seat on the floor. A boy came in carrying glasses of green tea and plates full of nuts, sweets and biscuits. I started eating and drinking straight away as it's customary in Afghanistan for the hosts not to take any food or drink before the guests. The businessman kicked off the meeting with a flattering introduction of Patcha Khan. He explained that the people of Zadran, Paktia, the surrounding provinces and all Pashtoons in Afghanistan regard Patcha Khan as a great chieftain. (Qadeer was translating so I knew whatever was being said was being conveyed accurately.)

I responded by telling Patcha Khan that I was honoured to have an individual audience with him and that I appreciated him taking time away from his parliamentary duties to meet with me – which led straight into my first question. Why did he become an MP?

Patcha Khan explained that his journey to parliament had started where we'd left off, in Zadran two and a half years earlier. Not long after his infamous road closure, American and Afghan forces launched a combined air attack and a ground assault against him in his own territory. Patcha Khan survived the onslaught, but members of his family, including his son and his brother, were killed.

Patcha Khan was convinced that the US had attacked him at the urging of Northern Alliance generals in government who wanted to eliminate him as a historic rival and a potential contender for US favour. He told me that after the attack he'd pleaded with Karzai to intervene so as to prevent more bloodshed. The President, he claimed, refused. Patcha Khan fled to the tribal areas of Pakistan but was quickly detained, flown back to Kabul and put under house arrest. Following an intervention with Karzai by tribal elders, Patcha Khan was allowed to return home to Zadran. In 2005, he said, his people convinced him to run for office and join the government that had tried to kill him.

As he spoke, it was clear from his expression that Patcha Khan was deeply affected by the death of his son. I asked him what he thought of the US, given that its forces had attacked him in his home and killed members of his family. Much to my surprise, rather than curse the Americans, Patcha Khan said he did not see them as the enemy. Though he still had differences with the US-led coalition, he genuinely believed that they were trying to help the Afghan people.

I asked him if there was anything about the US presence in Afghanistan that concerned him. Patcha Khan answered that what worried him most about the Americans was that they seemed in such a hurry to leave. He feared that if US and NATO troops were to withdraw from Afghanistan it would trigger a repeat of what happened when the Soviets left; in the absence of a dominating power, Afghanistan would plunge into civil war. Patcha Khan didn't feel the US-backed Afghan Government could hold the country together. He said he would like to see democracy take root and the Afghan Government prosper but parliament was too corrupt, MPs were interested only in serving themselves and he felt President Karzai was more concerned with pleasing his American masters than serving the best interests of his nation.

In Patcha Khan's view, Karzai's unwillingness to stand up to the Americans had already compromised the nation's future. Patcha Khan said he warned Karzai four years earlier that if America and its allies didn't send more troops to Afghanistan, the Taliban would regroup in the south, move east and start taking over provinces. Sadly, things were unfolding just as he'd predicted.

In the months leading up to my meeting with Patcha Khan, British forces had fought some fierce battles with the Taliban in the southern province of Helmund. The Brits were greatly undermanned when they assumed control of Helmund from US forces in early 2006 and the Taliban exploited this by taking over small villages one by one across the province. British forces managed to regain the territory, but in order to hold it they had to establish 'platoon houses' inside each village, spreading themselves even more thinly on the ground. It was only through sheer bravery and professionalism that the Brits were able to hold out in these places with so few numbers and so little support. But British lives were lost. When senior officers finally realized what a grave strategic error they'd made, they struck a 'ceasefire' deal with local tribesmen, who agreed to keep the Taliban away from their villages. As soon as the Brits withdrew, however, the Taliban moved right back in.

I later found out through local sources living in Helmund that most of the tribal leaders who'd struck deals with the British were executed by the Taliban. In addition to punishing the 'traitors', the executions served as warnings to others not to do business with the 'infidels'. Many of the villagers quickly switched loyalties.

By the end of 2006, Helmund wasn't the only province where the Taliban had regained their footing. They were engaging the Canadian Army in Kandahar and had even penetrated Kabul, where, according to my sources, local cells were very active.

The Taliban's resurgence begged my final question to Patcha Khan; did he think the Taliban would return to power officially? Patcha Khan took a deep breath and with a pained but wise expression declared that the Taliban would be running Kabul within two to three years. If not, then they would definitely control the south and east of Afghanistan.

'And the rest of the country?' I asked.

'Civil war,' he replied.

I asked him whether anything could be done to prevent this from happening. The answer, he said, was for the United States and its allies to get serious about their commitment to Afghanistan and send more troops – immediately.

All told, my meeting with Patcha Khan lasted just over an hour. I was extremely grateful to have had so much of his time. I said goodbye to the warlord in the darkened courtyard of his compound. He took my hand in both of his and told me I was welcome to come and see him again anytime.

Before Qadeer and I left, I made a point of saying goodbye to Patcha Khan's guards – just in case I ran into them again under less hospitable circumstances. I reached out in the dark to take one of their hands to shake it, only to find a stump. The guard withdrew it and offered me his left hand instead.

Scary in the Afghan darkness. These people certainly have been through it over the years.

CHAPTER 35

The timing couldn't have been better. It was March 2007 and I was just about to wrap a year-long training task in Kabul when an email from Nic Robertson landed in my inbox. He was on his way to Kabul and wanted to know if we could meet. Nic and I had kept in touch since I'd last worked with him two years earlier so he had a rough idea of what I'd been doing. I couldn't wait to talk to him. My Afghan contacts and my meeting with Patcha Khan a few months earlier had given me a wealth of insights into Afghanistan, but no outlet for sharing them. I knew Nic would put the information to good use.

We managed to link up at Dubai International Airport. Nic was flying into Kabul and I'd just flown out. Over a brew, he told me he was working on stories for an upcoming CNN special focusing on Afghanistan, the Taliban and the War on Terror. Nic wanted to know if I had any story ideas for him.

Not only did I have ideas – by that point, I had a list of Afghan contacts most journalists would kill for. I asked Nic what he'd already lined up. As usual, he was on a whirlwind tour. In addition to Kabul, he planned to travel to eastern Afghanistan to update the drugs story and then across to Pakistan. He had also submitted a request for a US military embed in the Afghan provinces of Kunar and Nuristan.

I asked him if he planned to take security with him on any of these assignments. He said he'd like to take me – if I was still doing media work.

Ten days later I was back in Kabul working with Nic.

*

Through my local contacts in Kabul, I was able to land Nic the first world exclusive of his trip: an interview with Mullah Abdul Salam Zaeef, the Taliban's former ambassador to Pakistan. I had tried to meet with Zaeef in December 2006. I wanted to know if he agreed with Patcha Khan's prediction that the Taliban would be running Kabul in a few years' time. Zaeef would certainly have some unique insights. He was a founding member of the Taliban, and the movement's public face.

As a high-profile Taliban, Zaeef was the object of special interest to the Americans. He had stayed in Pakistan following the 2001 US-led invasion of Afghanistan, but was soon handed over to US authorities and shipped off to Guantanamo Bay for three and a half years. Upon his release in 2005, Zaeef returned to Kabul where the Karzai government had a guest house waiting for him. The Afghan government claimed the house was part of an incentive programme aimed at reintegrating 'reformed' Taliban like Zaeef back into society. As I discovered, it was also a convenient way for Karzai and the Americans to keep tabs on the former Taliban ambassador.

Zaeef did agree to see me in 2006 but a pre-meeting recce revealed that the Afghan government had heavy surveillance on his house. I also suspected American intelligence was keeping an eye on who was coming and going. As much as I wanted to meet him face to face, I knew I'd be inviting trouble by visiting Zaeef without a good excuse (I doubted anyone would believe that I wanted to see him out of personal curiosity). A visit by a CNN crew, on the other hand, wouldn't be the least bit suspicious.

You might think that three years or more in Guantanamo Bay would have left Zaeef a frail, broken figure. On the contrary. When we arrived at his house for the interview, we were greeted by a six-foot-three monster who still looked every bit the Taliban – from his long black beard to the spotless black turban on his head.

Detention may not have left a mark on Zaeef physically, but

the interview revealed some deep mental scars. Nic questioned Zaeef at length about his arrest. You could tell by the way he recalled it that the experience had left him deeply traumatized, so much so that he had to stop several times and swallow before continuing his answer. Zaeef seemed to be choosing his words carefully, like a man still in hiding.

Zaeef said the most trying times of his captivity weren't the years in Guantanamo Bay but the months preceding it. Following his arrest in Pakistan, he was shuffled from an American naval ship in the Gulf to a military base in Kandahar and then to Bagram Airbase outside Kabul. Zaeef claimed that while in Bagram, he was beaten, deprived of food, stripped naked and forced to stand in the snow. Zaeef also claimed the Americans shaved his beard – sacrilege to a devout Muslim.

Zaeef said throughout his detention the Americans kept asking him the same questions over and over again: where is Mullah Omar and where is Osama bin Laden? Zaeef claims to this day he hasn't a clue where either man is hiding. He added that he kept telling his American captors that he was an ambassador and that they had no right under international law to detain him. The Americans would counter that since they'd never recognized the Taliban as a legitimate government, he wasn't entitled to diplomatic immunity.

Fascinating as his past was, what most interested me were Zaeef's thoughts on the Taliban's resurgence in Afghanistan. On this point, Zaeef was adamant that the Taliban he'd founded had been far less radical than the one which had regrouped. He said he could never get to grips, for example, with suicide bombings, a tactic embraced by the Taliban after the US-led invasion of Afghanistan. Zaeef felt suicide bombings were a clear indication that al-Qaeda was exerting a tremendous amount of influence over the movement.

As to whether the Taliban would return to power formally, Zaeef danced around the question. He did say, however, that the movement had got it wrong the first time around by being so strict and that if the Taliban were to join a unity government, they'd be much more moderate. Zaeef was understandably reluctant to comment at length about the Taliban's possible return to power. But from Helmund to Nuristan, the writing was on the wall: the Taliban was getting stronger by the day. One reason the Taliban was regrouping so effectively was drugs money. By 2007, Afghanistan's heroin trade was worth an estimated 3.1 billion US dollars, a fair portion of which was being funnelled into the Taliban's ever-expanding war chest.

Following the interview with Zaeef, we headed east to Jalalabad, where Nic had arranged to check in on Afghanistan's poppy eradication efforts. He would have liked to return to Helmund to update the story he'd reported in 2004, but the province had become far too dangerous to visit outside of a military embed. It didn't matter because Jalalabad's poppy eradication programme was pretty much a carbon copy of what we'd seen in Helmund two and half years earlier. Nic and his crew were taken to a token field to film a tractor ceremoniously ploughing through poppies. Just like Helmund, the local farmers had gathered to protest against the action and the local drug lords had assembled to make sure their fields weren't touched. The only difference was the landscape; instead of Helmund's flat valleys, the mountains of Tora Bora were visible in the distance.

Thanks to one of my local contacts, Nic was able to add a new element to his drugs coverage; an interview with a trafficker in Jalalabad. Not surprisingly, he told Nic it was very easy to run drugs out of Afghanistan and into Pakistan or up through China.

Between drugs and insurgency, it seemed the question was not if the Taliban would return to power formally but when. For years, the US-led coalition had been struggling to maintain the status quo in Afghanistan, let alone secure the ground and move the country forward. Afghanistan seemed dangerously close to plunging into warring autonomous regions; some controlled by 'moderate' Taliban, some by al-Qaeda-influenced

Taliban and some by former members of the Northern Alliance. By that point, I was convinced that barring radical action by the coalition, civil war had become inevitable.

In that respect, Nic's third interview of the trip would prove very telling. Nic secured a one-on-one with the new head of NATO in Afghanistan, US General Dan McNeill. McNeill had recently taken over from General David Richards, a British commander who at that point had overseen the bloodiest year in Afghanistan since the Taliban's fall in 2001.[25]

McNeill offered up a flannelling worthy of his rank. He dodged and weaved his way through the interview like a heavyweight champion. Whenever possible, McNeill would steer his answers back to the subject of reconstruction. NATO's efforts in Afghanistan were primarily focused on hearts and minds reconstruction projects as opposed to dominating the ground through military force. Though I wasn't in a position to tell him so, I disagreed with McNeill's priorities. They were not at all in keeping with the type of strategy I believe a true soldier should embrace. In my view, a true soldier focuses all of his energies into winning and securing the ground before pouring resources into goodwill projects.

Experience has left me of the opinion that most generals are politicians first and soldiers second. McNeill was no exception. Why else would he accept a military task that was almost surely destined to fail? Even I, a lowly former warrant officer, knew there weren't nearly enough NATO troops in Afghanistan to secure the ground. What's more, McNeill wasn't in full control of the soldiers under his command.

In order to be effective, a general must have the ability to move his troops around like pieces on a chessboard. The head of NATO in Afghanistan can't do that because many NATO countries provide troops to Afghanistan with the caveat that

---

25 In 2006, an estimated 4,000 people in Afghanistan died in insurgency-related violence.

they not be deployed to the southern or eastern provinces – dangerous places like Helmund where undermanned British forces had been bravely holding back the Taliban for over a year; and Kandahar, where Canadian soldiers had also been fighting courageously.

The Brits would have benefited tremendously, for example, if McNeill had had the authority to deploy New Zealand forces to Helmund. In my experience, Kiwis are some of the best infantry soldiers in the world. They are certainly one of the most professional fighting forces in Afghanistan. Yet in 2006 and 2007, instead of fighting alongside the British in Helmund where they were desperately needed, the Kiwis were up in Bamiyan, a soft province where the biggest enemy is poverty, not the Taliban and al-Qaeda.

Nic did hold McNeill's feet to the fire on the issue of caveats. McNeill admitted he was constrained by them but he claimed that some countries had suggested that 'there may be ways' for him to get around the deployment restrictions.

It sounded to me like political bullshit. Governments either agree to send their troops to hard areas or they don't. It's as simple as that.

After the interview, I was fairly certain that McNeill would probably preside over a worse year than his predecessor. Caveats are for the faint-hearted and McNeill (who had to contend with them) was fighting an enemy that was fully committed to achieving its aims by any means necessary, including suicide missions. In my view, it would be miraculous if McNeill even managed to maintain the status quo – no mean feat, considering that across the border Pakistan was in the throws of what some were calling 'Talibanization'.

CHAPTER 36

The War on Terror will be won or lost in two countries – neither of which are Iraq or Afghanistan. I believe that if western governments are to achieve a decisive victory over Islamic terrorism, they must crush it at its source. In 2004, I visited what I've called the premier hub for al-Qaeda recruitment: Saudi Arabia. In spring 2007, I travelled to the country which in my view runs a close second: Pakistan.

Pakistan and Saudi Arabia are worlds apart economically and culturally but they are similar in two crucial respects: both have Muslim populations rife with anti-western sentiment yet both have governments that are allied with the west in the War on Terror. By 2007, Saudi Arabia's ruling elite had managed to accommodate this contradiction by driving its radical Islamic elements underground. In Pakistan, the opposite was happening: Islamic militants were not only operating with impunity in the Afghan border areas; their influence was also growing in the moderate capital, Islamabad. Meanwhile, even moderate Muslims were calling for President Pervez Musharraf – the man charged with cracking down on extremism – to resign.

Though technically I had been to Pakistan previously, my experiences consisted solely of stopping over in Islamabad en route to Kabul. My trip with Nic and his crew would be my first proper assignment in Pakistan.

In addition to Nic and myself, our team included a seasoned cameraman named Scotty and a young British female producer I'll call Susan. Sometimes news crews can be at odds with one another from the word go – a real nightmare from a security standpoint. Fortunately, Nic had assembled himself a close-knit group. Having worked with Scotty on several occasions, I knew he was as talented as he was easy-going. I had not worked with Susan before, but from her pre-trip preparations, she struck me as well researched and highly organized; both assets in a producer.

It was important that our team be on the same page at all times. The type of hostile environment we'd be operating in was one of the most hazardous in my book. Like Saudi Arabia, Pakistan's dangers are largely concealed beneath a deceptively calm exterior. Take our accommodation, for instance. We were booked in at the Marriott Islamabad, one of the capital's top international hotels. When guests pull into the Marriott's gated entrance, they're greeted by doormen with red uniforms and smart turbans. They are then ushered past a big set of glass doors into an opulent, marble-floored lobby. It's easy to be blinded by the five-star luxury and forget that as a favourite destination for visiting diplomats and one of the few places in Pakistan with a licensed bar, the Marriott is a prime target for militants. In October 2004, an explosion in the hotel's lobby injured several people including a US diplomat. In January 2007, a suicide bombing outside the hotel's bar left two people dead.

The January attack on the Marriott had been carried out by Islamic extremists angered by Musharraf's pro-western policies. But discontent was also rife among Pakistan's moderate Muslims, who were growing increasingly frustrated with President Musharraf's authoritarian rule. Prior to our arrival, Musharraf suspended Pakistan's Chief Justice; a move viewed by many as an attempt to consolidate power before an expected election later that year. The Chief Justice had taken a tough line with Musharraf's government, particularly on the issue of human rights abuses by Pakistan's notorious Inter-Services Intelligence (ISI). Rather than bolster his position, Musharraf's suspension of the Chief Justice galvanized the opposition. Pakistan's legal community organized rallies throughout the nation calling for the Chief Justice to be reinstated and for Musharraf to step down. Some of the protests ended in violent clashes between police and members of Pakistan's legal community. There were reports that Pakistani authorities had stormed two privately owned news channels and suspended transmissions after pictures were broadcast of blood-soaked lawyers at a rally in Lahore.

Nic's first story in Islamabad had the potential to go the same way. The Chief Justice was scheduled to appear before the Supreme Court in Islamabad to challenge the legality of Musharraf's decision. Throngs of protesters were expected to turn out for the occasion. Nic wanted to get to the Supreme Court early in order to interview the demonstrators. We arrived to find a handful of local media and opposition representatives gathering on the grounds outside the gated Supreme Court complex. A heavy contingent of male and female riot police wearing face shields and carrying long sticks was also on hand. They had formed a human barricade outside the main gate of the complex to keep the protesters from getting too close.

It all appeared very orderly, but as the day wore on the crowd grew in size and intensity. Lawyers dressed in black suits, white shirts and black ties started arriving in groups of twenty and thirty. They had come from all over Pakistan to support the Chief Justice. Opposition groups, some as large as a hundred people, also began descending on the area. Within a few hours, the small clutch of demonstrators had swelled to a slogan-chanting, banner-waving mob of nearly a thousand.

It takes just one person to whip a crowd into a frenzy and when you've got hundreds crammed into a small area, the situation can turn dangerous in seconds. Luckily, Susan had agreed to stay back at the hotel so I'd have fewer bodies to look after should a riot break out. I kept reminding Scotty and Nic to please let me know their intentions, be it shooting b-roll, interviewing individuals or trying to report live.

The crowd was energized but still in control as the Chief Justice showed up in a convoy surrounded by black-suited members of his legal team. The protesters' chants grew deafening as the entourage inched its way past the crowd and through the gates into the main grounds of the Supreme Court complex. The demonstrators began storming the gate, demanding to be allowed in as well. The riot police tried to hold them back, but sticks proved no match for the mob. The gates were flung wide open and the protesters flooded inside. Nic, Scotty and I were right behind them.

CNN didn't have permission to film inside the Supreme Court building, but there was plenty to keep Scotty and Nic occupied outside in the courtyard. At one point, the lawyers appeared to turn on each other. Several men were beaten with fists and sticks and thrown over the fence to the crowds beyond. The police didn't intervene. I found out that the men who'd been assaulted were believed to be ISI agents, who, allegedly, had posed as lawyers to spy on the protesters.

The protest peaked without tipping into a full-scale riot. The crowd started to disperse and the situation calmed enough for Nic to file live reports. The Chief Justice made little headway in his case; he was given a ten-day adjournment. For the lawyers and opposition parties who'd turned out to support him, the battle to remove Musharraf from power would go on.

The erosion of moderate support was just one challenge facing Musharraf. The other had been dogging him for some time: the threat from Islamic extremists. Since 11 September 2001, fundamentalist activity in Pakistan had been largely confined to the tribal areas with the odd incursion into Islamabad. By 2007, however, the Pakistani capital was undergoing what the media were calling 'Talibanization'.

The Talibanization of Islamabad was being driven by the Lal Masjid or Red Mosque, a sprawling complex housing the largest female *madrasah* in the world and a male seminary with strong links to Pakistan's tribal areas. The Red Mosque always taught extremist views, which, over the years, its students exported throughout the world. The mosque was linked to Shehzad Tanweer, one of the 7 July London bombers.

In 2007, the mullahs encouraged the students to exercise their fundamentalist beliefs in their own backyard by imposing Sharia law on the residents of Islamabad. Female students from the Red Mosque reportedly stormed a local brothel and kidnapped the madam while male students cracked down on stores in the capital selling 'un-Islamic' DVDs.

The campaign to enforce Sharia law in Islamabad was a direct challenge to Musharraf's rule. Tensions between the Red Mosque and the country's security forces were mounting and the students and clerics were reportedly preparing for an armed confrontation. Nic wanted to investigate.

Nic had been following the Red Mosque for some time, having interviewed one of its chief clerics, Abdul Rashid Ghazi, the previous year. Ghazi was an unapologetic al-Qaeda sympathizer who publicly condemned Musharraf for supporting the War on Terror. At the time, few western journalists could secure an audience with Ghazi, but Nic's groundwork had paved the way for a second interview.

My primary security concern with the interview was timing. Should we be unfortunate enough to be in the mosque when the police decided to attack, it would be very hazardous indeed. The odds of that happening, however, were remote. The other possible pitfall was being abducted by the students and held as human shields or bargaining chips to be used against the authorities. Again, an unlikely scenario in my view. Ghazi wanted to get his message broadcast impartially on international TV. Kidnapping journalists would work against that goal.

The Red Mosque sits in a large, walled complex in the heart of Islamabad. As the crow flies, it's roughly a mile from the Presidential Palace but once you turn on to Masjid Road – a narrow, tree-lined street leading directly to the mosque – the hustle and bustle of the capital's daily life dissolves.

We arrived to find students and worshippers calmly going about their daily business. The serenity was surreal given the circumstances. Although the students looked quite radical with their long, flowing beards, everyone seemed to be at peace with one another. There were signs, however, that a siege mentality had taken hold of the place. The walls of the mosque compound were surrounded by guards armed with sticks and spears and guards were posted on the rooftops of the buildings inside. As soon as Scotty started filming, many of them covered their faces to conceal their identities.

The crew and I were led through the main gate of the complex and searched. While this was going on, one of the guards asked me if I was a Muslim. I had grown a very long beard during my assignments in Afghanistan which I'd kept for my tour with Nic. I told the guard I wasn't Muslim. He then asked if I was Christian. The follow-up question was a sticky one. As a child I thought religion was fantasy and as an adult I've seen it rip societies apart. I'm an atheist and in Muslim eyes being a *kafir* (a non-believer) is worse than being Christian or Jew. A kafir is the worst possible kind of infidel. I told the guard, 'No, I'm not a Christian and I'm not Jewish,' and left it at that.

Inside the mosque grounds there was total silence. As we walked to an administrative building to set up for the interview, I searched for signs of weapons. There were rumours that the students had amassed large caches, including AKs. I saw many sticks, the odd spear and even an axe, but no guns. I assumed that the guards posted outside the mosque and inside the courtyard were mere sentries. The hardcore jihadists were probably staying out of sight.

The interview was held in a small ten- by eight-foot office furnished with floor cushions and a desk covered in paperwork and DVDs of the mullah's sermons. Ghazi showed up barefoot, dressed in a simple tan khamis. A stocky man in his mid-forties with a long, bushy, grey beard, Ghazi's appearance was softened considerably by a pair of round, wire-rimmed glasses.

Ghazi gave the interview sitting down on the floor. His English was very good and he expressed himself with complete clarity. Like many of the rogues I'd met before him – Arafat, Yassin, Khalifa – Ghazi knew his days were numbered. He was completely resigned to the fact that Musharraf's security forces would eventually storm the Red Mosque and take him out. Ghazi vowed that he and his followers would fight to the death. If I'd learned anything by that point, it's that infamous figures like Ghazi rarely grandstand. I had no doubts he would go down fighting.[26]

The Talibanization of Islamabad combined with Musharraf's loss of moderate Muslim support had enormous implications for the War on Terror. If Musharraf couldn't control events within a mile of his own palace, what possible hope did he have of stopping radicals from launching cross-border raids into Afghanistan? It was no secret that Taliban fighters had regrouped along the border with Afghanistan, but Nic wasn't content to rely on second-hand reports. He wanted to see for himself whether the Taliban were operating there freely.

Nic had applied to the Pakistani authorities to travel to Quetta; a north-west border city which sits atop a plateau in Pakistan's Baluchistan province. Though ethnically Quetta is predominantly Baluchistani, with its large Pashtoon population and Afghan refugee communities, it was an easy place for Taliban to go underground and re-emerge at a later date.

Baluchi separatists had been conducting a violent independence campaign in Quetta and the city had grown so dangerous that Pakistani authorities wouldn't allow CNN to film there without a government minder and ring of police security present. Of course, the minder was also there to keep Nic from learning too much. During our first day of filming, the minder

26 In July 2007, Ghazi and dozens of his followers were killed when Pakistani security forces raided the Red Mosque.

would step in and interfere whenever Nic attempted to interview someone on the streets. When that happened, I would hang back a few yards and canvas the locals on the sly.

One thing I discovered is that the people of Quetta watch a lot of CNN. At least half a dozen locals recognized Nic from television. They were full of praise for his commitment to reporting on events in Afghanistan and Pakistan. They were also attuned to CNN's interest in Quetta. Several asked me if we were there to film the Taliban.

I looked around for overt signs of the Taliban, but if anything the centre of Quetta appeared moderate. Many of the men had western hairstyles and wore moustaches as opposed to long, flowing beards. This was the Quetta the Pakistani authorities wanted us to see. Nic knew from his contacts, however, that there were Afghan refugee camps in Quetta that were allegedly crawling with Taliban such as Pashtoonabad, on the city's eastern side, and Nawa Gari in the north-west.

At first, our minder and police escorts were reluctant to let us go to either camp, though they all insisted that there were no Taliban there. Nic kept pushing the issue and eventually the minder allowed us, under police escort, to travel to Pashtoonabad. As the police weren't a welcome sight in Pashtoonabad, it was decided that the best way to film the area was through the window of a moving vehicle under cover of darkness. The police and I agreed on a route that would lead us into the camp at one end and out through another. That way, we wouldn't have to backtrack or dismount our vehicles.

Though it was dark, Pashtoonabad reminded me of the refugee camps I'd seen in Gaza. The narrow dirt road through the camp was lined with one- and two-storey buildings. Several times we had to pull over to allow trucks to pass. The brief stops gave an opportunity to get a closer look at the side streets leading off the main road. Most of them were too narrow to drive up and could only be used as walkways.

I asked our police escorts if they ever patrolled the area on foot. They didn't – only by car, which meant that anything going on up the side streets was hidden from view. Madrasahs, mosques, homes – all were left to their own devices. We couldn't confirm that Taliban were present, but, given their limited view on the camp, the police couldn't rule it out either.

The next day, Nic got his best shot at securing concrete proof of the Taliban's presence in Quetta. Some Pakistani news agencies were reporting that Taliban fighters wounded in Afghanistan were being treated in a hospital located on the main road through Quetta. We were given permission to film there. The conditions in the hospital were dreadful: dirty wards, beds crammed close together, the sour smell of body fluids permeating the air. Nic asked the doctors if he could see some patients' charts. Sure enough, many of the injuries listed were consistent with shrapnel wounds. When Nic asked the doctors their opinion, they agreed; the wounds had most likely been sustained in battle. Short of the patients jumping on their beds and declaring themselves Taliban, it was a sure sign that Islamic radicals were moving freely over the border. If they were wounded in Afghanistan, they could limp back to Pakistan, receive medical treatment, and head back across the border to wage jihad against coalition forces.

Clearly, Musharraf had little control over the militants' movements. But if Pakistan lost its grip on the border completely, it could undermine everything the US-led coalition had achieved and hoped to achieve in Afghanistan. The coalition claimed it was making progress securing the border from the Afghan side, but Nic and I wanted to see this for ourselves. We would soon get the chance. While we were in Quetta, Nic got word that his Kunar/Nuristan embed was a go.

CHAPTER 37

Landing the Nuristan embed was yet another major coup for Nic. Not only would he be the first western television journalist to film there, but he'd be travelling to an area some believed harboured the War on Terror's most wanted man. Personally, I was over the moon about the embed as I'd been trying to find a way into Nuristan for some time. Tucked away in the north-east corner of Afghanistan on the south-western slopes of the Hindu Kush, Nuristan is perhaps the most rugged and inaccessible of all the Afghan provinces. Until the 1890s it was known as Kafiristan – land of the unbelievers – and was the setting for Rudyard Kipling's short story 'The Man Who Would Be King' on which the movie is based.

The Yanks were operating in Nuristan unilaterally as opposed to under NATO-led ISAF because when it came to fighting the War on Terror, Nuristan was the sharp end of the spear. Not only had Nuristan's porous border become a major conduit for al-Qaeda fighters travelling over the border to and from Pakistan, but the province's mountainous terrain was also thought to harbour Osama bin Laden. In 2003 a video was released showing bin Laden and his Lieutenant, Ayman al-Zawahiri, walking down a mountainside in what many believe is Nuristan. Some people think bin Laden is still hiding there (personally I think he's in Yemen, but that's for another story).

Fortunately for Nic – and for me – the US military was anxious to get press up to Nuristan to showcase its Provincial Reconstruction Teams or PRTs in the province. Staffed by professional soldiers and civilian experts, PRTs execute quick-impact development projects. At any given time there are roughly two to three dozen PRTs operating around Afghanistan: some administered by ISAF, some by NGOs and some directly by the US military. General McNeill had banged on about PRTs during his interview with Nic. Hardly surprising considering the US military had become positively evangelical about the ability of PRTs to win Afghan hearts and minds. Put simply: build a bridge, make a friend, win the war. It's a great theory, but one which I have yet to see work in practice. As usual, before deploying, I did some background research on recent events in Nuristan. The American mission there wasn't all about good works. In 2006 the US military launched Operation Mountain Fury in Nuristan to seal the border with Pakistan and root out al-Qaeda forces. If past reports were any indication, the US military was having a very tough time of it. The province shares a very lengthy border with Pakistan and is home to Taliban and al-Qaeda fighters who enjoyed local support in the form of Hizb-i-Islami, a rogue militia led by Gulbuddin Hekmatyar. Ironically, Hekmatyar, a lifelong Mujahid, was the biggest recipient of US funds and training during the 1980s insurgency against occupying Soviet forces.

Insurgents had engaged US forces in some very serious incidents in Nuristan. In 2006, fighters led by the Taliban Commander Ahmed Shah attacked a squad of US Navy Seals, killing three. Shah's fighters then shot down a helicopter full of US reinforcements, killing a further sixteen. If elite soldiers were getting hit like that, what kind of obstacles were the PRTs encountering? I concluded that the embed had the possibility of being quite hairy indeed.

Nic was told to report to Bagram Airbase the night before the embed for departure to Nuristan early the next morning. The main US base in Afghanistan, Bagram is approximately a one-hour drive north of Kabul city. In 2007, the dangers involved in making even that short journey underscored just how organized the insurgency had become in and around the Afghan capital.

The route I selected to Bagram would take us along the infamous Jalalabad Road. Before departing, I ran the drivers and crew through the SOPs including a new one I'd introduced since returning to media work. I instructed the CNN crew to put away their BlackBerries until we reached a secure environment. A combination mobile phone, email, SMS device and web browser, BlackBerries are a tremendous asset to journalists on the go, but in a hostile environment they can be a serious liability. It's impossible to be fully aware of your surroundings when your face is buried in a BlackBerry, and for the drive to Bagram I insisted all eyes be on the lookout for trouble.

We arrived at Bagram without incident but, as always, I refused to relax until my clients were safely inside the camp. A month earlier, a suicide bomber had killed more than a dozen people at Bagram's gates. The attack was staged during a visit by US Vice President Dick Cheney. The bomber managed to penetrate an outer cordon of security manned by Afghan police and strike at an inner checkpoint manned by American troops. Both the timing and execution of the attack revealed a lot about the Taliban's operations in Kabul. Cheney's visit was not pre-announced, which meant that the insurgents were able to get the bomb and driver to Bagram almost on a whim. It was the clearest evidence I'd seen that the Taliban had well-trained, organized cells in the Afghan capital.

A member of the PAO's office was waiting for us inside he gates. Luckily, he'd brought a minivan. Between Nic, Scotty, Susan and me, we had fifteen items of gear. Driving through Bagram is like driving through a small town in America. It has all the amenities of home: Burger King, coffee bars, pizza place, the best hospital in Afghanistan, a PX with great items at bargain prices. Most of the troops stationed in Bagram never see an angry char wallah and many are as good-natured as they are polite. You'd never guess you were in a hostile environment were it not for the signs on the perimeter reading 'Danger Mine Field'.

We were taken to the PAO's office for a quick brief on Bagram and an overview of our embed. We learned that our embed would last approximately six days and take us to three forward operations bases to observe three separate PRTs in action: two in Nuristan and one in Kunar. The PAO didn't have a tremendous amount of detail about the PRTs though he did warn us that there were few amenities at the FOBs and we should be prepared to rough it.

The PAO ended the brief by handing us reams of paperwork to sign. We were given form after form in triplicate; disclaimers stating that we understood the dangers involved in the embed and that we wouldn't hold the US military liable should we get injured or killed. I had not been required to sign anything on previous embeds. Then again, I hadn't been on one for over two years. I took it as yet another sign of how dangerous Afghanistan had become.

After the brief, the PAO showed us to our accommodation: a building the size of a garden hut kitted out with cots, air conditioning for the summer and heating for the winter. Clean, modern washing facilities were across the way and half a mile up the road was the best food in Afghanistan. You would never guess there was an insurgency raging all around us. We took the PAO at his word that we'd be in for some hardships in Nuristan and sat down to a dinner that really could feed an army. I tucked into a T-bone steak the size of a frisbee, crab, veggies and half a gallon of ice cream. I was well fed and mentally prepared for anything Nuristan had in store.

Then, it started to rain. Military transport in Afghanistan is seriously overstretched and if your flight is cancelled due to poor weather conditions, you can wait around for weeks to get another one. If our flight to Nuristan was grounded, the embed would be off.

By early morning, the rain had stopped and the skies had

cleared. It seemed we'd be on our way. I roused the crew at 5 a.m. sharp to drive ourselves and equipment the short distance across the road to the helipad. I wanted to be sure we were the first in line to board our aircraft.

We were scheduled to fly out on a CH 47 Chinook helicopter. As much as I was looking forward to the embed, I was nervous as hell about flying to it, especially in a Chinook. Chinooks are very old workhorses, having first come out in 1966 when I was only twelve years old. As I've said, I'm not a keen flyer in ideal circumstances, and I was well aware that in both Iraq and Afghanistan these huge, tandem-rotored monsters were falling out of the sky at an alarming rate; some downed due to mechanical failure and some shot down by insurgents.

For that reason, Chinooks operating in hostile environments are mounted with three 7.62 mm medium machine guns, one on either side of the fuselage, and a tail gunner who sits on the open ramp during flight. Chinooks also fly in pairs for mutual support. Even with the precautionary measures, though, operating a Chinook is among the most dangerous assignments in a theatre of war. The crews who man these helicopters are incredibly brave.

Our Chinook was full to the gunnels with troops and equipment all bound for the same destination: FOB Kala Gush, Nuristan. I braced myself for a stomach-churning flight but once airborne I found myself pleasantly distracted by the views sweeping past. We climbed out of Bagram through the saddle of two bald mountains, dropped into a desert valley, climbed into another mountain range and back down into a lush green valley. When you drive through Afghanistan the scenery changes every twenty minutes; from the air, it's every twenty seconds. The colours swirled underneath us like a shifting kaleidoscope: pale and tawny browns, emerald and deep moss greens.

The tree-lined, snowy-peaked mountains of the Hindu Kush rose in the distance as we approached our destination. FOB Kala Gush is at the top of a very flat valley and when approached by air it feels as if the mountains are literally closing in around you. The helicopter dropped us in the LZ (Landing Zone), and took off again. As the dust cleared I was dismayed to discover that the FOB was positioned right at the base of a two-thousand-foot mountain. I couldn't believe the Americans built a base so barefaced and open to attack. It wasn't as if the compound was large and imposing enough to deter insurgents; it was barely big enough for the two Chinooks to land.

I took a quick walk around to assess the base's defensive capabilities. I saw two 155 mm howitzer artillery pieces, which made me feel a bit better. The base also had a mortar pit and sentry posts with machine guns positioned at various points around a perimeter circled in blast walls and barbed wire. Unfortunately only two of the sentry posts were manned. It was just like the US base in Samarra, Iraq, only worse because Kala Gush was overlooked by a two-thousand-foot peak. It was really scary.

My discomfort was heightened by the sight of a dozen local Afghans holding court in the middle of the camp. Again, it was a repeat of the same mistakes I'd seen in Samarra, except these locals were guests and not detainees. Any one of them could have been an insurgent or a tout.

When I asked one of our military hosts about the group of Afghans, I was told by a captain that they were village elders who'd been invited there for a meeting. I asked him why the base hadn't set up a secured location outside the camp; one that would allow them to conduct meetings with locals without compromising security. The captain's answer was a familiar one: 'That's not how we do things here.' He explained that they wanted to show the locals that the US was on their side. I felt like saying that in due course he'd find out which side the locals were really on. But I'd only just arrived and I didn't want my big mouth reflecting badly on Nic and his crew.

Later that evening, the elders were invited into the cookhouse for a meal. I couldn't help but recall an attack in December

2004 in which a suicide bomber walked into a cookhouse in the middle of a US base in Mosul, Iraq. The attack killed twenty-six soldiers and wounded sixty. Nothing seemed to have been learned from that episode. I could only conclude that there's little to no cross-pollination of ideas between the US military in Iraq and Afghanistan. If there is, then the lessons are quickly forgotten.

Given the poor security at the base, it was vital that I keep the team close together. Should an incident occur, I didn't want them scattered. This presented a little mini-drama upon our arrival because it is US military policy to segregate the sexes into different tents. Nic and I had to fight tooth and nail to keep Susan with us. Finally our hosts relented after Nic argued that he needed Susan to help him cut stories late into the night.

Once we'd sorted the sleeping arrangements we were shown to our tent. Far from the 'rough' conditions advertised by the PAO in Bagram, our accommodation contained an abundance of cots and an air-conditioning unit. In fact, the Americans had managed to cram all sorts of amenities into FOB Kala Gush: showers with hot water, flush latrines, a cookhouse serving real food as opposed to just army rations, a laundry tent with huge washing machines and industrial driers, a small running track around the LZ and even a gym with Olympic weights. The US military didn't seem to know much about securing bases in an insurgent-rich environment but when it comes to making troops comfortable, the Yanks wrote the book.

Once settled, we went for a briefing with the commander of FOB Kala Gush. The commander was in good condition for a man of his age and spoke in a very mild-mannered tone. It was the complete opposite of the in-your-face bravado I'd experienced with some other US commanders. The commander had only been in his post a few weeks, and when he spoke of his PRT he did so with all the freshly minted enthusiasm one would expect from the uninitiated. The commander was assigned to his post for a year, during which time he was utterly determined to lay a road from Kala Gush all the way to the centre of Nuristan. If the flight to Kala Gush were any indication of the province's general topography, achieving that would be one incredible feat. Throw in the security issues – the proximity to the Pakistan border and the al-Qaeda foothold in the region – and the task seemed completely unworkable.

But the commander had absolute faith that his PRT would prevail. Prior to his deployment, he completed a six-month course in the States covering counter-insurgency tactics and other roles which he believed would enable him to produce a successful mission. He truly believed he and his men would build their road and secure the loyalty of the local population. He may have thought otherwise had his course included a lesson in recent Afghan history. The Soviets built brilliant roads all over Afghanistan – roads which they used to run back to Moscow with their tails between their legs. Yet, despite all the historical evidence, the US and NATO were convinced that PRTs held the key to defeating the insurgency.

The commander's commitment was genuine and quite touching. But for all his passion and preparation he spoke of his PRT as if there were no security hurdles to clear first. Rather than set his sights on completing the road, in my view it would have been far more realistic for him to spend his year laying the security groundwork for the project and then hand things over to another officer. I wondered if the commander had the energy to maintain his enthusiasm over the coming months. If he did encounter delays with the project, would he put the safety of his troops first or would he, like so many fofficers, allow himself and his men to be pushed to the limits by a senior echelon demanding results within an unrealistic timeframe?

As the sun dropped below the mountains, we moved into our tent and switched to red lights; white lights were banned after dark because they're visible from a distance and can act as bull's eyes to insurgents trying to target the base. The crew and I bedded down with the war looming above and beyond us. I fell asleep to the sound of fighter aircraft heading towards the Pakistan border to take out enemy positions deep within the mountains.

CHAPTER 38

We passed the night in relative peace, with the exception of one incident. Around 3 a.m. I woke to what sounded like the thump of a mortar round coming in to our tent. I thought the base was under attack. I sprang to my feet, ready to rouse the crew. It was then that I realized that the thump wasn't a mortar round but the sound of Nic's cot collapsing underneath him. I must have looked completely startled because Scotty, the cameraman, had a good laugh at my expense.

For our first full day in Kala Gush the commander invited CNN to join a half platoon on a clearance patrol in the mountains surrounding the base. I was very interested to see how the soldiers would perform. Clearance patrols, as the name suggests, involve clearing an area of possible hazards, such as IEDS and insurgents.

Before going outside the wire the troops asked us to take part in a 'rehearsal': a drill involving various patrolling scenarios. It sounded great to me, especially as I'd never seen, let alone participated in, a rehearsal on any of my previous embeds with the US military.

The half platoon was commanded by a very young first lieutenant. Although he had a captain and some seasoned sergeants on hand to guide him, the lieutenant was keen to establish his authority. He had obviously gone through his aide-memoire – sort of an idiot's guide to commanding – the night before to ensure that his patrol literally went by the book. The rehearsal was held in an open vehicle area where the unit's Humvees were parked. It was meant to simulate a withdrawal from a contact to the front. For the next three minutes the crew and I watched as the troops lifted their feet in double time while the lieutenant barked incomprehensible orders. None of the soldiers knew who was covering whom and the back of the patrol seemed completely lost as to how they should be responding.

I looked at Susan, our young producer. 'You got that?' I asked her.

'Got what?' she said.

I thought for sure the lieutenant would order the lads to do the drill again before going outside the wire, but he didn't. He'd ticked his rehearsals box and it was on to the next phase. I couldn't trust my clients' safety to that lot if we were ambushed, so I told the lieutenant that if anything happened during the clearance patrol I'd get the CNN team to the nearest point of cover and await his orders.

The lieutenant estimated the clearance patrol would last approximately four to five hours. We would be walking over some very steep and rugged terrain in extremely hot weather conditions. Factor in the altitude (we were operating at between 6,000 and 8,000 feet) and I was convinced that the major hazards we'd face wouldn't be incoming rounds or RPGs – it would be broken limbs and heat illness.

With that in mind I told Nic and the crew to wear their body armour but leave their helmets behind. The rest of the gear was all essential; Scotty carried his camera and ancillaries, Nic took the tripod, water, a GPS and satellite phone, plus his own individual medical pack and compact video camera (which he lugs with him everywhere). Susan carried water for herself and Scotty, and I had water, the team medical trauma pack, my own GPS and satellite phone and a few odds and sods. In addition, we all had power bars to munch on during the trip to keep our energy levels up. We were quite the little patrol on our own. The only thing we lacked was weapons.[27]

27 The US military does not permit journalists or security advisers to carry weapons on embeds, and rightly so.

Together with the platoon we shook out in a basic formation and stepped outside the wire. The patrol would travel to the peak of a mountain and back down to the camp. The lieutenant punched some coordinates in his GPS and gave the troops a reference point to walk towards. We travelled three quarters of a mile down a newly graded, dirt vehicle path and hung a sharp left at a re-entrant carved into a steep hillside. There were narrow goat tracks on either side of the re-entrant; one leading to a small community of poppy growers and the other climbing sharply up the hillside. Goat tracks, especially ones that don't lead directly to and from populated areas, are prime places to get ambushed or hit by IEDs or anti-personnel mines. Fortunately, the lieutenant was able to radio back to camp and call out a drone to recce the areas we couldn't see. Once we got the all clear, we moved up the hillside track for six hundred yards before moving off track for the rest of our journey to the summit.

About a third of the way up, the patrol spotted a white sedan and two motorbikes driving along a narrow dirt road. I was very concerned. White sedans are the vehicles of choice for suicide bombings in Afghanistan. The car stopped approximately three quarters of a mile from our position. The driver got out and disappeared behind a large boulder.

One of the soldiers next to me started observing the sedan through the scope of his sniper rifle. I asked the soldier if he could make out the wheels on the car.

'Mister, I could make out the whites of the guy's eyes if I could see him,' he said.

'Does the vehicle's chassis look like it's sitting close to the tyres?' I asked.

'What do you mean?' said the soldier.

'Does it look like it's carrying a heavy load?'

'Why?'

'Because what I'm wondering right now is did that vehicle stop so the driver can jump out and have a piss? Did he stop to plant an IED? Or, is the car rigged as a suicide bomb?'

The soldier looked up from his scope. 'Wow,' he said. 'I never would have thought of that.' Down in Helmund that would be the first thing on a British soldier's mind.

It saddened me that this great bunch of young lads seemed to have no in-depth counter-insurgency training whatsoever; not in basic tactics as evidenced by their abysmal rehearsal or in what to look for whilst out on patrol. To his credit, the young lad with the sniper rifle had the common sense to observe the sedan through his scope. I had no doubt that with the proper training he could be an excellent soldier.

The driver eventually popped back out from behind the boulder, climbed into his car and drove away. He must have been taking a piss. Lucky bastard. Had our patrol been full of nervous, trigger-happy soldiers, that piss could have cost him his life.

The rest of the way up the mountain was very slow going. We were scrambling over large boulders on a steep incline in temperatures topping ninety degrees Fahrenheit. In between huffing and puffing, the patrol made several stops to rest and take in the views. Scotty and Nic worked through these breaks, shooting b-roll and stand-ups explaining how the ground we were travelling resembled the mountainous terrain in bin Laden's 2003 video.

I was very proud of the CNN crew. Despite the rough conditions Nic, Scotty and Susan were holding their own. Some of the soldiers, meanwhile, were in a lot of distress. All of them were loaded down with mountain warfare kit including body armour, helmets, operational waistcoats, weapons, ammunition, comms and water bags fitted on their backs like day sacks. Half of the lads were coping well with the harsh conditions but the others were labouring intensively. A captain and a sergeant went down with heat-related problems.

It didn't help matters that the lieutenant was leading the patrol along a very difficult route. At times we almost needed mountaineering equipment to negotiate the huge boulders and overhangs. I didn't expect to travel along graded tracks the whole time but I did expect the lieutenant to set a course that would enable us to more easily break contact with the enemy should we be attacked.

I spotted several different routes we could have taken. I asked one of the sergeants why we were climbing such bad ground when there was easier terrain to travel.

The sergeant nodded towards the lieutenant. 'He has the GPS,' he said.

I took that to mean that the lieutenant was following a direct bearing to the top of the mountain. It was crazy. A soldier needs to use the ground to his or her advantage. Unlike a compass, a GPS enables a soldier to contour the ground and plot the most advantageous path. The lieutenant hadn't done that. He was following a bearing blindly.

The sergeant and I scanned the area again and soon agreed on an easier route for the journey down. He asked me if I had prior military experience. I told him I'd spent twenty years in the SAS. The Americans must have amazing communications skills because before we reached the top of the mountain, every member of the patrol knew my background.

The journey to the summit had been unnecessarily difficult but the view up top made it all worthwhile. We could see clear across the border into Pakistan where the mountains of the Hindu Kush rise up to 16,000 feet. It was an incredible feeling knowing that I was working with the first western TV news crew to film that view. The Circuit may have its considerable faults but at that moment I wouldn't have traded my job for anything.

We began our descent along a course determined by the young lieutenant. After a wee bit of cajoling on my part, he allowed us to take a break. During the stop, I asked the lieutenant, privately, how he'd decided on the route up. As I'd suspected, he answered that he had followed a direct bearing from our departure point. I mentioned in the most tactful way I could muster that if he'd factor in the contours of the ground as opposed to following what the GPS said was the quickest way, it could help his troops avoid heat problems. I also explained how he could use the ground to his advantage in a contact scenario.

I half expected the lieutenant to tell me to bugger off. Instead, he thanked me for my input and said he'd send a recce to find an easier path down the mountain. I told him not to bother; his sergeants and I had already agreed an alternative route. He grinned and told me he was still learning. I told him not to worry as I was in my fifties and I was still learning too.

Back at the base, I made myself a brew, sat outside my tent and looked through my binoculars at the ground we'd covered with the patrol. I was exceedingly grateful we hadn't encountered any insurgents that day. They could have hit our patrol and dissolved right back into the mountains. The soldiers stationed at the base may have had howitzers and air support at their disposal, but those are blunt instruments for taking out guerrillas, especially in steep, rocky terrain.

I could understand flying soldiers into Nuristan for border operations and flying them back out, but from where I was sat, establishing bases in the province seemed absolute madness. I seriously doubted whether the potential goodwill generated by PRTs justified the risks involved in executing them. There weren't even enough troops in Kala Gush to secure the immediate ground around them.

I woke early the next morning to the sound of Nic's cot buckling underneath him – again. I didn't get it. Nic's not a heavy lad. I jokingly told him to stop sleeping with his wallet in his back pocket; all that money he earned as a correspondent was putting him in danger.

The commander had set aside several hours that day to personally show CNN development projects his PRT was running in the area. The tasks included a girls' school located in the nearby village of Kowtalay and a medical day clinic the base's doctor and a few medics were holding in a neighbouring village. Before leaving the base, the commander assigned soldiers to look after each member of the CNN crew. I understood his motives and I didn't feel as if my toes had been stepped on. Still, I had every intention of doing my job. If things went pear-shaped, the soldiers' priorities could shift whereas my focus would stay fixed on my clients.

In addition to me and the CNN crew, our patrol included the commander, thirty-two troopers and two civilians attached to the PRT: a Nuristan specialist from the US State Department and an engineer. Both civvies were very nice grey-haired men in their late fifties. I may not have agreed with the strategic value of their projects, but hats off to them for spending what should have been their retirement years doing good deeds in one of Afghanistan's most dangerous provinces.

We all piled into a convoy of eight Hummers and headed toward Kowtalay. The village looked like a picture postcard in the distance; a clutch of quaint buildings nestled in an emerald valley along the banks of a crystal-clear, rapidly flowing river. The Hummers were too heavy to drive over a suspension bridge crossing the river into Kowtalay, so we parked on a hill and finished the journey on foot. Each vehicle was assigned two soldiers both to protect the Hummers and to cover us from the hilltop.

As soon as I dismounted my vehicle, a soldier walked up to me. 'I'm with you,' he said.

I didn't think anything of it. As we were going along, I stepped out of the line of march to look for possible signs of ambush ahead of the suspension bridge. The soldier stepped off with me.

'What are you doing?' I asked him.

The young soldier grinned at me self-consciously. 'Um, I'm your bodyguard, man.'

I laughed.

'Seriously,' he said.

I sized him up. He seemed a good-natured lad, definitely in

his early twenties and in very good physical condition. But that didn't make him a bodyguard.

'OK,' I said. 'If shit happens, how are you going to respond?'

'I'm going to get you to safety and cover you,' he said.

It was ridiculous. There were sixteen infanteers covering us from the hilltop and a further sixteen in our little patrol. If four soldiers were busy looking after me and the crew when a contact ensued, the foot patrol's defensive response would be reduced by a quarter.

'No, you're not, mate,' I said. 'There aren't many of you on the ground so if shit happens I'll get myself and my clients to safety while you return fire.'

The young soldier thought about it for a few seconds and smiled. 'Fair enough,' he said and we cracked on.

The girls' school in Kowtalay was still under construction. We arrived to find a group of girls dressed in brightly coloured clothing playing on a patch of waste ground next to what appeared to be a very well built shell. A group of tents nearby served as temporary classrooms until the building was finished.[28] The commander was beaming over his nearly completed school and the civilian engineer was also bursting with pride. He gushed, and rightly so, about the craftsmanship the local workforce had put into the building. Considering the obstacles the Americans were encountering daily in Nuristan, the project was a big feather in their caps. Whether it would actually secure the loyalty of Kowtalay was another matter. The PRT had assembled a group of local men for CNN to interview. From their expressions, the men didn't strike me as being particularly overjoyed by the American presence in their village or grateful for their new school.

---

28 There are tens of thousands of children in Afghanistan going to school in tents that provide little protection against the extreme cold of winter and blistering heat of summer. Erecting school buildings is extremely worthwhile, but the projects often suffer from a major oversight: very few have provision for a qualified teacher. The majority of teachers in Afghanistan are volunteers who have no formal training.

After Kowtalay, we walked to a neighbouring village where the medical PRT was in full swing. There was a large queue of locals outside the clinic, from the very young all the way up to the very old. The ailments were equally diverse, ranging in severity from toothaches to malaria, with a scattering of tuberculosis in between. A doctor and several medics from the base had been treating people for more than two hours when we arrived. They looked shattered. I asked the doctor how long he planned on staying. He told me that after the next patient it was vitamin pills only.

The day clinic was a nice gesture but it was doubtful it would have any real impact on the lives of the villagers. In a stable environment a clinic can go on for weeks if not months until a permanent medical facility is built. This doctor couldn't be on the ground longer than a few hours without endangering himself, his staff and the villagers. That's because an unintended consequence of PRTs is that they draw insurgents like a red rag to a bull. When insurgents first moved into Nuristan, they operated in the caves hidden deep within the mountainsides and left the villages alone. The PRTs were drawing them out. A few days after our tour, we learned that a suicide bomber killed seven Afghan police stationed near Kowtalay. It made me wonder about the future of the girls' school. It was by far the best building in the village. Girls' school one day, Taliban headquarters the next? Not an unrealistic scenario given the way Afghanistan was going.

CHAPTER 39

During my time in Afghanistan I befriended a man whose career read like a recent history of the country's rulers. He began by serving in the Soviet Army. When the Soviets' grip on power started to slip, he jumped to the Mujahudeen. Later, he put on a black turban and joined the Taliban. When the Taliban came under threat, he went to work for the American military as an interpreter. Last time I checked, the man was working as a police officer in Herat. He's a very charming character, but at the end of the day he has no loyalty – whoever is strongest wins his support.

The same is true of most Afghans. Over the years, I've worked side-by-side with many of them. A few were rogues but the majority I found to be courageous, honourable and trustworthy – to a point. Because for all their noble attributes, history has taught the Afghans that remaining loyal to a conquering power is a losing proposition. I can hardly blame them. It's self-preservation because conquerors always cut and run. The Soviets did it, the Taliban did it and many Afghans believe the coalition will as well. The only enduring allegiances Afghans have are to themselves, their families and their tribes, not to whoever happens to be in charge of their country. Yet the west, to its detriment, has failed to recognize this. It doesn't matter how many sweets are thrown at them – girls' schools, medical clinics, new roads – Afghans will always jump to the winning side.

For our final day in Kala Gush, the commander had lined up quite a field trip for CNN: a helicopter flight to the north of Nuristan to recce the proposed route for the road inland. Though the views promised to be spectacular, the decision to do the recce by air as opposed to overland wasn't entirely for our benefit. A few days before we arrived a PRT was ambushed by RPGs and small-arms fire while attempting to recce the route with Humvees. Three people were injured in the attack.

The heli-recce involved two UH60 Blackhawks supported by an AH64 Apache gunship. The Apache is a real mean machine with eight Hellfire missiles, over thirty rocket pods and a 30 mm chain gun that fires ammunition at an awesome rate. It may sound like overkill, but our airborne convoy needed all the firepower it could get. Blackhawks are little more than airborne soft-skin vehicles and even though they were fitted with machine guns, we would still be very vulnerable up there. The Apache circled overhead while the two Blackhawks touched down to collect us. I was impressed by how effortlessly the pilots dropped down into the narrow valley and landed in tandem on the constricted LZ.

Nic and Scotty were both thrilled to discover that the doors had been removed from the Blackhawks. Though it had been done to offer the commander and his staff a better view of the ground for their recce, it would also make Scotty's job of shooting the landscape much easier. Doors on Blackhawks don't provide much in the way of protection but they do make the helicopter easier to manoeuvre. I hoped our pilot was skilled enough to compensate for the deficit.

All three pilots kept in constant radio contact with each other throughout the flight. The Blackhawks were flying very close to the ground. Every so often, a valley would open out and I could see the insect-like underbelly of the Apache looming above us. It would shadow the Blackhawks, peel off and check a re-entrant and return to position. It was some of the best tactical flying I've ever seen.

Our pilot handled his Blackhawk with great skill, manoeuvring over summits and through mountain passes so narrow that the rotor blades were literally a few feet from the rock face. Blackhawk pilots have considerable courage. Day in and day out they risk their lives to get ground soldiers out of the shit. I couldn't get over how tiny ours was. I could only see the back of his helmet sticking up from the port seat – no sign of shoulders whatsoever.

It wasn't until the pilot looked back at us that I realized he was in fact a she. I should have guessed it from the sticker on the back of her helmet: *The louder you yell, the quicker I come.* With all due respect, she certainly gave me the ride of my life. For such a petite young lady to be flying a monster Blackhawk through such difficult terrain was something I never would have imagined. Working alongside some extremely professional women at CNN had gone a long way towards redefining my view on women in war zones. The young lassie piloting the Blackhawk cemented it; there are definitely roles women can execute with equal if not more skill than a man in a hostile environment.

We flew north through valleys, along re-entrants, up steep mountainsides and over snowy peaks. Now and again, we'd spot a tiny hamlet built somewhere you just wouldn't dream people could live: mountainsides with no apparent access in or out; cliffs perched 2,000 feet above valley floors. It was the harshest, most inaccessible terrain I'd ever seen. Building a road through it seemed a hell of a way to play hearts and minds. Getting whacked by insurgents would be the least of the PRT's problems. If it were my mission, I'd be far more concerned about driving off a mountain and plunging hundreds of feet into a rocky ravine. As for the other half of the US mission – finding bin Laden – forget it. Bin Laden could elect to live out his life in ten square miles of Nuristan and a thousand ground troops would struggle to find him.

The next morning we were scheduled to leave Kala Gush for the second leg of our embed – a two-day move to a US forward operations base in Naray on the northern edge of Kunar province, practically a stone's throw from the Pakistan border. The trip would include an overview of Naray's PRTs as well as a brief heli-recce to a US forward operations base in Kamdesh, Nuristan, perhaps the most dangerous military outpost in all of Afghanistan.

Before boarding a Chinook, Nic piled his fourth collapsed cot into the corner of our tent. He'd managed to break one every night of our embed. I do hope the troops at Kala Gush appreciated the sculpture CNN left behind.

It was early afternoon when our Chinook touched down at US FOB Naray. Located between the foot of a mountain and the Kunar River, the base was even more exposed and vulnerable than the one in Kala Gush. One side was overlooked by a village on the far bank of the river while the other was bordered by a narrow track that cut between the mountains and the blast walls surrounding the base.

The Commander of Naray was waiting at the helipad when we landed. He'd been in his post for twelve months and was anxious to show CNN how much progress his PRT had made over the course of a year. He treated Nic to a very detailed brief including a PowerPoint presentation complete with charts and graphs detailing how much money had been spent on various development projects in his area. The sums were impressive: tens of millions of dollars splashed out on things like roads, schools and recruiting and training local police. But for all the facts and figures, the brief revealed very little about what the PRTs had actually achieved strategically. For example, it didn't include information on how many troops and civilians had been killed or wounded working on the projects. The US military seemed to measure a PRT's success in terms of dollars spent rather than ground secured.

I couldn't wait to see what the Yanks had going in Kamdesh.

*

The next day felt like Christmas morning. I don't know who was more excited about the heli-recce to Kamdesh: Nic, as he'd be the first western television journalist to film there, or me, the ex-Special Forces soldier.

FOB Kamdesh is the northernmost American outpost in Afghanistan. The area is so remote that when the Americans arrived there to build their base in 2006, the locals asked if they were Russians. We were invited to Kamdesh to film PRTs but it's well known that the base is a jumping-off point for US Special Forces probing north and east and along the border with Pakistan. Operations of that nature require a very high degree of skill and training. If the Regiment were there, the lads would be ripping each other's arms off to get in on the action.

Following an RPG attack on a Chinook at Kamdesh in early 2007, the army temporarily halted all flights in and out of the base. Fortunately, the ban had been lifted in time for our embed. By air it took less than half an hour to travel the twenty-five miles north from Naray to Kamdesh. Overland, the journey would have taken up to nine hours. The only vehicle route connecting the two bases was a nearly impassable, narrow dirt track the Americans had nicknamed 'Ambush Alley'.

Similar to our heli-recce in Kala Gush, we flew to Kamdesh in two Blackhawks covered by an Apache. The views were a photographer's Valhalla. Soaring up to 16,000 feet, the smooth-rock mountains surrounding Kamdesh dwarfed the puny, 6,000-foot shale ranges near Kala Gush. Twenty minutes into the flight, we circled around the actual village of Kamdesh: a collection of modest stone and wood houses dominated by an intricately carved wooden mosque. From the air, the village looked like something out of a fantasy; it seemed to be teetering on the edge of a mountain slope.

Five minutes on from the village, we dropped down into a very steep gorge and landed on an LZ near the stony bank of a fast-flowing, trout-filled river. As soon as we dismounted, the crew and I were ushered to cover while the Blackhawks rose swiftly up and out of there. FOB Kamdesh wasn't a place for helicopters to hover. The base sits on a valley floor surrounded by 3,000-foot peaks. Once a pilot commits to landing, he or she has very little room to manoeuvre if fired on. It was a miracle the Americans were managing to survive there, let alone execute a PRT. Just prior to our visit, the base had been averaging three attacks a week.

We had approximately three hours on the ground to film Kamdesh's PRTs. Not surprisingly, the projects were modest compared to those we'd seen in Kala Gush. The first stop was a local police station the PRT had established in a village just over the riverbank from the base. The station was a small stone building the size of a double garage. Eight recruits were inside. Their uniforms didn't match and they looked more like a rag-tag militia than a proper police unit. It was humble but as the US soldier showing us around said, 'It's a start'. I agreed. It was amazing they'd managed to accomplish even that much.

Next we were shown a medical facility and a school. The Americans told us that a few weeks earlier both buildings had been attacked by insurgents, the school being hit by an RPG. Before the Americans showed up, insurgents had left the village alone. Just like Kala Gush, the development projects in and around Kamdesh were drawing al-Qaeda and Taliban fighters down from the mountains.

I felt sorry for the villagers and for the US troops assigned to help them. Both groups were being treated as pawns in the War on Terror. It was outrageous. The US ground troops and middle management I met in Kunar and Nuristan were good, professional lads. But their military leaders, no doubt spurred by politicians back home, had sent them on a losing mission. Instead of administering development projects from vulnerable bases on valley floors the troops should have been soldiering in the mountains. With the benefit of good OPs, the US military could dominate the high ground without ever disturbing the villages below.

The same applied to the rest of Afghanistan. PRTs are not silver bullets. The US and its coalition partners can lay roads and build schools all over Afghanistan and it still won't compensate for the fact that the number of troops needed to secure the country was grossly underestimated from the word go. The US and NATO need to come clean about their past mistakes and commit more soldiers, including highly trained troopers, to win and hold the ground.[29] Only then will the conditions exist for PRTs to have a lasting impact.

Even with a fundamental shift in strategy, however, total victory in Afghanistan could take decades. It's not an area a foreign army can secure in two to three years, hand over to local forces and withdraw from. Pursuing long-term objectives like winning a war isn't for the faint-hearted.

The soldiers in Kamdesh and the rest of Nuristan deserved better than to have their commitment, passion and, in some cases, their lives squandered on token gestures that probably wouldn't stick. In Kamdesh, the troops' faces seemed to reflect the impossibility of their task. Morale looked very low indeed. I found out that some of the soldiers were entering month fifteen of their Afghan tours. Talk about stretched to the limits! British soldiers would never spend more than six months at a time in a theatre of war. Anything beyond that risks psychological damage.

Three hours in Kamdesh was enough for me. The soldiers there were like fish in a barrel and though my heart went out to them, I had no desire to stay in there with them. While we were waiting for the helicopters to collect us, an infantry captain asked me what I thought of the PRT tour. Having seen how tough his mission was, I didn't want to bring him down with a totally honest critique.

---

29 The SAS spent six years fighting a counter-insurgency in Oman, mentoring local forces and forming units to help them dominate the ground. In the end the Regiment was successful because they won and held the land – not because they built roads for people. The good works came later – after the insurgents were driven out.

'It's the best embed I've ever been on,' I said. 'Thank you for looking after us so well.'

'What do you think of our location?' asked the captain.

Again, I didn't want to take the wind out of his sails, but for his own safety and that of his men, I couldn't hold back. 'To be honest, I feel very, very vulnerable here,' I said.

The captain tried to reassure me, saying that attacks on the base had subsided and that the insurgents appeared to have been contained.

'I take on board what you're saying,' I said. 'But please, don't let your guard down. Two men could unleash mass destruction on this place.'

'How so?' asked the captain.

I pointed to a ridgeline hanging 2,000 feet above us. 'See those boulders?' I asked. 'Twenty pounds of low explosives placed under one of those overhanging boulders by Mr Taliban and his cover man and this place would be buried.'

The captain turned white. 'Shit, man, we thought we'd looked at everything but we hadn't even considered that one.'

Within minutes he was sharing the scenario with his mates.

SUMMARY

In all my years on The Circuit I've never fired a shot in anger. I hope I never do. If you were expecting to read about a gun-toting madman shooting up terrorists from Baghdad to Kabul, I'm *not* sorry to disappoint.

I'm not a journalist and I'm not a spy. I'm an ordinary person whose work has enabled him to find out a few things. I wrote this book because I wanted to share my personal experiences and hopefully shed some light on an industry most people only know through the distorted lens of Hollywood or sensationalist novels.

I'm aware that some books written by security professionals centre on killing 'rag heads', a term I find incredibly offensive. Ninety-nine per cent of the indigenous people I've encountered in hostile environments – be they Palestinians, Iraqis or Afghans – have been absolutely delightful. The ones I've worked with directly would lay down their lives to save mine and vice versa.

Shoot-out stories misrepresent the nature of the threat in places like Kabul and Baghdad and warp the public's perception of how competent security professionals really behave on the ground. Knowledgeable security advisers don't go looking for a fight. They don't wave weapons at crowds – or worse, shoot into crowds – on the off chance there may be a terrorist lurking within. Experienced security advisers use proactive skills to spot trouble in sufficient time to get clients to safety without having to draw a weapon.

I certainly don't hold myself up as the ultimate role model.

I've had occasions during my time on The Circuit when I've messed up big style, like my drama with the Russian–Israeli soldier. I've tried to learn from my mistakes and thankfully my clients have never picked up the tab. Furthermore, I don't pretend for a second that I haven't benefited from a bit of luck. It doesn't matter who you are or what your skill level, if you're in the wrong place at the wrong time, you're going to get it.

Some situations are unavoidable. But an element of luck is one thing; it's quite another when your entire proactive regime consists of crossing your fingers and hoping you don't get whacked.

Today there are tens of thousands of security professionals working in Iraq, Afghanistan and other flashpoints in the War on Terror who lack the proper skills, equipment and/or training to perform their tasks effectively. It is a despicable state of affairs, one that compromises the lives of security professionals on the ground, their clients and the legitimate militaries operating in these areas.

Since 2003, The Circuit has grown fat on outsourced military jobs. The industry and its political backers argue that commercial security companies help stabilize conflict areas by freeing up soldiers for other tasks. Bullshit.

I've read the political spin, the annual reports, the Whitehall papers written by CSCs to influence government policy. Trust me: they have no bearing whatsoever on what's really happening on the ground. Rather than aid stability, CSCs contribute to instability in places like Iraq and Afghanistan by making the military's primary job – securing the ground – more difficult. Put simply, The Circuit is *undermining* the War on Terror.

How does it do this? First and foremost by enabling politicians to continue implementing flawed policies. I don't mean to belabour the point but it bears repeating: the primary objective of any military campaign is to dominate the ground and hold it. The US-led coalition didn't commit enough troops to dominate the ground in Iraq or Afghanistan at the start of either campaign. When faced with declining security and an escalating manpower gap, rather than admit its errors and send more troops, the coalition used The Circuit to cover up its mistakes.

Troop deployments are headline news. Images of brave young soldiers waving goodbye to their families tend to weigh heavily on the public conscience; flag-draped coffins returning home even more so. Hence, why so many military jobs have been outsourced to The Circuit; it's far more politically palatable than troop deployments. I have yet to see a TV news report on a security adviser shipping out to Iraq or Afghanistan, let alone one of them returning home – in a body bag. Were the lives of the Edinburgh Risk lads who died on Baghdad's airport road worth less than the life of a soldier?

As I write this, there are approximately 150,000 American soldiers in Iraq. The number of private security personnel working on US government contracts there isn't far behind: 126,000 men and women.[30] I wish I could tell you the total number of private security personnel working in Iraq and Afghanistan but no one knows.[31] Even with half the picture, however, it's clear that what began as a gap has widened into a chasm.

Until the middle of 2006 government leaders and top-ranking officers from Washington to Whitehall argued that things were improving in Iraq. Do you think anyone would have believed that had the US been forced to up its legitimate military presence from 150,000 to 276,000 troops? I have no doubt that had it not been for The Circuit, public calls for a radical rethink on Iraq would have come much, much sooner.

Another way in which The Circuit has enabled the White House and Downing Street to conceal the true cost of the campaigns in Iraq and Afghanistan is by perpetuating the illusion

---

30 John M. Broder and James Risen, 'Contractor Deaths in Iraq Soar to Record', *New York Times*, 19 May 2007.

31 The US only keeps track of people working on its government contracts and CSCs aren't required to disclose any information about their personnel including the names and job descriptions of those killed and maimed in hostile environments.

that both countries are stable enough for civilians to operate in. I haven't worked in Iraq since late autumn 2004, not because it became unstable – that's the nature of hostile environments. I called it a day because Iraq had degenerated into absolute anarchy and chaos and it's impossible to operate proactively under those conditions. I believe it is unethical to accept money to look after clients in areas where the best I can offer is reactive security.

The commercial security companies that stayed in Iraq after 2004 may label me overly cautious. By 2007, however, Iraq was clearly no place for foreign civilians, including security professionals, to operate. In May of that year dozens of armed insurgents dressed as Iraqi police commandos surrounded the Finance Ministry in Baghdad and kidnapped a civilian computer consultant and four members of his British CP team. Let me be clear, the CP team did nothing wrong other than agree to work an impossible task. What chance does a private, unsupported CP team have against an organized, sophisticated, deeply entrenched insurgency?

That episode and others like it not only impact the people directly involved. Each time a security adviser and/or a client are kidnapped in a hostile environment, it makes the job of securing the ground that much more difficult for the military. Civilians should steer clear of Iraq and Afghanistan until the security situations improve – drastically.

I'm convinced that if Iraq was an impoverished African nation with no exploitable natural resources, the US and UK would have evacuated their nationals from there years ago. But Iraq isn't a marginalized African nation, nor is Afghanistan, and politicians are under enormous pressure to show progress is being made in both countries. In this respect, The Circuit has also helped perpetuate misguided policies.

Reconstruction projects shouldn't begin until the military has secured the ground – which can take years. That's why politicians and military brass boast about how many reconstruction projects have been *implemented* in Iraq and Afghanistan as opposed to how many have been completed. It maintains the illusion that things are moving forward.

The experience of Bechtel is very instructive in this respect. In 2003, the US engineering giant was awarded a US$2.3 billion contract to rebuild Iraq's physical infrastructure: water, sewage, electricity and so forth. In November 2006, Bechtel announced it was leaving Iraq. Given what its employees endured, it was amazing the firm hung in there as long as it did. On a Bechtel project in Basra, for example, the site security manager was murdered, the site manager received death threats, a senior engineer's daughter was kidnapped, twelve employees of the electrical-plumbing subcontractor were killed, as were eleven employees of the concrete supplier – and that was one project.[32]

During its three years in Iraq, Bechtel spent enormous sums beefing up security for its employees; hiring CP teams, investing in armoured vehicles and fortifying installations. It's estimated that of the US$21 billion allocated for Iraqi reconstruction, 34 per cent was spent on commercial security.[33] Money that should have gone towards improving the lives of Iraqis wound up lining the pockets of CSC executives and shareholders.

Another popular benchmark politicians and the military hierarchy love to reference as an example of progress is the number of national police and army recruited and trained in Afghanistan and Iraq. Here again, The Circuit is facilitating damaging policies.

Training local police and military in Iraq and Afghanistan is a job largely outsourced to The Circuit. As pressure mounts in the US and Britain to hand over more responsibilities to local security forces, so too does the drive to rush recruiting and training timetables. If the government tells a commercial security company to cut a ten-week training course down to five

32 David Baker, 'Bechtel Pulling Out After 3 Rough Years of Building Work', *San Francisco Chronicle*, 1 Nov 2006.

33 David Pallister, 'A Multibillion Dollar Industry Built on the Most Dangerous Jobs in the World', *Guardian*, 30 May 2007.

weeks, do you think the CSC is going to say no to the client, or take the money?

Squeezed timetables have already resulted in poorly trained and sometimes poorly vetted local recruits. Before the British took over Helmund in 2006, US forces were in charge there. According to several of my Afghan sources, in 2004, in an effort to step up the handover of security to Afghan forces, the Yanks recruited 500 local police in Helmund. In addition to training, the recruits received uniforms, weapons, vehicles and other equipment to do their jobs. Within eighteen months of completing the programme, 450 of the original 500 recruits had either switched allegiance to the Taliban, left the police to apply their skills in Afghanistan's booming drugs trade (which funds the Taliban), or formed private armies to wreak havoc in their own little fiefdoms. I wonder how many of them turned their weapons on British soldiers.

I get very upset when I think about what's happened in Iraq and Afghanistan; how many brave soldiers have died or been maimed as a result of flawed policies and poor leadership. It's outrageous that not a single serving general, British or American, has resigned over the handling of the conflicts. Penning best-selling retirement memoirs criticizing government policy is too little, too late. The troops deserve better . . . *now*.

I see The Circuit in much the same way. When contracts aren't administered ethically and competently, lives are lost. It hurts me to know that there are executives on The Circuit receiving big fat bonuses funded by the deaths and maiming of brave men and women on the ground. It has to stop.

I strongly believe that things wouldn't have got so bad were it not for the fact that The Circuit is largely unregulated.[34] Thus far, The Circuit's independence has suited the US and

---

34 CSCs incorporated in the United States are regulated to a degree. However, they are not required by US law to issue the names or job descriptions of security personnel injured or killed in hostile environments.

UK strategies in Iraq and Afghanistan. It comes as no surprise then that cleaning up The Circuit would go a long way towards forcing both governments to admit their mistakes and, hopefully, not repeat them.

First, let me state that it would be impossible to regulate every CSC operating worldwide. That would require the establishment of an international regulatory body with real powers. If the United Nations is any guide, regulation at the global level would be at best symbolic and ultimately a huge waste of time and resources.

Regulating CSCs incorporated in Britain, however, is absolutely achievable and in my opinion the way ahead for the whole industry. The military feeds The Circuit and British soldiers are the best in the world. I'd like to see that same level of professionalism carried over to the commercial sector. Britain can set the standard by implementing three key reforms: first, limit British CSCs to servicing only commercial contracts; secondly, require British CSCs to perform due diligence on all employees, including independent contractors, to ensure that only properly qualified personnel are assigned to specific tasks; thirdly, establish an independent, regulatory body to draft, implement and enforce a code of conduct for the industry.

I know my first suggestion – limiting CSCs to commercial contracts – will be greeted with collective moans from both government and the industry. Obviously, if the government can't outsource military jobs, it will have to commit more troops to Iraq and Afghanistan. It will also prevent the implementation of poor exit strategies in these countries by eliminating the option of replacing professional soldiers with commercial security personnel. But the real benefits will be felt in future. If the government can't turn to The Circuit, odds are it will think twice before committing to policies not justified by our military strength.

The loudest objections to the idea of limiting CSCs to commercial contracts will most likely come from inside The Circuit. Outsourced military jobs in hostile environments are a goldmine; looking after government personnel, providing security for government installations, running convoys and security sector reform (training military and police in places like Iraq and Afghanistan) – all these tasks are incredibly lucrative.

There's enough evidence in the preceding pages to demonstrate that when it comes to hostile environments, The Circuit will never operate with the same level of professionalism as the military. Take, for example, looking after government personnel in hostile environments. Commercial Close Protection teams are cap in hand so when a client wants to do something stupid – like dine at an international restaurant in Kabul – it's very hard for the CP team to say no or to get the support of its managers back in the UK. The pressure to keep revenues flowing at CSCs is enormous and in the end most firms will cave in to the client's wishes rather than risk losing the contract.

That wouldn't happen with a military CP team. If a British diplomat wanted to ignore his CP team and engage in a reckless activity, the military CP team could take up the issue with its superiors in the UK who can then go across to the diplomat's bosses and nip the whole scenario in the bud. In most instances, the military chain of command ensures best practices are maintained. That chain of command doesn't exist on The Circuit.

One of the biggest outsourced moneyspinners for British CSCs is running military convoys in Iraq. Again, it's difficult to quantify exactly how many people have died doing this job because CSCs are not required to disclose the information. Nevertheless, it's well known on The Circuit that running convoys is one of the most dangerous jobs out there. According to one estimate, up to 60 per cent of all convoys in Iraq are attacked.[35]

Commercial security personnel don't enjoy the same level of firepower as military convoy operators. Most crucially, commercial operators can't call for backup if they're attacked; the military can. For that reason alone, British CSCs should be

---

35 Broder & Risen, op. cit.

barred from accepting all military convoy contracts, British, American or otherwise.

Of all the jobs the military has pushed out to The Circuit none has more wide-reaching ramifications for national security than the outsourcing of security sector reform in places like Iraq and Afghanistan. It's too easy for CSCs to agree to unrealistic recruiting and training schedules for the sake of keeping a contract. The practice also insulates the government from any negative fallout; if recruits switch sides and turn their weapons on British soldiers the CSC becomes the scapegoat for the government's poor policies.

I do understand that British troops are stretched thinly and there are not enough warm bodies to oversee security sector reform. There is, however, a solution to this dilemma: the army can offer extra financial incentives to recently retired military instructors to re-enlist for one-year tours focusing exclusively on training tasks. This would keep the entire operation in the hands of the military, ensure quality instruction and probably work out to be much less expensive.

So what jobs can CSCs do in hostile environments if military contracts are off limits? Plenty. Looking after journalists is one task that should never fall to the military (and that includes rescuing journalists who get themselves kidnapped); securing energy sector operations such as oil and gas installations; providing security to international aid agencies and NGOs; looking after business executives. There are many contracts, perhaps not enough to fill the gap left by outsourced military jobs, but enough to keep quality British CSCs in business.

Limiting British CSCs to commercial contracts is the first step towards reforming the industry; the second step involves what I like to call 'horses for courses'. In the army people are given specialist training to perform specific tasks. As I've said, a driver drives, a signaller communicates, an engineer constructs, an infantry man fights and a policeman polices. The same should apply to the commercial world – but it doesn't.

Take the example of a trained army vehicle mechanic. There's a role for this person in the commercial security world: keeping armoured vehicles on the road. The mechanic should not, however, be inside the armoured vehicle working as part of a CP team because mechanics are not trained in Close Protection.

As with so many things on The Circuit, it's impossible to quantify exactly how many security personnel lack the proper training for their assigned tasks (remember the ex-Royal Logistic Corps lads who lost the Greek ambassador on Baghdad's airport road?). I can, however, share with you anecdotal evidence suggesting that the problem is widespread.

During a training task in 2006, I had the opportunity to hold classes in my spare time to help CP advisers working for one of Britain's biggest CSCs. One evening I began my lecture by asking a classroom of almost sixty advisers for a show of hands; I wanted to know who among them felt they were doing their current CP task correctly. Not one hand went up.

CP work is among the most lucrative on The Circuit for a reason; it requires a very high level of skill to master. Paying a few thousand pounds to sit an SIA course doesn't prepare a person adequately for the task. As things stand, there are no externally regulated UK-approved courses that teach CP in hostile environments. If there were, and they were any good, I can tell you one thing: the courses would last more than three weeks.

A good commercial CP team should have the following: at least one ex-Special Forces soldier or ex-Royal Military Police CP, preferably in the role of team leader, backed up by a smattering of ex-infantry.

Who should ensure this mix of skills? The CSCs. They collect a management fee. CSCs should be required by law to perform due diligence including verifiable reference checks on all advisers deployed to hostile environments. For too long now, shoddy outfits have got away with shoving any warm body into specialized jobs.

Some British CSCs have recognized that reform of the

industry is inevitable. Rather than place their fate in the hands of an independent body charged with drafting, implementing and enforcing a code of conduct, some British CSCs have clubbed together to push their case for internal regulation. In 2006, the British Association of Private Security Companies or BAPSC was established. It's stated mission: influence the political process that will shape a regulatory structure for British CSCs operating abroad.

On paper, the BAPSC seems a good idea. According to its charter, its members agree to be governed by the following principals: to build and promote open and transparent relations with UK government departments and relevant international organizations; to promote compliance with UK values and interests and with the laws of countries in which its members operate; to issue guidance on the substance of and the need to comply with international legal statutes; to decline contracts that may conflict with international human rights laws, UK values and interests, or that may involve criminal activity; to not provide security services that may adversely affect the military or political balance in the country where they are delivered; to not provide lethal equipment to clients when there is a possibility of human rights infringement; to ensure that employees avoid any armed exchange whilst operational except in self-defence; to ensure that all appropriate staff are properly trained for each assignment; and to ensure 'that all reasonable precautions are taken to protect relevant staff in high risk and/or life threatening operations including the provision of protective equipment, adequate weapons and ammunition, medical support and insurance.'[36]

The BASPC is pushing for what it calls 'a matrix' of controls for British CSCs operating abroad including international codes of conduct, national regulation and industry *self*-regulation based on the association's charter; '. . . the industry understands itself better than the government' states one of its policy

---

36 www.bapsc.org.uk.

papers.[37] It argues that if a member violates the BASPC charter, the trade body 'can exercise pressure on its members, impose financial sanctions and suspend or withdraw membership rights'. Meanwhile, BASPC's idea of national regulation is limited to 'an ombudsman in a government department' charged with collecting, investigating and processing complaints against CSCs. The administration of punishment, however, would still fall to the BASPC.

On paper, it really does sound above board and totally efficient. In practice, however, the BASPC failed to police at least one of its members effectively.

Remember that charter provision to ensure 'that all reasonable precautions are taken to protect relevant staff in high risk and/or life threatening operations including the provision of protective equipment, adequate weapons and ammunition, medical support and insurance'? I quoted that directly from the BAPSC's own website because I wanted to make sure I got the words exactly right. Why? Because the commercial security company that held the Kabul embassy contract I resigned from in 2006 is a BASPC member; the same CSC which failed to provide its CP team on the ground with weapons or an armoured vehicle for over a year; the same CSC which time and again dispatched CP advisers to Kabul who had no background whatsoever in Close Protection; the same CSC which advised me to allow the client to pursue dangerous activities in order to keep the contract.

Allowing British CSCs to self-regulate is tantamount to allowing Afghan drugs traffickers to police the border with Pakistan. It's a very bad idea. The only way to ensure British CSCs operating abroad offer professional, reliable and high-quality services is to establish an external regulatory body chaired by an appointed MP with no financial ties whatsoever to the industry.

37 Bearpark & Shulz, op. cit.

The external regulatory body should have sweeping powers. Forget slap-on-the-wrist fines and sanctions; if a CSC violates the industry's codes on conduct, the regulators should have the authority to dissolve the offending firm and ban its senior managers from participating in Britain's commercial security industry – for life.

I have no doubts that Britain has the talent pool to set the standard for The Circuit worldwide. The question is – does it have the will? I hope some of the stories I've recounted in this book will drive home the message that The Circuit cannot continue to operate in the shadows; it's bad for clients and bad for the security personnel on the ground, many of whom have died and continue to die unnecessarily. Most of all, it's bad for Britain.

If the worst-case scenario does happen and British CSCs succeed in their bid for self-regulation, I do hope the men and women risking their lives on The Circuit will fight for what they deserve: adequate operational equipment to execute their tasks, the support of their managers back home and, above all, fair pay. Sometimes it takes a very big person to stand up to their employer, especially in an industry oversaturated with warm bodies. But remember, in the commercial world, it's better to lose your job than lose your life.